DECISION SUPPORT SYSTEMS

FOR

PRODUCTION AND OPERATIONS MANAGEMENT (DSSPOM)

SECOND EDITION

Vahid LOTFI, Ph.D.

The University of Michigan-Flint
Flint, Michigan 48502

C. Carl PEGELS, Ph.D.

State University of New York at Buffalo
Buffalo, New York 14260

IRWIN

Homewood, IL 60430
Boston, MA 02116

To my parents
V.L.

PREFACE

The material covered in the introductory production and operations management (POM) course is ideally suited to the development and utilization of computer-assisted planning aids. With the arrival of the personal computer, the availability and accessibility of computers has become much easier for both instructor and student. Whereas the mainframe computer has always had a tendency to appear to be distant or removed from the user (as it actually was), the personal computer is more like a typewriter, telephone or slide rule in its function to the user.

The availability of the fourteen software programs that accompany this volume provides both the instructor and student the opportunity to utilize these programs as learning tools of the respective POM techniques.

One of the prime considerations in the development of these programs has been the notion of user friendliness. Many of the POM techniques that are programmed in this software package have previously been available in mainframe software packages. However, the user friendliness of these packages frequently was not quite up to desirable levels. Also the packages were usually developed as individual packages and user rules for one package usually had little relationship to user rules for another package.

The software programs described in this volume are not only user friendly but the operating instructions for each program are virtually identical for each package. Hence, once the user becomes familiar with one program, whatever he has learned is directly applicable to all other programs in this volume.

The student who is expected to experiment with the fourteen computer programs and who does the assignments at the end of each chapter will be thoroughly trained in the use of the techniques and will also gain a deeper understanding of all material in the Production and Operations Management course.

Becoming familiar with these programs and the techniques they represent will also enable the student/user to appreciate the benefits and advantages that are provided by in-depth exploration of POM problems, especially those that can be modeled by one of the programs available in this volume.

We wish to thank Valerie Limpert who was responsible for assisting in the typing and preparation of several drafts of the book.

We also wish to thank the following reviewers who provided many suggestions and refinements:

Warren Fisher, Stephen F. Austin State University
Bob Landeros, Western Michigan University
Hal Langford, University of Southwestern Louisiana
Jack Matthews, University of Wisconsin-Madison
Saeed Mohaghegh, Assumption College
Joseph Ormsby, Stephen F. Austin State University
Stephen Peek, Utica College
Fred Raafat, San Diego State University
Richard A. Reid, University of New Mexico
Sam Seward, University of Texas-Tyler
M.A. Shaikh, Florida Institute of Technology
Mahesh Sharma, Concordia University, Montreal
Fred Silverman, Pace University-White Plains Campus
Kalyan Singhal, University of Baltimore
Dwight Smith-Daniels, Arizona State University
William J. Stevenson, Rochester Institute of Technology
James Storbeck, Ohio State University
Paul Swamidass, Indiana University
Paul Van Ness, Rochester Institute of Technology
Educational Software Services at Richard D. Irwin, Inc.

TABLE OF CONTENTS

OVERVIEW OF DECISION SUPPORT SYSTEMS FOR PRODUCTION AND OPERATIONS MANAGEMENT

Decision Support Systems for Production and Operations Management (DSSPOM) is a software package designed to be used in a Production/Operations Management (POM) course. The package consists of two 5 1/4 inch diskettes (or one 3 1/2 inch diskette) which contains the computer programs and this book. This text serves as the instruction manual for using the programs and also provides summary descriptions of each of the underlying models. The diskette contains fourteen programs for modeling, solving and analyzing the most commonly encountered problems in POM. The fourteen POM modules are listed below. A more detailed description is presented at the end of this chapter.

Module Name	Short Description
Time Series Analysis	Time series analysis with five forecasting techniques
Multiple Regression	Multiple regression with up to 10 independent variables
Decision Analysis	Decision analysis using decision trees and decision tables
Linear Programming	Simplex method with MIN/MAX and $<$, $>$, and $=$ constraints
Transportation Method	Transportation method for balanced and unbalanced problems
Assignment Method	Assignment method for MIN/MAX and unbalanced problems
Location Analysis	Location analysis using work flows and location distances
Layout Analysis	Layout analysis using preference ratings
Line Balancing	Line balancing using four heuristics
Aggregate Planning	Multi-item, multi-period production scheduling
Inventory Analysis	Deterministic and stochastic inventory models
Materials Planning	Multi-item problems with scheduled receipts
Project Management	Deterministic and probabilistic models with time-cost tradeoffs
Quality Assurance	Acceptance sampling and quality control charts

SYSTEM REQUIREMENTS

The programs have been developed and compiled in the Quick Basic[1] language for the IBM[2] Personal Computer (PC) or a PS/2 with a minimum of 512K bytes of RAM, and one or two disk drives. The package can be used on a machine with either a *Color* or a *Monochrome* Display. No graphics capability is required. Use of the Color Display is highly recommended since the display screens, in all of the programs, have been color coded to present information more effectively.

---

[1]Quick Basic is a Copyrighted product of Microsoft Corporation

[2]IBM is a registered trademark of International Business Machines Corporation

Disk Operating Systems (DOS) version 2.1 or higher is required. The package can also be installed on a hard disk. Use of a hard disk can substantially improve the performance of the programs. In addition, the programs have file management capability for more efficient file processing.

Throughout, it is assumed that the user has some familiarity with the use of a PC and DOS. In particular, the user should know how to boot the PC with DOS and be familiar with DOS file naming conventions. Those using a PC with the hard disk drive, should know the various sub-directory commands such as DIR, CD (Change Directory), and file referencing using drive and path.

PREPARING A BACKUP COPY OF DISKETTE

The DSSPOM diskettes contain the programs for fourteen POM models. The diskettes have not been copy protected and may be copied for backup. An easy way of doing this is to perform the three steps outlined below. You will need either one 3 1/2 diskette or two 5 1/4 inch diskettes.

    1 - Place the DOS disk in drive A:
    2 - Type DISKCOPY A: A:
    3 - Follow the prompts from the DISKCOPY program.

Repeat the above three steps for both System Disk #1 and System Disk #2, if you have the two diskette version.

HARD DISK INSTALLATION

The DSSPOM diskettes include various batch files which are designed to install DSSPOM on a hard disk. If you are already familiar with DOS directory commands, you may create a sub-directory, call it "DSSPOM", and then copy all of the files from the system disks to that sub-directory. If you are installing the system from the 5 1/4 inch diskettes, you should also perform the following DOS copy command,

COPY MENUH.EXE MENU.EXE

Alternatively, you may use the batch file provided in the system disk to perform the hard disk installation as described below. The batch file will install the package on a sub-directory called DSSPOM.

3 1/2 inch System

To install the package on the hard disk, place System Disk in one of the floppy drives. These drives are usually referred to as A: or B:. Make this drive the default drive by typing the drive letter followed by a ":" and press <ENTER>. For example, if the floppy drive is A, then type,

    A:

Next, type,

    INSTC X: Y:

where X is the name of the floppy drive and Y is the name of the hard disk drive. For example, to install the package on C: drive from the A: drive, type,

    INSTC A: C:

Then follow the prompts from the installation program to complete the installation procedure.

5 1/4 inch System

To install the package on the hard disk, place System Disk #1 in one of the floppy drives. These drives are usually referred to as A: or B:. Make this drive the default drive by typing the drive letter followed by a ":" and press <ENTER>. For example, if the floppy drive is A, then type,

    A:

Next, type,

    INSTC X: Y:

where X is the name of the floppy drive and Y is the name of the hard disk drive. For example, to install the package on C: drive from the A: drive, type,

    INSTC A: C:

Then follow the prompts from the installation program to complete the installation procedure.

HOW TO LOAD THE PROGRAMS

DSSPOM may be loaded from any floppy drive (e.g., A:, B:, etc.). To load DSSPOM, you must first boot the system with a DOS version 2.1 or higher. Then, place System Disk #1 (or the 3 1/2 inch System Disk) in one of the floppy drives. If this drive is not the default drive already, make it the default drive by typing the drive letter followed by a ":". For example, if you wish to run DSSPOM from drive B and your boot drive is A, first place System Disk #1 in drive B: then type,

B:

Next type,

DSSPOM

Note that for the 5 1/4 inch system (the two floppy version), DSSPOM must be loaded by using System Disk #1.

Hard Disk

Turn the system on and wait for the hard disk prompt (systems with a hard disk are self booting and do not require the DOS disk). Then change the sub-directory to DSSPOM by typing,

CD \DSSPOM

Next, load the package by typing,

DSSPOM

THE DSS-POM MAIN MENU

The DSSPOM Main Menu enables you to select and run the module of interest. Fourteen common POM techniques are available. Below, we will illustrate the use of the Main Menu. We assume that you have prepared a working copy of the DSSPOM diskette or it has been installed on your hard disk.

Load the DSSPOM into the computer (see "HOW TO LOAD DSSPOM"). The computer will take a few seconds to load the library of the routines. The time it takes for the computer to load the programs is dependent on the speed of your system and may take several seconds. The computer will then display the first introductory screen as shown below.

```
DECISION SUPPORT SYSTEMS
FOR
PRODUCTION AND OPERATIONS MANAGEMENT
(DSS-POM)


Second Edition


Vahid Lotfi   and   C. Carl Pegels




Version 2.1

Copyright Richard D. Irwin, Inc. 1990
```

The computer will ask that you press a key to continue. Press any key to continue with the copyright message as shown below.

```
Decision Support Systems for Production and Operations Management


  This software  package is provided in a  copyable format

  for your convenience.   You are permitted to make backup

  copies, copies for students who are enrolled in a course

  and for teaching assistants and other faculty teaching a

  course for which the book:  DECISION SUPPORT SYSTEMS FOR

  PRODUCTION AND OPERATIONS MANAGEMENT  by Vahid Lotfi and

  Carl  C.  Pegels  is a required textbook.  This software

  package may not be  copied,  distributed and/or used for

  any other purpose.
```

The computer will ask you to press a key again. Press a key to continue with the Main Menu as shown below.

```
                        DSS-POM   Version 2.1


   * * * MAIN  MENU * * *              * * * OVERVIEW * * *

  ╔═══════════════════════╗   ╔═══════════════════════════════════╗
  ║ Time Series Analysis  ║   ║      TIME SERIES FORECASTING      ║
  ║ Multiple Regression   ║   ║ This program  performs  forecasting for ║
  ║ Decision Analysis     ║   ║ time series data with up to 50 points. ║
  ║ Linear Programming    ║   ║ The forecasting techniques include: ║
  ║ Transportation Method ║   ║ Weighted Moving Average(WMA), Exponential ║
  ║ Assignment Method     ║   ║ Smoothing(ES) without trend, Double ║
  ║ Location Analysis     ║   ║ Smoothing (with trend).  Decomposition ║
  ║ Layout Analysis       ║   ║ Method (additive  model), and Adaptive ║
  ║ Line Balancing        ║   ║ Exponential  Smoothing.   In each case, ║
  ║ Aggregate Planning    ║   ║ Mean-Squared Error (MSE), Mean Absolute ║
  ║ Inventory Analysis    ║   ║ Deviation (MAD), Bias of the forecast, ║
  ║ Materials Planning    ║   ║ Coefficient  of  Variation, and Tracking ║
  ║ Project Management    ║   ║ Signal are reported. ║
  ║ Quality Assurance     ║   ║                                   ║
  ║ Exit DSS-POM          ║   ║                                   ║
  ╚═══════════════════════╝   ╚═══════════════════════════════════╝

       Use ↑ and ↓ to highlight and press Enter (<--|) to select.
```

As seen from the above display screen, the screen consists of two distinct areas enclosed in double-lined squares. The square on the left side of the screen is a vertical menu system, entitled "MAIN MENU". The square to the right is entitled "OVERVIEW" and contains a short overview of the highlighted option. A highlighted option, in the MAIN MENU as well as other menus throughout the package, is either displayed in a different color (usually Red) or reverse video. Throughout this text, the highlighted option will be referred to as the *Pointer*. For example, the phrase "move the *pointer*" implies using an arrow key to highlight another option as instructed.

Initially, the first option, "Time Series Analysis" is highlighted and the OVERVIEW section displays a short description of the Time Series Module. As you use the up and down arrow keys to highlight other options (move the *Pointer* up or down) in the MAIN MENU, the OVERVIEW section is updated and presents the description for the highlighted option.

To select an option, move the pointer to a desired option and press the <ENTER> key. To exit from DSSPOM and return to DOS, move the pointer to the last option "Exit DSSPOM" and press <ENTER>.

BYPASSING THE LOGO AND/OR MAIN MENU: QUICK LOAD

After using DSSPOM several times, you may wish to bypass the introductory screens containing the Logo and Copyright message. The advanced user can also bypass the MAIN MENU and execute the desired module directly at the DOS prompt.

To bypass the introductory screens and execute the MAIN MENU directly, change the sub-directory to DSSPOM then type MENU (hard disk system). If you are running the programs from floppy system, place the System Disk (3 1/2 inch version) or System Disk #1 (5 1/4 inch version) in a floppy drive. Make the drive the default drive, then type MENU.

You may also bypass the MAIN MENU (only hard disk and 3 1/2 inch disk users) and execute a particular program directly. To do this, change the sub-directory to DSSPOM (for hard disk system) then type the program name (see below) for the desired module. If you have a 3 1/2 inch system, boot the system with DOS. Then place your System Disk in a floppy drive. Make that drive the default drive then type the program name (see below) for the desired module.

Module Name	Program Name
Time Series Analysis	FORCAST
Multiple Regression	REGRESS
Decision Analysis	DECISION
Linear Programming	LINPRO
Transportation Method	TRANSPT
Assignment Method	ASSIGN
Location Analysis	LOCATION
Layout Analysis	LAYOUT
Line Balancing	BALANCE
Aggregate Planning	AGGPLAN
Inventory Analysis	INVENT
Materials Planning	MRP
Project Management	PERT
Quality Assurance	QUALITY

For example, to execute the Location Analysis program directly, without going through the introductory screens and MAIN MENU, place the System Disk in the default drive and type LOCATION. Note that the computer will require several seconds to first load the program library and then execute the desired module.

USING THE MODULES: A TUTORIAL

In order to minimize the amount of time a user must spend in learning how to operate each new program, we have tried to keep the instructions for each program similar. For this reason each program operates through the same six-option menu. We will refer to this menu as the common menu. Most of the programs also utilize the same spread sheet editor for data entry and edit process. This example utilizes the Assignment Module to illustrates the use of the common menu and the spread sheet editor. For this example, you need not be familiar with the details of the Assignment Method at this time. Just follow the instructions in this tutorial to become familiar with loading a module, using the common menu, and using the spread sheet editor to enter the problem data.

The example problem involves assigning three candidates; Joe, Marry, and Bob to three jobs; A, B, and C so as to minimize the total training time. The training times (in hours) for the three candidates and three jobs are as follows.

	A	B	C
Joe	20	10	8
Marry	25	15	25
Bob	15	20	17

To solve the problem, load DSSPOM into the computer and press a key twice to display the MAIN MENU. Next, press the down arrow key several times to move the pointer to the Assignment Method. The computer will update the OVERVIEW section as shown below.

```
                    DSS-POM   Version 2.1


* * * MAIN  MENU * * *              * * * OVERVIEW * * *

  ┌─────────────────────┐      ┌──────────────────────────────┐
  │ Time Series Analysis│      │      ASSIGNMENT METHOD        │
  │ Multiple Regression │      │ This program solves the       │
  │ Decision Analysis   │      │ assignment problem. The       │
  │ Linear Programming  │      │ problem may include up to 30  │
  │ Transportation Method│     │ rows (candidates) and 30      │
  │ Assignment Method   │      │ columns (jobs).               │
  │ Location Analysis   │      │ The solution method consists  │
  │ Layout Analysis     │      │ of the standard assignment    │
  │ Line Balancing      │      │ algorithm. The program        │
  │ Aggregate Planning  │      │ solves maximization and       │
  │ Inventory Analysis  │      │ minimization problems. If     │
  │ Materials Planning  │      │ the problem is unbalanced     │
  │ Project Management  │      │ dummy candidates or dummy     │
  │ Quality Assurance   │      │ jobs are added. The input     │
  │ Exit DSS-POM        │      │ data consists of the number   │
  └─────────────────────┘      │ of candidates, the number of  │
                               │ jobs, and the assignment      │
                               │ costs for each candidate-job  │
                               │ combination.                  │
                               └──────────────────────────────┘

      Use ↑ and ↓ to highlight and press Enter (<--|) to select.
```

8

Press the <ENTER> key to load the Assignment Module. The computer will pause for a few seconds and then displays the common menu (for the Assignment Method) as shown below.

```
≡  Input  Edit  Print  File  Solve  Quit




                                                                    

 F1-Help F2-Calculator          ASSIGNMENT METHOD            File:
```

As seen from the above display screen, the common menu screen contains two non-blank lines; the top line (row 1 of the display), and the bottom line (row 25 of the display). The items in the top line (except for the first one ≡) are the six menu options. These six options are common throughout all of the fourteen modules. Below, we describe each item separately.

≡   Pressing the <ENTER> key while the pointer is on this option will give general directions on how to use the common menu.

Input   This menu option is used to enter input data for a new problem from the keyboard. If a model already exists, the computer will give a warning message and ask whether it should erase the current model and begin a new one.

Edit   This menu option is used to edit and/or view problem data. The edit option is used as a view mechanism for a problem which has been loaded from a disk file. In certain modules this option has several sub-options to edit various parameters of a problem independently. In other modules, including the Assignment Method, it does not have any sub-options. Choosing this option will trace the problem parameters, starting with the first one. To keep the values which are not being changed, just press the <ENTER> key to proceed.

Print   This option is used to send problem data to a printer. As with the Edit option, it has several sub-options for certain modules to allow printing separate parameters independently. Upon choosing this option, the computer will ask you to make sure that the Printer is On and Ready (or "On Line").

File   This option provides several file management commands as shown below:

Retrieve a file: To load a previously saved data file from disk
Save current file: To save the current model on disk
Copy a file: To make a backup copy of a file

9

Erase a file: To delete a file from disk
Rename a file: To rename a data file
List current DIR: To display a list of files in current directory (or disk)
Change the DIR: To change the current sub-directory (mainly for hard disk)

Solve This option is used to solve the problem. It has three sub-options:

Display output: To solve the problem and display the results on the screen
Print output: To solve the problem and print the results on printer
Save output: To solve the problem and save the results in a text file

Quit This option is used to exit from the current module. It has two sub-options:

Return to DOS: End from the module and return to DOS
*DSS-POM Main Menu:*End the module and return to DSSPOM Main Menu

The bottom line (row 25 of the display screen) is the help and message area. It contains four items. The first two are function key definitions as described below.

F1:Help   Throughout DSSPOM, function key <F1> is used as the help key. The help facility is context sensitive. That is, pressing the help key <F1> will provide information for the menu option or sub-option which is highlighted by the pointer.

F2:calculator Pressing the function key <F2> from the common menu will invoke a calculator.

The third item (middle of the line) is the name of the current module (in this case *Assignment Method*). The last item, *File:* is used to display the name of the current data file. It remains blank until the current model is saved on disk or a new model is retrieved from disk.

To solve the assignment problem, move the pointer to the *Input* option by pressing the right arrow key once and press <ENTER>. The computer will begin the data entry process by asking you to enter a problem title. Type TUTORIAL EXAMPLE and press the <ENTER> key to continue with the next item. If you make a typing mistake before pressing the <ENTER> key, you can use either the backspace key or the left arrow key to correct the mistake. If you have already pressed the <ENTER> key, do not worry, there is a way to return to this item and correct it later.

After pressing the <ENTER> key, the computer will ask you to enter the "Objective type". For this example problem, the objective is to minimize the total training time, hence type "MIN" and press <ENTER>. Note that the computer will not accept values other than "MIN"

10

or "MAX". Before pressing the <ENTER> key (after typing the last letter of "MIN"), you may press the up arrow key to backtrack to the title field and correct any mistakes.

The computer will then ask you to enter the number of candidates. The number of candidates for this problem is 3. Be sure to type "03" and then press <ENTER>. Alternatively, you can press the right arrow key once to move the cursor one position to the right, then type "3".

The next query involves the number of jobs. The number of jobs is 3. Type "03" and press <ENTER>. The completed screen is shown below.

```
┌────────────────────────────────────────────────────────────────┐
│  ≡  Input  Edit  Print  File  Solve  Quit                      │
│                                                                  │
│                                                                  │
│      Problem title: TUTORIAL EXAMPLE                            │
│                                                                  │
│      Objective type (MIN/MAX): MIN                             │
│                                                                  │
│      Number of candidates (rows): 03                           │
│                                                                  │
│      Number of jobs (columns): 03                              │
│                                                                  │
│                                                                  │
│    ┌──────────────────────────────────────────────────────┐   │
│    │ Enter problem parameters as requested.  Press RETURN to │  │
│    │ accept, or ESC to exit.   Maximum problem size is 30 by 30, │
│    │ assignment costs should be within 0 and 9999.          │   │
│    └──────────────────────────────────────────────────────┘   │
│                                                                  │
└────────────────────────────────────────────────────────────────┘
```

After pressing the <ENTER> key, the computer will ask if you wish to continue with the assignment costs as shown below.

```
┌──────────────────────────────────────────────┐
│  Continue with assignment costs (Y/N) Y       │
└──────────────────────────────────────────────┘
```

Spread Sheet Editor

Before resuming with the tutorial, we will present a more detailed description of the spread sheet editor. The spread sheet editor is used for entering problem data in most of the modules. Becoming familiar with it at this point will save you much search for information later. We will present the spread sheet editor in the context of the tutorial example.

After pressing the <ENTER> key, the computer will invoke the spread sheet editor for entering the assignment costs. The initial spread sheet is presented below.

```
≡  Input  Edit  Print  File  Solve  Quit
                                                    ⊣READY⊢
A1
          A       B     C     D
1               Job1  Job2  Job3
2   Candid1        0     0     0
3   Candid2        0     0     0
4   Candid3        0     0     0



  F1:Help  F2:Edit  F5:Goto   HOME:Cell A1  ESC:Exit no save  F10:Exit.
```

As seen from the above display screen, the spread sheet has several rows and columns. The rows are identified by integer numbers and the columns are identified by the letters of alphabet. The cells are referenced through their addresses. A cell address consists of its column letter followed by its row number. For example, the address of the top left corner cell is A1. A pointer is utilized to move from one cell to another and update its contents. Initially, the pointer is located in cell A1 (in the above display, cell A1 is empty). The contents of the pointed cell is displayed in front of its address in the top row of the spread sheet.

Cell Content

Cell contents are either *labels* (a series of alpha-numeric characters) or *values* (real or integer numbers). A label must be preceded with either a single quote (') or a carat sign (^). Labels preceded by single quotes will be left-justified and labels preceded by carat signs will be centered. Even though, a label can be preceded by a double quote ("), which will be right-justified, double quotes should not be used (labels preceded by double quotes will cause unpredictable results when saving files). When entering a label which begin with a letter, it need not be preceded by (') or (^). The spread sheet will automatically recognize it as a label and will left justify it (precede it with a single quote).

A *value* is numeric entity and must be preceded by plus or minus sign, a period (.), or a digit. For some modules, ceratin cells have been formatted to display the value in a special way. For example, if a cell value represents dollar amount, the cell may have been formatted to display the value using two decimal places.

For this solved example, the job titles (A, B, and C), and the candidates' names (Joe, Marry, and Bob) are labels and the training costs are values.

12

Function Keys

The last line (row 25 of the display screen) presents the definitions of various function keys which are used within the spread sheet editor. The description of the keys are as follows.

F1:Help   Pressing the function key < F1 > will produce general information about cell data entry and format.

F2:Edit   Pressing the function key < F2 > will invoke the cell editor. The contents of the cell where the pointer is located can be edited. Note that in the above display screen, the pointer is located in cell A1 as indicated by the cell address in the top left corner of the spread sheet.

F5:Goto   Function key < F5 > is designed for quick movement through the spread sheet. For example, to move the pointer to cell G20, press < F5 > then enter G20 and press < ENTER >. The pointer will be placed in cell G20.

HOME   The < HOME > key is used to return to the top left corner (cell A1) of the spread sheet using one key stroke.

ESC   The < ESC > key is used to exit from the spread sheet without updating the contents (various problem parameters). This key is especially useful when the spread sheet editor is used to view a problem data or invoked by mistake.

F10   The < F10 > function key is used to exit from the spread sheet and update the problem parameters.

Resuming the Tutorial

Begin the data entry process for the tutorial example by entering the job titles and the candidates' names as described below.

Use the down arrow key to move the pointer to cell A2 and type "Joe" (recall that Joe begins with a letter and will be entered as a label)

Use the down arrow key to move the pointer to cell A3 (it is not necessary to press < ENTER > after typing the letter "e".) and type "Marry"

Press the down arrow key again, type "Bob" and press < ENTER >

Press < F5 > to move the pointer to cell B2. The computer will ask you to enter the cell address. Type B2 and press < ENTER >

13

Type the letter "A" and press <ENTER> (note that pressing the <ENTER> key here is necessary because using the right arrow key will move the cursor (not the pointer) one space to the right)

Press the right arrow key and type the letter "B" and press <ENTER>

Press the right arrow once more and type the letter "C" and press <ENTER>.

After completing the data entry for the job titles and candidates' names, you can proceed with the data entry for the assignment costs as described below.

Move the pointer to cell B2, type 20, then press the down arrow key.
Type 25, then press the down arrow key.
Type 15, then press <ENTER>.
Press <F5>, then enter C2 and press <ENTER>.
Type 10, then press the down arrow key.
Type 15, then press the down arrow key.
Type 20, then press <ENTER>.
Press <F5>, then enter D2 and press <ENTER>.
Type 8, then press the down arrow key.
Type 25, then press the down arrow key.
Type 17, then press <ENTER>.

While entering the problem data, the computer may display the message "Working! Press any key to continue." This message is not an error message and has been incorporated into the programs as a safety mechanism for preventing a system halt when DOS performs memory management operations. If you encounter this message, just press the space bar once and resume with the data entry process.

The data entry for the assignment costs have been completed. Check the cell entries to make sure there is no mistake. In case of an error, move the pointer to that cell and re-enter the value. Alternatively, move the pointer to the cell in error and press <F2>. You can edit the contents, using the right and left arrow keys, the <DEL>, and Backspace keys. The competed spread sheet is presented below.

```
                                                            ⊣READY⊢
 D4    17
               A      B      C      D
  1                 A      B      C
  2    Joe         20     10      8
  3    Marry       25     15     25
  4    Bob         15     20     17
```

Press <F10> to exit from the spread sheet editor and keep the problem data in memory. Note that you have not saved the problem data on disk at this time and exiting from DSSPOM or turning the machine off will result in loss of problem data. The computer will terminate the spread sheet editor and display the Assignment Menu again.

Saving the Problem on Disk

You can now save the problem data on disk for future reference. To do so, move the pointer to the FILE option by pressing the right arrow key several times. The computer will display the FILE option sub-menu as shown below.

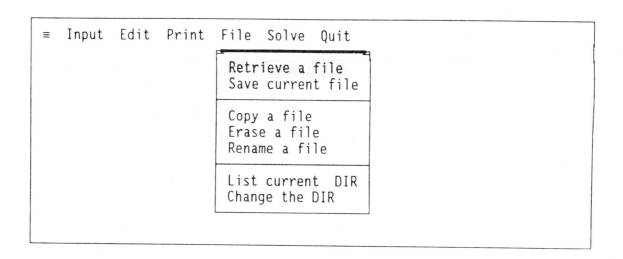

As seen from the above display, the pointer initially points to the first sub-option "Retrieve a file". Press the down arrow key once to move the pointer to the "Save current file" option and press <ENTER>. The computer will respond by asking you to enter a file name as shown below.

```
Enter file name   C:\DSSPOM\TUTOR.ASN
```

Note that the computer will display the current drive and sub-directory. In this case, the current drive is "C" and the sub-directory is "\DSSPOM". Use the right arrow key to move the cursor to the first position after the second back slash. Then type "TUTOR.ASN" and press <ENTER>. The problem data will be saved in a file named "TUTOR.ASN".

The last three characters of a file name (after the period) are called a file extension (or suffix). Using meaningful suffixes results in easier file search later during the file retrieve process. For example, using the suffix "ASN" for files containing assignment problem data will make the retrieval process easier later on (see Retrieving Data Files below).

You are now ready to solve the assignment problem. Move the pointer to the SOLVE option by pressing the right arrow key several times. The computer will display the following menu.

```
≡   Input  Edit  Print  File  Solve  Quit
                                ┌─────────────────┐
                                │ Display output  │
                                │ Print output    │
                                │ Save output     │
                                └─────────────────┘
```

The SOLVE option has three sub-options as shown above. The first choice, entitled "Display output" is designed to solve the problem and display the results on the secern. The other two choices will send the results to the printer or a disk file, respectively.

Since the pointer is already on the "Display output" sub-option, press <ENTER> to select this choice. The computer will pause for a few seconds and then display the solution as shown below.

```
                    Problem Title: TUTORIAL EXAMPLE
                    Optimal Solution: Objective value = 38

        Joe         assigned to    C
        Marry       assigned to    B
        Bob         assigned to    A
```

The above solution indicates that the total optimal training time is 38 hours. Further, Joe should be assigned to job C, Marry to job B, and Bob to job A. Press a key to return to the Assignment Menu.

You have completed the data entry and solution process for the example problem. At this point you may exit from the Assignment Module by moving the pointer to the QUIT option. the computer will display the following two choices.

16

```
≡  Input  Edit  Print  File  Solve  Quit

                              ┌─────────────────────┐
                              │ Return to DOS       │
                              │ DSS-POM Main Menu   │
                              └─────────────────────┘



        ┌──────────────────────────────────────────┐
        │ Return to DSS-POM Main Menu (Y/N) N       │
        └──────────────────────────────────────────┘
```

The default choice is to "Return to DOS". In the above screen, the pointer has been moved down to the seconds choice "DSS-POM Main Menu". Pressing the <ENTER> key will result in the computer asking if you to verify terminating the Assignment Module (<u>do not exit from the Assignment Module at this time</u>). You may end the Assignment Module by pressing the <Y> key. Alternatively, you may press <ENTER> to remain within the assignment module. Press <ENTER> to return to the Assignment Module and resume with the next exercise involving file retrieval.

<u>Retrieving Data Files</u>

Although, the assignment problem is still in memory, we will retrieve the "TUTOR.ASN" file, saved earlier to illustrate the file retrieve option. Move the pointer to the FILE option and select the "Retrieve a file" sub-option by pressing the <ENTER> key. Since there is a model in memory already, the computer will ask if you wish to begin a new problem as shown below.

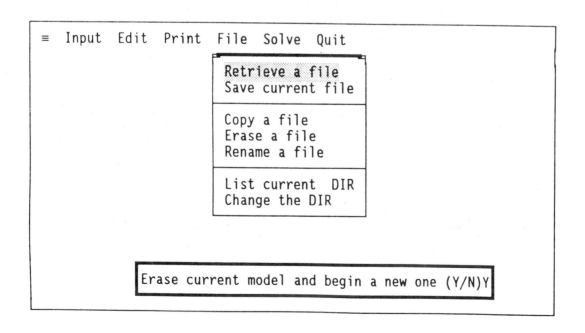

```
≡  Input   Edit   Print   File   Solve   Quit

                    ┌──────────────────────┐
                    │ Retrieve a file      │
                    │ Save current file    │
                    ├──────────────────────┤
                    │ Copy a file          │
                    │ Erase a file         │
                    │ Rename a file        │
                    ├──────────────────────┤
                    │ List current  DIR    │
                    │ Change the DIR       │
                    └──────────────────────┘


        ┌────────────────────────────────────────────┐
        │ Erase current model and begin a new one (Y/N)Y│
        └────────────────────────────────────────────┘
```

Press <Y> to erase the current model and retrieve a new one. The computer will display the current drive and path and ask you to enter the file specification as shown below.

```
Enter file spec. C:\DSSPOM\*.*
```

The file specification may be a specific file name such as "TUTOR.ASN" or an expression using the DOS wild characters "?" and "*". For example, to display the list of files having the suffix "ASN", the file specification would be "*.ASN". As mentioned earlier, when saving data files, using an appropriate suffix greatly improves the file retrieve process through the use of "*" and the suffix.

Move the cursor to the first position after the last character "*" by pressing the <END> key. Now press the <Backspace> key once to delete the last "*". Then type the three characters "ASN" and press <ENTER> as shown below.

```
Enter file spec. C:\DSSPOM\*.ASN
```

The computer will display a vertical menu containing a list of all file names having the suffix "ASN" as shown below.

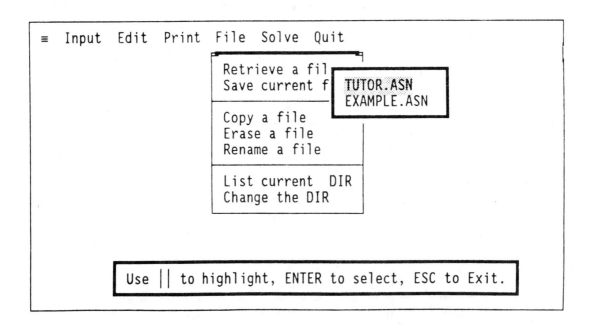

18

Note that in this case, there are two files having the suffix "ASN". These include "EXAMPLE.ASN" and "TUTOR.ASN" ("EXAMPLE.ASN" is another assignment problem that the author had saved earlier).

To retrieve "TUTOR.ASN", use the arrow keys to highlight the file name and press the <ENTER> key. Since the pointer is already on this file name, press the <ENTER> key to retrieve it. The computer will pause for a few seconds and then load the data file. Note that the "File:" section of the bottom line is immediately updated and contains the file name.

SUMMARY DESCRIPTION OF THE MODULES

The fourteen programs included in DSSPOM Version 2.1, are among the most commonly used techniques in POM and may be found in nearly all POM textbooks. The fourteen programs consist of:

1. Time Series Analysis
2. Multiple Regression
3. Decision Analysis
4. Linear Programming
5. Transportation Method
6. Assignment Method
7. Location Analysis
8. Layout Analysis
9. Line Balancing
10. Aggregate Planning
11. Inventory Analysis
12. Materials Planning
13. Project Management
14. Quality Assurance

Below we present a brief summary for each program to familiarize the user with its contents and limitations.

Time Series Analysis

The first module, called "Time Series Analysis," is designed to perform time series forecasting. The program includes five forecasting methods consisting of exponential smoothing with and without trend, weighted moving averages, adaptive smoothing, and the decomposition method involving seasonality. The program can solve problems with up to 50 data points. It will report mean square error, mean absolute deviation, bias of the forecast, coefficient of variation, and the tracking signal.

Multiple Regression

The second module performs multiple regression with up to 10 independent variables and 60 observations. The output consists of the regression function coefficients, standard deviations of coefficients, and t-statistics. It also provides the analysis of variance table, coefficients of determination, and predicted values.

Decision Analysis

The third module solves decision analysis problems utilizing decision trees and decision tables. For decision trees, with up to 50 branches, the conditional payoffs as well as the optimum alternative is provided. For decision tables, with up to 20 alternatives and 20 states of nature, decision analysis under uncertainty and under risk is performed. A decision matrix is used for decision tables with the rows representing the alternative actions and the columns representing the states of nature.

Linear Programming

The Linear Programming module uses the regular simplex method to solve problems of up to 50 variables and 30 constraints. The problem can be in MIN or MAX form, subject to equality, less than or equal to, and/or greater than or equal to constraints. The output consists of the optimal objective value, values for the decision variables, and the associated reduced costs. Also reported are the values of the slack variables and their shadow prices. Sensitivity analysis of the right-hand values as well as of the objective function coefficients are provided.

Transportation Method

This module solves the transportation problem, using the transportation simplex method. The program solves problems with up to 20 sources (plants) and 20 destinations (warehouses). If the problem is unbalanced a dummy warehouse or dummy plant is added. Initial solution is obtained by using the northwest corner method. The program reports the intermediate solutions, presenting the cost as well as the quantities to be shipped for each route.

Assignment Method

The Assignment Module solves the assignment problem. The problem may include up to 30 rows (candidates) and 30 columns (jobs). The solution method consists of the standard assignment algorithm. The program solves maximization and minimization problems. If the problem is unbalanced dummy candidates or dummy jobs are added. The input data consists of the number of candidates, the number of jobs, and the assignment costs for each candidate-job combination.

Location Analysis

The Location Analysis module solves the location analysis problem which consists of assigning n departments or facilities to n locations while minimizing the total transportation cost. The problem can include up to 25 facilities. The solution methods consist of a random assignment heuristic and a pairwise exchange heuristic. The user may also request pairwise exchanges of selected department pairs. The input data consists of number of departments, number of locations, the inter-departmental work-flows, and the inter-location distances.

Layout Analysis

This module solves the layout design problem which consists of developing a layout design for departments or facilities while maximizing the total adjacency preference ratings. The problem may include up to 30 facilities. The solution methods consist of a random assignment heuristic and a pairwise exchange heuristic. The user may also request pairwise exchanges of selected department pairs. The input data consist of number of facilities, grid size, and pairwise adjacency ratings using an adjacency preference scale.

Assembly Line Balancing

The Line Balancing module solves the assembly line balancing problem with up to 30 tasks. The solution methods consist of four heuristic rules which prescribe the task that should be scheduled first. The rules are:

1- Longest processing time
2- Largest number of following tasks
3- Largest number of predecessor tasks
4- Largest positional weight.

The output consists of the minimum cycle time, number of work stations required, and the assembly line efficiency.

Aggregate Planning

The Aggregate Planning module solves the multi-product aggregate or intermediate production planning problem with up to 4 products and 12 periods. The problem may include regular time, overtime, sub-contracting, and backlogs. The solution methods consist of an optimizing procedure based on the transportation model formulation. The output consists of the optimal production schedule and cost report for each product. An overall cost summary report is also provided.

Inventory Analysis

The Inventory Analysis module provides the minimum cost solutions for the following inventory models:

A-Economic Lot Size without shortage
B-Economic Lot Size with shortage
C-Economic Run Size without shortage
D-Economic Run Size with shortage
E-Economic Lot Size model with quantity discounts
F-Stochastic Demand model with lead-time

For each model, the program reports the optimum order quantity, total cost, holding cost, setup or order cost, and length of the cycle.

Material Requirements Planning

This module solves the multi-item material requirements planning (MRP) problem. The problem may include up to 5 end-items, 30 parts, and 26 periods. Components may include up to 4 sub-components. The input data consist of the master production schedule, bill of materials, inventory record file, and scheduled receipts. Items can be ordered according to lot-for-lot, lot-size, and/or period order quantity policy. Output consists of the time phase plan and cost report for all components or a selected component.

Project Management

The Project Management module solves project management problems using the activity on arc method for up to 30 events and 50 activities using PERT/CPM. Both deterministic activity times and three level time estimate problems can be solved. Events (nodes) must be numbered from 1 to N, with the beginning event as node 1 and the ending event as node N. Each activity also receives a separate number although it can also be identified by its two end nodes. To speed up a project, individual activities can be speeded up (crashed) through time cost trade-offs.

Quality Assurance

The Quality Assurance module provides the parameters and helps solve two quality control models: the acceptance sampling model and the process control model. The acceptance sampling model provides data to plot the operating characteristics curve and the average outgoing quality curve on the basis of the inputs: lot size, sample size and number of acceptable defectives in sample. The process control model provides the mean and the lower and upper control limits for mean, range, and p and c control charts on the basis of number of defectives found in each of the specified samples.

CHANGES FROM THE FIRST EDITION

Based on the feedback from the users, we have modified and extended DSSPOM extensively. In revising the package, our main goals have been to make the software more user friendly, add to the substance, and increase the number and quality of the end-of-chapter problems. The major modifications are described below.

Data Entry Modifications

The primary change in the data entry process is the replacement of the prompted input with a spread sheet type data input process. Using a spread sheet, for the data entry process, is both easy to learn and easy to use. The spread sheet data editor, incorporated in the new version, is almost self-explanatory and does not require referring to the text. More importantly, the same spread sheet editor is used in all of the modules. Consequently, learning the spread sheet data entry process in one module will significantly decrease the amount of time needed to learn its use in other modules.

Another improvement in the data entry process involves using various mechanisms to avoid unnecessary typing. For example, in the Layout Analysis and Location Analysis modules, when the matrix is symmetric, the mirror image need not be entered. As another example, in the Aggregate Planning module, when the demand forecasts (or other parameters) for all of the time periods are the same, the value for the first time period is entered and the remaining values are left as default "^.". The editor will recognize the default values as being the same as that of the first period.

Program Extensions

Several new features have been added to the modules in the first edition and a new module "Decision Analysis" has been added. The new features are extensive, we present a summary of the major improvements below.

An important improvement, common to all of the modules, includes the ability to both print the solution output on the printer and save the output in a disk file. A file management utility has been added which provides file copying, file renaming, file deleting, listing the directory, and changing the directory.

Another improvement, common to all of the modules, consists of availability of a "context sensitive" help facility. The function key <F1> has been used to provide help for all of the menu options and sub-options. The user can obtain help by moving the pointer to a desired option or sub-option and press <F1>. A calculator is also available for you convenience. To invoke the calculator, press <F2> while the common menu is being displayed.

The Time Series Analysis module includes three new forecasting techniques and also reports various error terms. The Multiple Regression module allows the user to input their own variable names.

Both Transportation and Assignment modules allow the user to input row names and column names. Further, the user can request the intermediate solutions.

The new Decision Analysis module provides decision trees and decision tables. The user can input his/her own alternative names and states of nature.

The Location Analysis and Layout Analysis modules allow user defined row and column labels. Further, a new solution option is available which enables the user to perform pairwise exchanges of the departments to perform "what if" analysis.

The Line Balancing module allows user defined labels and also provides for entering the desired cycle time.

The Aggregate Planning modules has been extended to allow multiple product problems. The solution output consists of the production schedules as well as cost summary. Various type of capacities such as regular time, overtime, and sub-contracting are available.

The Inventory Analysis includes new stochastic demand model. The solution output has been extended to include reports of various cost components.

The MRP module has been extended to include multi-product problems. It also allows lot-size, lot-for-lot, and period order quantity ordering. The solution output has been extended to include various cost components.

The Project Management module now includes time cost tradeoffs (or crashing). The Quality Assurance module now reports the samples which are out of control.

CHAPTER 1

FORECASTING ANALYSIS - TIME SERIES

INTRODUCTION

There are a variety of techniques for forecasting on the basis of past historical data. These historical data are usually referred to as time series since they consist of a series of actual figures over a past time period.

Much research has been done to find the best forecasting method based on the squared error minimization criterion. The search for the best method has been difficult because some forecasting methods work better on certain sets of historical data than other methods. Hence, the best forecasting method can usually be found after the data has been generated, not before.

Not all forecasting methods are equally easy to apply. Some are more difficult to apply as well as to understand. Some of the complex forecasting methods may give only marginally lower forecast error rates than the easier-to-apply and easier-to-understand methods. Because of their ease of application, the easier-to-apply and easier-to-understand forecasting techniques are usually more popular.

In this chapter we shall present computer models for time series forecasting which use relatively easy to understand methods. They consist of the weighted moving average, the exponential smoothing method without trend, and the exponential smoothing method with trend effects. Also included are the decomposition method and the adaptive exponential smoothing method. The user thus has a choice of five techniques for application to production problems.

We shall explain how each method works starting with weighted moving average forecasting method.

WEIGHTED MOVING AVERAGE FORECASTING

Weighted moving average forecasting uses the weighted average of the most recent n periods. The value for n must be determined by the decision maker but is usually relatively small, say 3 or 4. The term "moving" is used because as each subsequent period forecast is made, it is based on the most recent n periods and the n periods thus move along the time series chain. The weights can be equal for each of the n periods or the weights can vary in each of the n periods. However, if the weights vary, the weights must sum to one (1).

Suppose that we need to make a forecast for period 4 on the basis of historical data for the prior three periods (i.e., n = 3). Also suppose that the weight for period 1 is 0.2, for period 2 is 0.3, and for period 3 is 0.5. The actual observed values for periods 1, 2, and 3 are 25, 30 and 28 respectively. What is the forecast for period 4 using the weighted moving average forecasting method? The forecast for period 4 will then be determined by the formula,

$$F_4 - 0.2(25) + 0.3(30) + 0.5(28) - 28$$

F_4 or 28 is the forecast for period 4.

EXPONENTIAL SMOOTHING FORECASTING WITHOUT TREND

Exponential smoothing is a more complex form of moving average forecasting. In exponential smoothing, theoretically, all actual historical values are considered in the forecast. Hence, instead of just basing a forecast on the most recent three or four periods, a much longer history of data is considered. Features of exponential smoothing are the relative ease of calculation, and the small amount of historical data needed to calculate the next term in the forecast.

The formula for exponential smoothing forecast is of the following form,

$$F_t - \alpha A_{t-1} + (1 - \alpha) F_{t-1}$$

where F_t is the forecast for period t, A_{t-1} is the actual observed value in the previous period (t - 1) and F_{t-1} is the forecast made for the previous period. The coefficient α is a weight between 0 and 1, and is usually set at 0.1 or 0.2. Larger values of α attach more importance to more recent actual values and smaller values of α use a larger sequence of historical data.

To begin using the exponential forecasting method it is necessary to have a beginning value for F_{t-1}. One way of estimating the value for F_{t-1} is to use the actual observed value of A_{t-2}. Then the first forecast will be based on the last two actual observed values.

To illustrate the exponential smoothing forecasting method we shall use the actual observed values of the previous example. The actual observed values for periods 1, 2, and

26

3 were 25, 30, and 28 respectively. Using an α value of 0.2 we shall now use the exponential smoothing method to forecast F_3 for period 3. We then find,

$$F_3 = \alpha A_2 + (1-\alpha)F_2$$

but since we let $F_2 = A_1$ the formula becomes,

$$F_3 = \alpha A_2 + (1-\alpha)A_1$$
$$F_3 = 0.2(30) + 0.8(25) = 26$$

Since the actual observed value for period 3 is 28, the forecast for period 4, F_4, can be determined by the formula,

$$F_4 = \alpha A_3 + (1-\alpha)F_3$$
$$F_4 = 0.2(28) + 0.8(26) = 26.4.$$

As one can observe from the above examples, the three items of data that enter each exponential smoothing forecasting equation are the most recent actual observed values (A_{t-1}), the smoothing constant (α), and the previous forecasted value (F_{t-1}). Hence, once the forecasting process has begun, it is rather straightforward to continue it each period.

DOUBLE EXPONENTIAL SMOOTHING - TREND EFFECTS

Double exponential smoothing will smooth the variation in the forecast more and pick up trend changes quicker than the single exponential smoothing method shown in the previous section. The double exponential smoothing forecast for period t is F_t. It is found by the formula,

$$F_t = 2S'_{t-1} - S''_{t-2}$$

where S'_{t-1} is the single exponential smoothed value. It is found by the formula,

$$S'_{t-1} = \alpha A_{t-1} + (1-\alpha)S'_{t-2}$$

Similarly, the double exponential smoothed value S''_{t-2} can be found by the formula,

$$S''_{t-2} = \beta S'_{t-2} + (1 - \beta)S''_{t-3}.$$

In the above formulas α and β are the single and double smoothing constants respectively. Each constant has a value between 0 and 1, and each is usually set at 0.1 or 0.2. Note that to start up the forecasting sequence requires estimates for S'_{t-2} and S''_{t-3}. One way to obtain these estimates is to set S'_{t-2} equal to S''_{t-3} and use the average of the actual values over the past three or four periods.

To illustrate the double exponential smoothing forecasting method we shall continue with the actual observed values of the previous example. The observed values for periods 1, 2 and 3 are 25, 30 and 28 respectively. Using double exponential smoothing we will forecast demand in period 4, F_4, with the formula,

$$F_4 = 2S'_3 - S''_2.$$

First we must determine S'_3 and S''_2 by their respective formulas. We use values of 0.2 and 0.1 for α and β respectively. The formula for S'_3 is,

$$S'_3 = \alpha A_3 + (1 - \beta)S'_2$$

and the formula for S''_2 is,

$$S''_2 = \beta S'_2 + (1 - \beta) S''_1.$$

For estimates of S'_2 and S''_1 we will use the value 30, which is based on recent actual sales levels. We then obtain,

$$S'_3 = 0.2(28) + 0.8(30) = 29.6$$
$$S''_2 = 0.1(30) + 0.9(30) = 30$$
$$F_4 = 2(29.6) - 30 = 29.2$$

where F_4 is the forecast for period 4.

DECOMPOSITION METHOD

The decomposition method takes into account both additive trend effects and multiplicative seasonal effects. The method decomposes the time series into a component for each season from which a seasonal index or seasonal relative can be generated. For applications where seasonality is critical decomposition is an important and often used method. Other techniques which do not consider seasonal effects will give inaccurate results.

The decomposition method uses linear regression whereby the slope of the linear regression line determines the additive trend. Alternatively, a centered moving average can also be used. The forecast then provides the seasonal index or seasonal relative for each season, the trend value, the ratio of actual to trend, the deseasonalized data, the forecast, the forecast error and the tracking signal. Also provided for the entire forecast horizon are the mean squared error (MSE), the mean absolute deviation (MAD), the bias of the forecast (BIAS), and the coefficient of variation. If requested, a plot of the data and of the forecasts can also be displayed (error measures are discussed below).

The above information is all based on a historical time series of data which must be provided to DSS. Based on the historical data, estimates of the parameters are calculated as stated above. If a forecast for a future period is required, the forecaster then only needs to provide the computer with the time period for which the forecast is required.

ADAPTIVE EXPONENTIAL SMOOTHING

In adaptive exponential smoothing the computer program determines the value of the smoothing constant on the basis of past forecast errors. The constant itself is then adjusted by applying exponential smoothing to a modified form of the forecast error as well as to a modified form of the absolute value of the forecast error.

The forecast equation is given as,

$$F_{t+1} - F_t + \alpha_t(A_t - F_t)$$

where F_t is the forecast for period t, A_t is the actual value for period t, and α_t is the smoothing constant in period t. The smoothing constant α_t is determined by the formula,

$$\alpha_{t+1} - \frac{|E_t|}{|M_t|}$$

where E_t is a modified form of the forecast error and M_t is a modified form of the absolute value of the forecast error. As a result E_t can be any value and M_t can only be non-negative. However, since absolute values are used for E_t and M_t, the value for α_t will always be positive. α_t is also ≤ 1. The modified form of the forecast error, E_t, can be

29

determined by the formula,

$$E_t - \beta(A_t - F_t) + (1 - \beta)E_{t-1}$$

where β is a value between 0 and 1.

Similarly, the modified form of the absolute value of the forecast error can be determined by the formula,

$$M_t - \beta|A_t - F_t| + (1 - \beta)M_{t-1}$$

where β is again a value between 0 and 1. Selection of the value for β is determined by the forecaster. A reasonable value is 0.1 or 0.2. With $\beta = 0.2$, the weight given to the most recent forecast error is 20 percent and the aggregate of earlier errors is given a weight of 80 percent.

To apply the adaptive exponential smoothing method the forecaster must provide an initial forecast value. Otherwise, the DSS program will use the initial data as the initial forecast.

Suppose the following data is available for actual sales of a product in periods 1 through 8. That is $A_1 = 150$, $A_2 = 160$, $A_3 = 145$, $A_4 = 155$, $A_5 = 165$, $A_6 = 150$, $A_7 = 170$, and $A_8 = 175$. Also let $\beta = 0.2$, and set $F_1 = E_0 = M_0 = A_1 = 150$, and $\alpha_1 = 1.0$. Then,

$$F_2 - \alpha_1 A_1 + (1 - \alpha_1)F_1 - 150 + 0 - 150$$

$$E_1 - \beta(A_1 - F_1) + (1 - \beta)E_0 - 0.2(150 - 150) + 0.8(150) - 120$$

$$M_1 - \beta|A_1 - F_1| + (1 - \beta)M_0 - 0.2|150 - 150| + 0.8(150) - 120$$

$$\alpha_2 - \frac{|E_1|}{|M_1|} - \frac{|120|}{|120|} - 1$$

$$F_3 - \alpha_2 A_2 + (1 - \alpha_2)F_2 - 160 + 0 - 160$$

The forecast for period 3 is therefore 160 units. We now proceed to make the forecast for period 4 by the same approach as shown above.

$$E_2 = \beta(A_2 - F_2) + (1-\beta)E_1 = 0.2(160-150) + 0.8(120) = 98$$

$$M_2 = \beta|A_2 - F_2| + (1-\beta)M_1 = 0.2|160-150| + 0.8(120) = 98$$

$$\alpha_3 = \frac{|E_2|}{|M_2|} = \frac{|98|}{|98|} = 1$$

$$F_4 = \alpha_3 A_3 + (1-\alpha_3)F_3 = 145 + 0 = 145$$

The forecast for period 4 is then 145 units. The computations for periods 5, 6, 7, and 8 are shown in Table 1-1.

Period t	Actual observed A_t	Forecast F_t	Smoothed error E_t	Modified error M_t	Adjusted constant α_t
1	150	150.00	120.0	120.0	
2	160	150.00	98.0	98.0	1.000
3	145	160.00	75.4	81.4	1.000
4	155	145.00	62.3	67.1	0.926
5	165	154.26	52.0	55.8	0.928
6	150	164.23	38.7	47.5	0.931
7	170	150.98	34.8	41.8	0.815
8	175	166.49	29.5	35.1	0.832
9		173.57			0.841

Table 1-1: Illustration of Adaptive Exponential Smoothing

From the above illustration, one may observe that initially the smoothing constant, a_t, has a rather high value which then declines to lower values. If the difference between the actual and the forecast remains small over a period of time, the value of a_t will increase towards its maximum value of 1.

MEASURES OF ERROR

The Forecasting program will present several error measures. These measures will be illustrated below. We shall present six forecasts for six periods, the actual values for the six periods, and the forecast errors and their measures for the six periods.

The table shows data points for the six periods. Note that the error measure, E_t, is the difference between the actual value and the forecast.

Period (t)	Actual (A_t)	Forecast (F_t)	Forecast Error (E_t)
1	177	180	-3
2	206	185	+21
3	182	190	-8
4	193	186	+7
5	175	187	-12
6	201	182	+19
Totals	1134	1110	+24

The first error measure is the mean squared error (MSE) which is determined from the actual observations (A_t), the forecasts (F_t) and the number of observations n. The formula used is,

$$MSE - \frac{\sum (A_t - F_t)^2}{n-1} - \frac{1068}{5} - 213.6$$

The mean squared error provides a measure of the squares of the errors. In other words large errors carry more weight than small errors.

The second error measure is the mean absolute deviation (MAD). It is determined by the formula,

$$MAD - \frac{\sum |A_t - F_t|}{n} - \frac{70}{6} - 11.67.$$

32

The mean absolute deviation is the average of each error regardless of whether the forecast was too high or too low.

The third error measure identifies the bias of the forecast (BIAS). It identifies to what extent the forecast is too high or too low, on average. It is determined by the formula,

$$BIAS = \frac{\sum (F_t - A_t)}{n} = -\frac{24}{6} = -4$$

If the BIAS is positive the forecast is too high on average, while if the BIAS is negative, the forecast is too low on average.

The fourth error measure is the tracking signal (TS). The tracking signal focuses on the <u>ratio</u> of the cumulative forecast error to the corresponding value of the mean absolute deviation (MAD). It is found by the formula,

$$TS_t = \frac{\sum (A_k - F_k)}{MAD_t}$$

for t = 3,

$$TS_3 = \frac{-3 + 21 - 8}{(3 + 21 + 8)/3} = 0.94.$$

The fifth error measure is the coefficient of variation (CV). The coefficient of variation is the ratio between the standard deviation and the mean of the actual observed values. It is determined by the formula,

$$CV = \frac{\sqrt{MSE}}{\sum (A_t)/n} = \frac{\sqrt{213.6}}{1134/6} = 0.077$$

The coefficient of variation <u>modifies</u> the square root of the errors by the average magnitude of the actual variation in observed values. As such, it is used as a comparison measure when comparing forecasts based on different sets of data.

SOLVED EXAMPLE - TIME SERIES FORECASTING

To demonstrate the use of the Time Series Forecasting Program, suppose the sales for a software package over the past 12 months are shown below. The objective of this program is to forecast the sales volume for the software for the 13th month using the methods of Moving Averages, Decomposition Method, Exponential Smoothing (with and without trend), and Adaptive Exponential Smoothing.

Month	Sales Volume (Units)
1	700
2	725
3	720
4	730
5	740
6	745
7	760
8	755
9	770
10	785
11	780
12	800

To begin the forecasting process, load the DSSPOM program into the computer and select the "Time Series Forecasting" program from the Main Menu. The computer will pause for a few seconds and then display the Forecast Menu. Move the pointer to the INPUT option and press <ENTER> to select this option. The program will begin the data input process by moving the pointer to the title field. Type "SOFTWARE SALES" and press <ENTER>. The program will then ask for the number of data points. This problem has 12 data points, enter "12" and press <ENTER>. The input data screen is shown below.

```
Problem title: SOFTWARE SALES


Number of observations: 12



┌──────────────────────────────────────────────────────────┐
│ Enter problem parameters as requested.  Press RETURN to  │
│ accept, or ESC to exit.   Maximum problem size is 50 data│
│ points, observations should be within -9999 and 9999.    │
└──────────────────────────────────────────────────────────┘
```

The computer will then ask if you wish to continue to enter the data points as shown below.

```
┌──────────────────────────────────────────────┐
│ Continue with the observations (Y/N) Y        │
└──────────────────────────────────────────────┘
```

Press < Y > to continue with the data entry process. The computer will then display a spread sheet editor for the data entry. The first column of the spread sheet (column A) has been initialized with the 12 time periods and contains numbers 1,2,..,12. The second column (column B) is entitled "Value". Move the pointer to cell B2 to enter the first data point. Press the < ENTER > key and move the pointer to cell B3 to enter the second data point. Repeat the process and enter all of the 12 data points. The completed spread sheet data entry screen is shown below.

```
                                                      ⊣READY⊢
Al Period
          A         B
1      Period Value
2          1   700.00
3          2   725.00
4          3   720.00
5          4   730.00
6          5   740.00
7          6   745.00
8          7   760.00
9          8   755.00
10         9   770.00
11        10   785.00
12        11   780.00
13        12   800.00
```

After completing the data entry process, press <F10> to keep the data in memory and exit the spread sheet editor.

You may obtain a hard copy printout of the input data by moving the pointer to the PRINT option and press <ENTER>. Be sure that the printer is ON and Ready. After obtaining a hard copy printout, examine it carefully for possible typing mistakes. If the input data contains an error, move the pointer to the EDIT option and press the <ENTER> key. The program will resume the edit process. The edit process is exactly the same as the initial data input process. Complete the editing and return to the Forecast Menu.

You are now ready to solve the problem. Begin the forecasting process by moving the pointer to the SOLVE option. The program will display three sub-options: 1- Display output; 2-Print output; and 3-Save output. Initially the first option is high-lighted. Press the <ENTER> key to choose this option as shown below.

```
Input  Edit  Print  File  Solve  Quit
                          ┌──────────────────┐
                          │ Display output   │
                          │ Print output     │
                          │ Save output      │
                          └──────────────────┘
```

The computer will begin the solution process by displaying several solution techniques as shown below.

```
┌──────────────────────────┐
│ Weighted Moving Average  │
│ Decomposition Method     │
│ Exponential Smoothing    │
│ Expon. Smooth. & Trend   │
│ Adaptive Expon. Smooth.  │
└──────────────────────────┘
```

```
┌────────────────────────────────────────────────────────┐
│ Use the arrow keys to highlight a method,  press the ENTER │
│ key to forecast ESC to exit.                           │
└────────────────────────────────────────────────────────┘
```

The first forecasting option is weighted moving average. Select this option by pressing the <ENTER> key. The computer will request the number of terms and also inquire if the weights are equal. Use a 4-period equally weighted forecast. The completed screen is shown below.

```
┌──────────────────────────────────────────────────────┐
│                                                      │
│  Number of terms to average   4                      │
│                                                      │
│                                                      │
│              ┌──────────────────────────┐            │
│              │ Are the weights equal (Y/N) Y │         │
│              └──────────────────────────┘            │
│                                                      │
└──────────────────────────────────────────────────────┘
```

The computer will resume the solution process by displaying the following output report.

```
                    Problem Title: SOFTWARE SALES

                                              Tracking
    Time    Actual     Forecast    Error      Signal
    ----    --------   ---------   -------    --------
     1      700.000
     2      725.000
     3      720.000
     4      730.000
     5      740.000    718.750     21.25       1.00
     6      745.000    728.750     16.25       2.00
     7      760.000    733.750     26.25       3.00
     8      755.000    743.750     11.25       4.00
     9      770.000    750.000     20.00       5.00
    10      785.000    757.500     27.50       6.00
```

```
                    Problem Title: SOFTWARE SALES

                                              Tracking
    Time    Actual     Forecast    Error      Signal
    ----    --------   ---------   -------    --------
    11      780.000    767.500     12.50       7.00
    12      800.000    772.500     27.50       8.00
    13                 783.750




    MSE =      514.29  MAD =        20.31  Bias =     -20.31
    Coefficient of variation =      0.03
```

Based on the above report, the forecast for time period 13 is 783.75. The forecast has mean squared error equal 514.29, mean absolute deviation is 20.31, a bias of -20.31, and the coefficient of variation is 0.03.

EXAMPLE 2 - USING EXPONENTIAL SMOOTHING

The previous forecast appears to have a relatively large MSE. Try to obtain a better forecast by utilizing exponential smoothing. Move the pointer to the SOLVE option and select the "Display output" sub-option. When presented with the menu of the solution techniques, pull the bar down two levels to "Exponential Smoothing", and press the <ENTER> key (process not shown here). The computer will continue the solution process by asking you to enter a smoothing constant. Use a smoothing constant of 0.40 and press <N> to indicate that there is no initial forecast as shown below.

```
Enter the Smoothing Constant    0.40



        Do you have an initial forecast (Y/N) N
```

The computer will report that the initial data will be used as the initial forecast as shown below.

```
Initial data will be used as initial forecast.
```

Press a key to continue and obtain the following solution report.

```
                     Problem Title: SOFTWARE SALES

                                                 Tracking
    Time      Actual      Forecast     Error      Signal
    ----    ---------    ---------    -------    --------
      1      700.000
      2      725.000      700.000      25.00       1.00
      3      720.000      710.000      10.00       2.00
      4      730.000      714.000      16.00       3.00
      5      740.000      720.400      19.60       4.00
      6      745.000      728.240      16.76       5.00
      7      760.000      734.944      25.06       6.00
      8      755.000      744.966      10.03       7.00
      9      770.000      748.980      21.02       8.00
     10      785.000      757.388      27.61       9.00
```

```
                    Problem Title: SOFTWARE SALES

                                                    Tracking
                                                    Signal
    Time      Actual      Forecast      Error
    ----      ----------  ----------    --------    --------
     11       780.000     768.433       11.57       10.00
     12       800.000     773.060       26.94       11.00
     13                   783.836



    MSE =      443.84  MAD =        19.05   Bias =    -19.05
    Coefficient of variation =       0.03
```

As seen from the above output reports, the exponential smoothing forecast with a constant of 0.4 is performing better than the earlier forecast. In this case, MSE is 443.84 and MAD is 19.05. The BIAS of the forecast is also slightly better than the earlier forecast and is equal -19.05.

EXAMPLE 3 - USING EXPONENTIAL SMOOTHING WITH TREND

This example involves using the exponential smoothing technique again but this time include a trend component. Move the pointer to the SOLVE option and select the display output sub-option. From the menu of solution techniques, select the 'Expon. Smooth. & Trend" option. The computer will ask you to enter two smoothing constants: one for single smoothing; and a second for double smoothing. Enter 0.40 for both as shown below.

```
    Enter the Single Smoothing Constant    0.40

    Enter the Double Smoothing Constant    0.40


        Do you have an initial forecast (Y/N) N
```

39

The computer will report that the initial data will be used as initial forecast. It will then present the output report as shown below.

```
+--------------------------------------------------------------------+
|                   Problem Title: SOFTWARE SALES                     |
|                                                                    |
|                                                      Tracking       |
|     Time      Actual      Forecast      Error        Signal         |
|     ----      ----------  ----------    -------       --------       |
|      1        700.000                                               |
|      2        725.000     700.000       25.00         1.00          |
|      3        720.000     720.000        0.00         2.00          |
|      4        730.000     724.000        6.00         3.00          |
|      5        740.000     732.800        7.20         4.00          |
|      6        745.000     743.520        1.48         5.00          |
|      7        760.000     750.816        9.18         6.00          |
|      8        755.000     764.512       -9.51         4.72          |
|      9        770.000     764.721        5.28         5.61          |
|     10        785.000     775.240        9.76         6.67          |
|                                                                    |
+--------------------------------------------------------------------+
```

```
+--------------------------------------------------------------------+
|                   Problem Title: SOFTWARE SALES                     |
|                                                                    |
|                                                      Tracking       |
|     Time      Actual      Forecast      Error        Signal         |
|     ----      ----------  ----------    -------       --------       |
|     11        780.000     790.189      -10.19         5.29          |
|     12        800.000     790.740        9.26         6.33          |
|     13                    805.220                                  |
|                                                                    |
|                                                                    |
|   MSE =     120.25  MAD =        8.44  Bias =       -4.86           |
|   Coefficient of variation =     0.01                              |
+--------------------------------------------------------------------+
```

Note that the above forecast is even more accurate than the previous two. The mean squared error is about 120 with a mean absolute deviation of 8.44. The forecast for time period 13 is 805.22.

EXAMPLE 4 - TIME SERIES DECOMPOSITION

When time series data is influenced by variations due change in seasons, a time series decomposition, accounting for seasonal variations, may result in a better forecast. For the above example, suppose that the data represent quarterly sales, collected over a 3 year period. Obtain a seasonally-adjusted forecast for the first quarter of the fourth year (time period 13).

To solve this problem, move the pointer to the SOLVE option and select the display output sub-option. When presented with the menu of solution techniques, select the "Decomposition Method". The computer will ask you to enter the number of seasons per year. Enter 4 for this value and press <ENTER> as shown below.

```
Number of seasons per year  4
```

The computer will continue the solution process by reporting the seasonal indexes as shown below.

```
The seasonal indices are:
Season      Index
------      -----
  1         0.997
  2         1.007
  3         0.998
  4         0.998
```

Seasonal indexes indicate the variation in the data as a percentage of trend. For example, the first seasonal index is 0.997. This value implies that the sales during the first quarter is about 99.7 percent of the trend. The four seasonal relatives presented above, indicate that variation in sales due to seasonality is not substantial (all four indexes are close to 1). Press <ENTER> to continue with the solution process. The computer will ask if you wish to see the deseasonalized data as shown below.

41

```
                    Problem Title: SOFTWARE SALES



        Do you wish to see the deseasonalized data (Y/N) Y
```

Press <Y> to obtain a report of the deseasonalized data as shown below.

```
                    Problem Title: SOFTWARE SALES
                                            Deseason
Time      Actual       Trend        Ratio    alized
----      ---------    ---------    -------- ---------
  1       700.000      706.410       0.99     702.03
  2       725.000      714.487       1.01     720.23
  3       720.000      722.564       1.00     721.41
  4       730.000      730.641       1.00     731.30
  5       740.000      738.718       1.00     742.14
  6       745.000      746.795       1.00     740.10
  7       760.000      754.872       1.01     761.49
  8       755.000      762.949       0.99     756.34
  9       770.000      771.026       1.00     772.23
 10       785.000      779.103       1.01     779.83
 11       780.000      787.179       0.99     781.53
 12       800.000      795.256       1.01     801.42
```

The next output report includes the trend equation. This equation is the usual linear regression line through the data points as shown below.

```
                    Problem Title: SOFTWARE SALES
                                            Deseason
Time      Actual       Trend        Ratio    alized
----      ---------    ---------    -------- ---------


   The trend equation is: Intercept =    698.333  , Slope =    8.077
```

The slope of the regression line represents the annual rate of growth in sales. The computer will then ask if you wish to forecast for another time period. Press <Y> to continue.

```
+------------------------------------------------------------+
|              Problem Title: SOFTWARE SALES                 |
|                                                            |
|        +-------------------------------------------+       |
|        | Forecast for another time period (Y/N) Y  |       |
|        +-------------------------------------------+       |
|                                                            |
+------------------------------------------------------------+
```

Next, enter 13 and press <ENTER> to obtain the forecast for time period 13 as shown below.

```
+------------------------------------------------------------+
|              Problem Title: SOFTWARE SALES                 |
|                                                            |
|                                                            |
|                                                            |
|     Enter the time period: 13                              |
|                                                            |
|     For time period:  13                                   |
|                                                            |
|     Trend =      803.33                                    |
|                                                            |
|     Forecast =    801.01                                   |
|                                                            |
|                                                            |
|          +-------------------------------------------+     |
|          | Forecast for another time period (Y/N) N  |     |
|          +-------------------------------------------+     |
|                                                            |
|                                                            |
+------------------------------------------------------------+
```

As seen from the above output report, the forecast for time period 13, or the first quarter of the fourth year, is 801.01 with a trend value of 803.33. Next, press <N> to continue with the solution process as shown below.

```
                    Problem Title: SOFTWARE SALES

                                                  Tracking
              Actual        Forecast     Error     Signal
 Time         ------        --------     -----    --------
 ----
  1           700.000       704.369      -4.37     -1.00
  2           725.000       719.222       5.78      0.28
  3           720.000       721.149      -1.15      0.07
  4           730.000       729.343       0.66      0.31
  5           740.000       736.583       3.42      1.41
  6           745.000       751.744      -6.74     -0.65
  7           760.000       753.393       6.61      1.02
  8           755.000       761.593      -6.59     -0.54
  9           770.000       768.798       1.20     -0.29
 10           785.000       784.265       0.73     -0.12
```

```
                    Problem Title: SOFTWARE SALES

                                                  Tracking
              Actual        Forecast     Error     Signal
 Time         ------        --------     -----    --------
 ----
 11           780.000       785.638      -5.64     -1.56
 12           800.000       793.843       6.16      0.01
 13                         801.906



 MSE =         24.56  MAD =        4.09  Bias =     -0.01
 Coefficient of variation =        0.01
```

As seen from the above output report, the decomposition technique is by far the most accurate forecasting technique (for the time series data at hand) than those used in earlier examples. The value of MSE in this case is 24.56 with a MAD of 4.09 and bias equal -0.01.

EXAMPLE 5 - ADAPTIVE SMOOTHING

This example involves the use of adaptive smoothing to obtain a forecast for the software sales data. Move the pointer the SOLVE option and select the display output sub-option. When presented with the menu of solution techniques, move the bar to the last row, "Adaptive Expon. Smooth.", and press <ENTER>. The computer will ask if you have an initial forecast. Press <N> to continue. The computer will then inform you that the first data point will be used as the initial forecast. Press <ENTER> to continue with the output report as shown below.

Problem Title: SOFTWARE SALES

Time	Actual	Forecast	Error	Tracking Signal	Alpha
1	700.000				
2	725.000	700.000	25.00	1.00	1.000
3	720.000	725.000	-5.00	1.33	1.000
4	730.000	720.000	10.00	2.25	0.994
5	740.000	729.945	10.06	3.20	0.995
6	745.000	739.945	5.05	4.09	0.995
7	760.000	744.973	15.03	5.14	0.995
8	755.000	759.919	-4.92	5.15	0.995
9	770.000	755.026	14.97	6.24	0.979
10	785.000	769.686	15.31	7.31	0.980

Problem Title: SOFTWARE SALES

Time	Actual	Forecast	Error	Tracking Signal	Alpha
11	780.000	784.688	-4.69	7.34	0.980
12	800.000	780.092	19.91	8.53	0.954
13		799.075			0.957

MSE = 200.37 MAD = 11.81 Bias = -9.16
Coefficient of variation = 0.02

As seen from the above report, the adaptive exponential smoothing is not as appropriate as the previous forecasting technique for the time series data at hand. The mean squared error is much larger and the forecast is somewhat more biased.

45

PROBLEMS

1. Apply all forecasting methods, except the decomposition method, to the actual observed values of 20, 25, 27, 24, 23, 29, 26, 27, 28, and 26 for periods 1 to 10 respectively. Set the initial value of the forecast equal to 25 when requested. Use α and β values of 0.3 and 0.4 respectively and use from 3, 4 and 5 periods in your moving average. Do not use weighting in moving average method.

2. For the data in problem 1 develop a table to show the comparison between the forecast errors of the four forecasting methods as shown below.

Method	MSE	MAD	BIAS	CV
Weighted Moving Average				
Exponential Smoothing No Trend				
Double Exponential Smoothing				
Adaptive Exponential Smoothing				

3. Repeat problem 2 but use the following parameter values, $\alpha = 0.2$ and $\beta = 0.3$. Also for the weighted moving average method use three periods with weights of 0.2 for the most distant period, 0.3 for the middle period and 0.5 for the most recent period.

4. For the set of actual observed data shown below, evaluate the four forecasting methods in the forecasting module. For the moving average method use five periods and equal weights, for the no-trend exponential method use a smoothing constant (α) value of 0.2, for the exponential forecasting method with trend use a smoothing constant value of $\alpha = 0.2$ and a trend smoothing constant of $\beta = 0.1$, and for adaptive smoothing set the initial forecast to 100. The actual observed data for periods 1 to 10 are respectively: 110, 95, 85, 110, 100, 98, 97, 108, 106, and 104.

5. You are provided with historical monthly sales figures for the year 1987 consisting of 85, 90, 95, 98, 100, 110, 115, 112, 106, 120, 125, and 124 units respectively for the months January through December. Using a trend adjusted exponential smoothing model, what is the sales forecast for January, 1988? Would you recommend a trend or a no-trend exponential smoothing forecasting method for the data in this problem? Use $\alpha = 0.3$ and $\beta = 0.2$.

6. For problem 5 use an adaptive smoothing forecasting model with initial forecast equal to 100. Compare the error measures with problem 5 error measures.

7. Apply the decomposition forecasting method to the following set of historical data.

Year	Quarter	Units	Year	Quarter	Units
1	1	1020	2	3	1600
1	2	900	2	4	240
1	3	1500	3	1	1160
1	4	210	3	2	950
2	1	1080	3	3	1700
2	2	910	3	4	250

8.   A canning factory contracts with local tomato growers for a specified acreage of tomatoes every year. The number of acres contracted has increased at the rate of about 10 percent per year and management of the canning factory plans to continue the 10 percent annual increase in acreage in the future. Based on the contracted acreage, the tomato growers can deliver their entire crop to the canning factory at an agreed upon price. Management of the canning factory would like to project a trend of tomato processing volume into the future to determine what plant additions are required in the future. The tomato supply in tons per year is shown below for the past 10 years.

a)   Using four year moving average what will supply be in 1989?

b)   Using exponential smoothing with trend what will supply be in the year 1989? Use smoothing constants of 0.2.

c)   What is mean absolute deviation, mean squared error and tracking signal in part b?

Year	Tons(000)	Year	Tons(000)
1979	5.60	1984	8.30
1980	6.10	1985	8.90
1981	6.30	1986	9.50
1982	7.00	1987	10.50
1983	7.50	1988	10.60

9. A health maintenance organization is attempting to project its membership growth over the next three years. Over the past three years it has kept track of quarterly net membership growth. Net membership growth consists of new members, less members who resigned. The net membership growth is shown below.

a)   Using a moving average with four quarters determine what the net membership projections will be in the four quarters of 1989?

b)   Using exponential smoothing with and without trend what will net membership growth be in the first quarter of 1989? Use smoothing constants of 0.3.

c)   What is mean absolute deviation, mean squared error, and tracking signal for the historical data?

Quarter	Membership(000)
1-86	70.119
2-86	73.467
3-86	78.835
4-86	83.911
1-87	85.716
2-87	86.481
3-87	87.329
4-87	92.916
1-88	96.980
2-88	97.453
3-88	97.314
4-88	97.193

10. The Oxford Company is in the process of evaluating its demand forecasting methods. Up through December 1988, the company has used a five month moving average forecast unadjusted for trend. For 1989, it is considering using an exponential smoothing approach adjusted for trend. It is planning to use a smoothing constant of 0.2 for the basic component and 0.4 for the trend component. The following is a history of demand during 1988 for the Oxford Company.

t	Year 1988	Sales in Units
1	January	100
2	February	105
3	March	95
4	April	100
5	May	100
6	June	140
7	July	105
8	August	110
9	September	110
10	October	115
11	November	120
12	December	125

Compute the sales forecast (trend adjusted) for June to December 1988 using both the moving average and the exponential smoothing techniques.

11. Determine Mean Absolute Deviation (MAD) and Bias for both the five month moving average and the exponential smoothing model forecasts of the Oxford Company (previous problem).

12.   Hannie Harmer Candy Company sells its products through a chain of specialty chocolate stores. It has been prone to high production variation due to forecasting errors by inexperienced management. Below are the demands for pounds of Coconut Clusters in the past 4 weeks. The manufacturing plant is closed on Saturday, so Friday's production must meet the demand for Saturday and Sunday.

Forecast the demand for next week based on the following:

a)   Daily demand using a 3 week moving average.

b)   Daily demand using a weighted average of 0.4, 0.2, and 0.4 for the past 3 weeks.

c)   Hannie Harmer is also trying to plan its purchasing requirements for its chocolate fudge. Managers had forecasted a stable weekly demand of 16,000 pounds, but only 14,500 were sold last week and 17,000 were sold the week before. Determine what Hannie Harmer's forecast for the week should be using a smoothing constant of 0.10.

d)   The production team went with your forecast in (c) and actual demand turned out to be 16,500 pounds. What forecast will you provide the team with for the following week?

	4 wks. ago	3 wks. ago	2 wks. ago	Last Week
Monday	1800	2000	1900	2000
Tuesday	1600	1700	1800	1800
Wednesday	1900	2000	1900	2100
Thursday	1400	1500	1400	1600
Friday	1500	1400	1700	1600
Saturday	1200	1200	1200	1300
Sunday	1200	1100	1400	1200

13.   Lerned Industries cannot decide which forecasting method is best suited to their needs. Demand for the past 11 months is shown below.

a)   Forecast demand for June through November using a 3 month moving average.

b)   Forecast the demand for June through November using exponential smoothing without trend and a smoothing constant of 0.10. Use actual data as the initial forecast.

c)   Compare estimated demand with the actual demand . Based on MAD and MSE, choose the best method and state your reasons.

MONTH	ACTUAL DEMAND	MONTH	ACTUAL DEMAND
January	150	September	130
February	120	October	140
March	110	November	145
April	130		
May	145		
June	105		
July	125		
August	150		

14. Afreka Corporation is involved in their yearly planning session in which they forecast revenues and profits for the remaining part of the year. They have called you in to provide a forecast of weekly and monthly sales figures. Actual sales data from the first half of the year is given below.

a) Give a monthly forecast for each month in the third quarter of this year. Use an exponential smoothing approach with $\alpha = 0.10$ and $\beta = 0.30$.

b) Calculate a weekly forecast for the third quarter using the same approach as in (a).

c) Do both methods produce the same monthly results? If not, which forecasts would you rather have? Why?

	WEEKLY SALES(000)	MONTHLY SALES(000)
January		50.0
1	15.0	
2	7.9	
3	8.1	
4	19.0	
February		56.0
1	21.0	
2	17.0	
3	10.0	
4	8.0	
March		53.0
1	9.5	
2	13.0	
3	14.0	
4	16.5	
April		58.0
1	18.0	
2	16.0	
3	12.0	
4	12.0	
May		56.0
1	12.0	
2	17.0	
3	11.0	
4	16.0	
June		54.0
1	14.0	
2	12.0	
3	11.0	
4	17.0	

CHAPTER 2

MULTIPLE REGRESSION

INTRODUCTION

Multiple regression allows one to evaluate the statistical relationship between two or more variables. The method also allows the establishment of prediction equations such that one variable, the dependent variable, can be predicted on the basis of one or more other, independent variables. The multiple regression method can be used to forecast sales, costs and other numeric values on the basis of other numeric variables.

Although the statistical relationship between two or more variables is evaluated by the multiple regression technique, the causal relationship is not. Hence, the user of multiple regression must assure him or herself of the relevance of the relationship between two variables. In some cases this is easy and straightforward. In other cases this is not so. For instance, the relationship between price of a product and demand for a product is clearly related, and a solid causal relationship can be assured. The multiple regression analysis will then be able to tell you if a statistical relationship also exists. Sometimes a statistical relationship may exist but a causal relationship cannot be explained or assumed. In that case the relationship should not be used.

MULTIPLE REGRESSION ANALYSIS

Multiple regression can be symbolically stated as follows,

$$Y = f(X_1, X_2, ..., X_n)$$

where Y is the dependent variable which is predicted on the basis of the independent variables $X_1, X_2, ..., X_n$.

For four independent variables the symbolic equation above would be expressed as follows,

$$Y = \beta_0 + \beta_1 X_1 + \beta_2 X_2 + \beta_3 X_3 + \beta_4 X_4.$$

The coefficients consist of β_0, the intercept and β_1, β_2, β_3, and β_4.

The purpose of the multiple regression calculation is to estimate the values of the coefficients. Estimates of the coefficients β_0, β_1, β_2, β_3, and β_4 are usually written as b_0, b_1, b_2, b_3, and b_4.

To estimate the coefficients we need a certain number of observations on the values of

Y, $X_1, X_2, X_3,$ and X_4. The recommended number of observations is usually about five times the number of independent variables. Hence in the above case one would need about twenty observations. The program described below will take up to 60 observations and will be able to apply the multiple regression technique to up to ten independent variables.

EXAMPLE 1 - MULTIPLE REGRESSION

In this example you will use multiple regression to explore the statistical relationship between cholesterol level and age and height. In case there is a significant relation, you can use multiple regression to predict the cholesterol level of a new observation. The data for this example problem is presented in Table 2-1 below.

Table 2-1: Cholesterol Level for 12 Individuals

Cholesterol Level (units)	Age (years)	Height (inches)
50	20	67
100	25	67
150	20	65
157	33	60
600	60	65
300	26	67
175	35	78
476	36	61
243	41	70
250	44	71
198	27	78
200	33	60

Load the DSSPOM into the computer and select Multiple Regression from the Main Menu. After the program has been loaded, move the pointer to the right one level to select the INPUT option. Press <ENTER> to select this option and continue with data entry process as shown below.

```
 Problem title: MULTIPLE REGRESSION

 Number of independent variables:  2

 Number of observations: 12




              | Continue with observations (Y/N) Y |
```

As seen from the above display screen, there are 2 independent variables and 12 observations. The two independent variables correspond to AGE and HEIGHT. Press the <ENTER> key to continue with data entry process. The completed spread sheet is shown below.

```
                                                              =|READY|=
A1
            A          B         C         D
1                    CHOLES     AGE      HEIGHT
2     Obs1           50.00     20.00     67.00
3     Obs2          100.00     25.00     67.00
4     Obs3          150.00     20.00     65.00
5     Obs4          157.00     33.00     60.00
6     Obs5          600.00     60.00     65.00
7     Obs6          300.00     26.00     67.00
8     Obs7          175.00     35.00     78.00
9     Obs8          476.00     36.00     61.00
10    Obs9          243.00     41.00     70.00
11    Obs10         250.00     44.00     71.00
12    Obs11         198.00     27.00     78.00
13    Obs12         200.00     33.00     60.00
```

Check the data carefully and make sure there are no typing mistakes. Press <F10> to keep the data and exit from the spread sheet editor.

You can now obtain a hard copy printout of the input data by moving the pointer two levels to the right to the PRINT option and press <ENTER>. Make sure that the printer is on and ready before you proceed.

To save the input data on disk, move the pointer to the FILE option and pull the bar down to the "Save current file" sub-option. Now press the <ENTER> key to select this option. The computer will display the current drive and path and will ask you to enter a file name. Press the <END> function to move the cursor to the end of the edit field. Enter a DOS file name to save the data and press <ENTER>. The computer will save the data on disk for future sessions.

You are now ready to solve the problem. Move the pointer to the SOLVE option and select the "Display Output" sub-option. The computer will take a few moments to solve the problem and display the following results.

```
                   Problem Title: MULTIPLE REGRESSION
                 Regression Function Coefficients:

      Coeff.        Value          St. Dev.        T-Ratio
      ------       ----------     -----------     ----------
        B0          218.193        364.956          0.598
        B1           10.549          2.777          3.798
        B2           -4.869          5.175         -0.941
```

The first screen (above) reports the regression function equation. That is, the estimated value of intercept (b_0), and the coefficients of the two independent variables AGE (b_1) and HEIGHT (b_2) are reported as well as their standard deviations and t scores. As seen from the above report, the intercept is 218.192, the coefficient of AGE is 10.549, and that of HEIGHT is -4.869. The regression function equation is therefore:

Cholesterol = 218.198 + 10.549 (AGE) - 4.869 (HEIGHT).

Press the <ENTER> key to continue with additional output report as shown below.

```
                    Problem Title: MULTIPLE REGRESSION
                    Analysis  of  Variance  Table

      Source      DF           SS              MS
      ------      --------     -----------     -----------
      Regress.    2            169285.847      84642.924

      Residual    9             97967.069      10885.230
      ------      --------     -----------     -----------
      Total       11           267252.917

      Coefficient of Determination R-Squared =        0.633

      Residual Standard Deviation =       104.332

                    +--------------------------------+
                    | Predicted Y Values (Y/N) Y     |
                    +--------------------------------+
```

The second output screen consists of the analysis of variance table. In this report you will find a measure of the strength of the relation namely, the coefficient of determination, R-squared. This value is 0.633 which implies that about 63.3 percent of the variance (in Cholesterol) can be explained by variation in AGE and person's HEIGHT.

To examine the predicted values, press < Y >. The following output report will be displayed.

```
                    Problem Title: MULTIPLE REGRESSION

   Observ.     Actual (Y)     Predicted     Error      ST. Error
   --------    ----------     ---------     ------     ---------
   Obs1          50.00        102.96        -52.96       -0.51
   Obs2         100.00        155.70        -55.70       -0.53
   Obs3         150.00        112.69         37.31        0.36
   Obs4         157.00        274.18       -117.18       -1.12
   Obs5         600.00        534.66         65.34        0.63
   Obs6         300.00        166.25        133.75        1.28
   Obs7         175.00        207.64        -32.64       -0.31
   Obs8         476.00        300.96        175.04        1.68
   Obs9         243.00        309.88        -66.88       -0.64
   Obs10        250.00        336.66        -86.66       -0.83
   Obs11        198.00        123.24         74.76        0.72
   Obs12        200.00        274.18        -74.18       -0.71
```

The computer will then ask you if you wish to predict for another observation.

```
Wish to determine Y value for an observation (Y/N) Y
```

To find the cholesterol level for a person of age 55 and 62 inch tall, press <Y> and enter the data in appropriate fields as shown below.

```
                  Problem Title: MULTIPLE REGRESSION


    Enter value for AGE:            55

    Enter value for HEIGHT:         62

    The value of Y is      496.522



                              More (Y/N) N
```

Press <N> to return to the Regression Menu and continue with the next solved example.

EXAMPLE 2 - ADDING ANOTHER VARIABLE

Suppose you have data on an additional variable (i.e., WEIGHT) for 12 individuals in the above example. The values are 85, 110, 121, 150, 317, 230, 130, 268, 147, 160, 132, and 150 for individuals 1 through 12, respectively. In order to add this new variable to the model, you can invoke the model editor and enter the data. To begin, move the pointer to the EDIT option. The EDIT option has three sub-options, the first one is labeled "Input Data". Press <ENTER> to select this option. The computer will respond by placing the pointer in the existing fields on the screen. You may edit these fields one at a time as desired.

Press the <ENTER> key to accept the current title and move to the next field. Move the cursor one position to the right and type <3> as the number of independent variables. Press <ENTER> once to enter 3 and one more time to accept 12 as the number of observations. The completed display screen is presented below.

```
 ┌─────────────────────────────────────────────────────────────┐
 │                                                             │
 │   Problem title: MULTIPLE REGRESSION                        │
 │                                                             │
 │   Number of independent variables:  3                       │
 │                                                             │
 │   Number of observations: 12                                │
 │                                                             │
 │            ┌────────────────────────────────────────┐       │
 │            │  Continue with observations (Y/N) Y     │       │
 │            └────────────────────────────────────────┘       │
 │                                                             │
 └─────────────────────────────────────────────────────────────┘
```

Press < Y > to continue with the spread sheet data entry. Note that the spread sheet now contains one more variable labeled "VAR3" with all observations equal 0. Move the pointer to the variable heading (cell E1) and change it to "WEIGHT". Now move the pointer down and enter the data values for the 12 observations under WEIGHT. The completed spread sheet is presented below.

```
                                                           ╡READY╞
┌──────────────────────────────────────────────────────────────┐
│E13    150                                                     │
│          A         B         C         D         E            │
│1                CHOLES     AGE     HEIGHT    WEIGHT            │
│2     Obs1        50.00    20.00    67.00     85.00            │
│3     Obs2       100.00    25.00    67.00    110.00            │
│4     Obs3       150.00    20.00    65.00    121.00            │
│5     Obs4       157.00    33.00    60.00    150.00            │
│6     Obs5       600.00    60.00    65.00    317.00            │
│7     Obs6       300.00    26.00    67.00    230.00            │
│8     Obs7       175.00    35.00    78.00    130.00            │
│9     Obs8       476.00    36.00    61.00    268.00            │
│10    Obs9       243.00    41.00    70.00    147.00            │
│11    Obs10      250.00    44.00    71.00    160.00            │
│12    Obs11      198.00    27.00    78.00    132.00            │
│13    Obs12      200.00    33.00    60.00    150.00            │
└──────────────────────────────────────────────────────────────┘
```

After completeing the data entry, press <F10> to keep the data and exit from the spread sheet editor.

You are now ready to solve the revised problem. Move the pointer to SOLVE option and select the display output as before. The output reports are shown below.

58

```
                    Problem Title: MULTIPLE REGRESSION
                    Regression Function Coefficients:

    Coeff.       Value          St. Dev.        T-Ratio
    ------       -----          --------        -------
     B0         -283.844        120.878         -2.348
     B1            2.335          1.190           1.962
     B2            1.738          1.692           1.028
     B3            1.982          0.206           9.632
```

The revised regression function equation is:

Cholesterol = -283.844 + 2.335 (AGE) + 1.738 (HEIGHT) + 1.982 (WEIGHT).

The next report will present the analysis of variance table as shown below.

```
                    Problem Title: MULTIPLE REGRESSION
                    Analysis  of  Variance  Table

    Source      DF            SS              MS
    ------      --            --              --
    Regress.     3        259476.076       86492.025

    Residual     8          7776.841         972.105
    ------      --          --------         -------
    Total       11        267252.917

    Coefficient of Determination R-Squared =      0.971

    Residual Standard Deviation =       31.179

              Predicted Y Values (Y/N) N
```

Notice the increase in the value of R-squared due to the inclusion of the new variable. The regression model can now explain about 97 percent of variance.

EXAMPLE 3 - FORECASTING WITH MULTIPLE REGRESSION

This example involves the use of multiple regression in time series forecasting. In particular, multiple regression will be used to account for seasonality in time series analysis. The data in Table 2-2 represents quarterly demand for a seasonal component, collected over a three year period. You will use this data to forecast the demand for the first quarter of the fourth year.

To solve the problem, you must first find the regression function equation which represents the demand. Because the data has been collected on a quarterly basis, you hypothesize that the demand may vary depending on the season as represented by each quarterly period. The forecasting equation then becomes:

$$Y_t = b_0 + b_1 t + b_2 X_1 + b_3 X_2 + b_4 X_3,$$

where, Y_t is the demand at time t, X_1, X_2, and X_3 are three binary variables used to represent the seasonal (quarter) effect. For example, for time periods corresponding to the first quarter (e.g., t = 1, t = 5, t = 9, etc.), let $X_1 = 1$, $X_2 = X_3 = 0$. For time periods corresponding to the second quarters (e.g., t = 2, t = 6, t = 10, etc.) let $X_1 = 0$, $X_2 = 1$,

Table 2-2: Quarterly Demands

Year	Quarter	Demand (in 000)
1	1	10.5
	2	12.0
	3	15.8
	4	13.2
2	1	12.7
	2	14.6
	3	17.9
	4	15.2
3	1	14.3
	2	16.7
	3	19.1
	4	17.4

Table 7-3: Input Data for Multiple Regression

Demand(Y)	Time(t)	X1	X2	X3
10.5	1	1	0	0
12.0	2	0	1	0
15.8	3	0	0	1
13.2	4	0	0	0
12.7	5	1	0	0
14.6	6	0	1	0
17.9	7	0	0	1
15.2	8	0	0	0
14.3	9	1	0	0
16.7	10	0	1	0
19.1	11	0	0	1
17.4	12	0	0	0

and $X_3 = 0$. For the third quarters, let $X_1 = X_2 = 0$, and $X_3 = 1$, and for the fourth quarters let $X_1 = X_2 = X_3 = 0$. Table 2-3 represents the completed data which will be entered into the multiple regression program. Note that the problem has 4 independent variables and 12 observations. The initial data entry screen is presented below.

```
Problem title: FORECASTING

Number of independent variables:  4

Number of observations: 12



        ┌─────────────────────────────────────┐
        │  Continue with observations (Y/N) Y  │
        └─────────────────────────────────────┘
```

Press <ENTER> to continue with the spread sheet data entry. The completed spread sheet is shown below.

61

```
A1
         A              B         C        D        E        F
                     DEMAND     TIME      X1       X2       X3
1
2      Obs1          10.50     1.00     1.00     0.00     0.00
3      Obs2          12.00     2.00     0.00     1.00     0.00
4      Obs3          15.80     3.00     0.00     0.00     1.00
5      Obs4          13.20     4.00     0.00     0.00     0.00
6      Obs5          12.70     5.00     1.00     0.00     0.00
7      Obs6          14.60     6.00     0.00     1.00     0.00
8      Obs7          17.90     7.00     0.00     0.00     1.00
9      Obs8          15.20     8.00     0.00     0.00     0.00
10     Obs9          14.30     9.00     1.00     0.00     0.00
11     Obs10         16.70    10.00     0.00     1.00     0.00
12     Obs11         19.10    11.00     0.00     0.00     1.00
13     Obs12         17.40    12.00     0.00     0.00     0.00
```

After completing the spread sheet data entry, press <F10> to keep the data and exit from the spread sheet. You can now print the data on the printer to obtain a hard copy printout of the problem and then save the problem on disk for future sessions.

To solve the problem, move the pointer to the SOLVE option and select the Display Output sub-option to display the output reports on the screen. The first display screen reports the regression function coefficients as shown below.

```
                    Problem Title: FORECASTING
                  Regression Function Coefficients:

        Coeff.         Value        St. Dev.      T-Ratio
        ------      -----------    -----------   -----------
          B0          11.267         0.303         37.132
          B1           0.500         0.029         17.019
          B2          -1.267         0.285         -4.439
          B3           0.167         0.278          0.600
          B4           2.833         0.273         10.380
```

As seen from the above report, the regression function equation is:

Demand $= 11.267 + 0.5\,t - 1.267\,X_1 + 0.167\,X_2 + 2.833\,X_3$.

Press the $<$ENTER$>$ key to continue with the ANOVA table report.

```
                Problem Title: FORECASTING
              Analysis  of  Variance  Table

     Source      DF           SS           MS
     ------      --------     -----------  -----------
     Regress.    4            72.177       18.044

     Residual    7            0.773        0.110
     ------      --------     -----------  -----------
     Total       11           72.950

     Coefficient of Determination R-Squared =    0.989

     Residual Standard Deviation =       0.332

          ┌─────────────────────────────────┐
          │ Predicted Y Values (Y/N) N      │
          └─────────────────────────────────┘
```

The above results indicate that the regression model is quite strong with a R-squared value of 0.989.

If you wish to examine the predicted values press $<$Y$>$. The computer will display the predicted values and associated error terms. (This report is skipped in this solved example.)

The program will then ask if you wish to predict another observation. Press $<$Y$>$ to continue with obtaining the forecast for the desired time period. Note that in this case you wish to forecast the demand during the first quarter of the fourth year. Hence, the values of the independent variables are:

$t = 13,\ X_1 = 1,\ X_2 = X_3 = 0.$

The completed data entry screen is shown below.

```
┌──────────────────────────────────────────────────────────────┐
│                 Problem Title: FORECASTING                     │
│                                                                │
│    Enter value for TIME:              13                       │
│    Enter value for X1: :              1                        │
│    Enter value for X2: :              0                        │
│    Enter value for X3: :              0                        │
│                                                                │
│    The value of Y is      16.500                               │
│                                    ┌────────────────┐          │
│                                    │ More (Y/N) N   │          │
│                                    └────────────────┘          │
│                                                                │
└──────────────────────────────────────────────────────────────┘
```

The forecast for the demand during the first quarter of the fourth year is therefore 16.5. Press <ENTER> to exit the SOLVE option and return to the Regression Menu. At this point, you may move the pointer to QUIT option and either exit to DSSPOM and return to DOS or return to the Main Menu and select another DSSPOM program.

PROBLEMS

1. You are asked to see if there is a statistical relationship between absentee rate (days absent), years employed, and age of employee. Run the Multiple Regression program with the data below. Interpret.

Observa-tion	Days Absent (Y)	Years Employed (X1)	Age (X2)
1	5	5	30
2	4	15	45
3	2	10	42
4	6	6	30
5	8	8	32
6	6	7	35
7	5	10	40
8	3	2	28
9	7	5	50
10	2	19	54

2. You are asked to check the statistical relationship between annual sales (Y), age of salesperson (X1), years of higher education of salesperson (X2), and days absent (X3) . The data are shown below. Interpret.

Observa-tion	Sales (Y)	Age (X1)	Education (X2)	Absence (X3)
1	75	40	4	2
2	65	35	3	5
3	60	50	6	6
4	85	45	2	3
5	80	40	4	2
6	75	40	1	6
7	45	60	6	18
8	90	35	5	2
9	75	35	2	7
10	50	60	4	14
11	45	65	2	9
12	65	50	3	7

3. Run problem 2 again but with the *absent* variable deleted.

4. The daily rates of rejection of a manufactured product are listed below together with the ambient temperature measured from the optimum of 65 degree F., and with the ambient humidity rate also measured from the optimum of 55% of relative humidity.

Observation	Rejects	Temperature	Humidity
1	14	-5	+1
2	12	-8	+1
3	16	+1	+4
4	20	+6	+6
5	24	+8	+7
6	29	+12	+14
7	24	+3	+17
8	14	-2	+2
9	16	-7	+1
10	10	-3	-1
11	14	-8	-2
12	8	-2	+3

Run the multiple regression program with the above data to investigate the relation between daily rejection rate and temperature and humidity.

5. For problem 4, suppose you have a third independent variable, batch size. The observations on batch size are (1 to 12) 510, 460, 600, 650, 720, 770, 600, 550, 400, 475, 525, 375. Run the multiple regression program with the added variable, batch size.

6. For problem 2, suppose you have a fourth independent variable, cigarettes smoked per day on average. The number of cigarettes smoked by each of the 12 salesreps are 30, 20, 15, 25, 30, 35, 30, 10, 40, 10, 0, 5. Run the multiple regression program with the added variable, cigarettes smoked per day.

7. State College has decided to do a study of the relationship between college admission tests, performance in school and reported family household income. The question is whether or not there is a statistical relationship between school performance and college admission tests and family income. The results of a random sample of 20 students is shown below. Can school performance be predicted? How?

Student	Test Score	School Performance	Family Income(000)
1	700	3.95	$60.0
2	550	3.05	45.0
3	540	3.10	47.0
4	590	3.10	47.0
5	610	3.65	52.3
6	620	3.75	55.0
7	615	3.70	53.0
8	605	3.45	47.5
9	695	3.85	48.5
10	645	3.90	65.0
11	585	3.60	60.0
12	545	3.40	55.5
13	515	3.50	56.0
14	560	3.20	40.0
15	640	3.80	57.0
16	510	3.10	35.0
17	595	3.50	40.0
18	590	3.60	42.0
19	610	3.80	59.0
20	540	3.10	48.5

8. A health spa provides ongoing health evaluation services for its members. At each checkup data is collected on, age, weight, height, blood pressure and blood cholesterol. The health spa has collected data on 20 members as shown below. Is there a statistical relationship among the five variables? Can cholesterol level be predicted? Which variables are statistically significant for predicting cholesterol level, if any?

Member	Age	Weight	Height	Blood Pressure	Cholesterol Level
1	25	165	71	110	130
2	27	150	69	120	125
3	39	140	70	140	140
4	35	175	73	130	135
5	42	163	70	120	160
6	26	162	69	110	140
7	38	181	73	115	180

8	31	172	68	105	170
9	29	139	65	135	160
10	25	145	64	140	150
11	23	162	69	115	150
12	52	166	72	125	220
13	51	159	68	135	240
14	48	182	73	140	210
15	47	143	64	110	200
16	36	162	70	125	190
17	33	172	71	125	160
18	31	181	71	140	170
19	29	149	69	135	150
20	48	159	69	130	190

9. Girard Drug, a drug chain with 84 stores wants to forecast sales on the basis of approximate population in each sales territory and on advertising expenditures in each territory. Girard's stores are located in seven separate territories, each of which consists of a large metropolitan area. For the data given below predict the territory sales of Girard Drug on the basis of population in each territory and advertising expenditures using multiple regression with population and advertising expenditures as independent variables.

Territory	Sales in Millions	Population in Millions	Advertising Expenditures in Tens of Thousands
	y	x_1	x_2
1	$6.8	5.4	$ 5.2
2	7.8	4.6	4.7
3	8.3	8.9	10.2
4	2.2	2.4	2.7
5	7.4	3.8	5.2
6	3.7	1.7	3.3
7	6.9	4.3	5.2

68

10. The Holsam Corporation wants to know if disposable personal income and industry sales were reliable indicators for forecasting Holsam Corporation sales. Over a period of ten years it had accumulated the data listed below.

Year	Holsam Sales in Millions y	Disposable Personal Income in Billions x_1	Industry Sales in Millions x_2
1	$5.35	1.253	$51
2	5.40	1.331	53
3	5.55	1.406	56
4	5.65	1.487	58
5	5.65	1.569	59
6	5.75	1.644	60
7	4.95	1.701	62
8	5.20	1.783	63
9	5.25	1.854	62
10	5.35	1.932	65

Using multiple regression, forecast Holsam's sales for the eleventh year if industry sales are expected to increase to 67 million dollars and disposable income is expected to rise to two billion dollars.

11.   You are a budding artist just waiting to make your first million dollars. In order to begin your career, you have decided to draw cartoons to be placed in the Sunday newspaper and an area magazine. Your income level depends on the circulation of the newspaper, circulation of the magazine, and the number of cartoons you get published each week.

Based on the information in the following table, project your income for the next four months (October to January).

	INCOME	NEWSPAPERS	MAGAZINES	STRIPS PRODUCED
January	4	10	8	.02
February	4.5	11	10	.05
March	3.8	12	7	.04
April	3	13	6	.03
May	3.7	14	7	.05
June	4	15	8	.06
July	4.4	12	8	.04
August	3.9	11	7	.02
September	3.8	10	7	.04
October		15	10	.04
November		13	11	.03
December		10	9	.01
January		12	8	.04

NOTE: All numbers are in hundreds.

12.   An experiment was conducted for three weeks to study the effect of refrigerator temperature and refrigerator storage density on refrigerator power usage (in kilowatt hours) for a certain type of residential refrigerator. Temperature and storage density are measured in standard deviations from the levels normally used. For example, in the first observation the temperature setting was 15 degrees below the normal setting and the storage density was 15% points below the normal density. The results of the study are given below.

a)   Run the multiple regression program on this data. State the resulting equation.

b)   How confident are you in this predictive function?

DAY	TEMPERATURE	DENSITY	POWER USED
1	-15	-15	250
2	0	-15	190
3	+15	-15	160
4	-10	-10	230
5	0	-10	180

6	+10	-10	175
7	-10	0	259
8	-10	+10	287
9	0	+10	189
10	0	0	207
11	-5	-5	204
12	-5	+5	253
13	+5	-5	182
14	+5	+5	161
15	0	-5	159

13. Below are statistics from St. Elsewhere Hospital during last year's flu season. St. Elsewhere is trying to determine how to stock the hospital in order to be prepared for this year's flu outbreak. Doctors have reason to believe that the number of outbreaks this year will be similar to last year. Doctors also believe the number of outbreaks is contingent on the number of flu shots given and the amount of aspirin sold. Actual data from last year is shown below.

a) Find a regression equation to fit the data that will predict the number of flu outbreaks for this year.

b) How good is this equation?

c) Based on this equation, predict the number of flu outbreaks St. Elsewhere can expect over the 7 week season.

WEEK	FLU OUTBREAKS	NUMBER OF SHOTS	ASPIRIN SOLD
1	100	50	600
2	200	100	700
3	300	150	800
4	500	200	900
5	400	250	900
6	200	100	700
7	50	50	500
1		75	700
2		100	750
3		150	800
4		200	850
5		225	900
6		275	800
7		100	700

14. Collins University would like to revise its admission standards. Administrators have found that college GPA is correlated with high school averages, SAT scores, and ACT scores. They base their findings on the data below which was acquired over the past several years. This, of course, is not the entire data base, but is a representative sample.

a) Calculate a regression equation that will help the Administrators decide on the best students to accept.

b) The second table shows data on 5 students wishing to attend Collins University. The school can only admit 3 of these students. Use the regression equation calculated in (a) to decide which students should be accepted.

STUDENT	GPA	H.S. AVERAGE	SAT	ACT
1	3.9	98	1300	28
2	3.2	92	1270	27
3	3.7	93	1310	27
4	2.6	88	900	19
5	2.9	85	1100	23
6	3.3	87	1300	24
7	2.7	80	1000	21
8	2.2	82	850	15

STUDENT	H.S. AVERAGE	SAT	ACT
Sue	90	1000	26
Bob	88	1100	24
Joe	93	1050	26
Todd	94	1300	20
Sara	85	1200	27

CHAPTER 3

DECISION ANALYSIS

INTRODUCTION

Decision analysis is concerned with finding the most desirable alternative from several alternative actions within a setting or scenario in which outcomes are dependent on several potential states of nature. A state of nature is essentially an environmental condition which produces a certain specified outcome depending on the alternative action.

This concept can best be illustrated by a simple example. Suppose you decide to go on a long walk and you know that there is a slight probability of rain. You can take your umbrella along to keep you dry if it rains. However, the umbrella is a nuisance to carry around especially if it turns out to be dry on your long walk.

In this example, the setting explains the alternative actions, the states of nature and hints at the outcomes. The two alternative actions are: 1. to take along an umbrella; and 2. to leave the umbrella at home. The two states of nature are: 1. no rain will fall on you during your walk; and 2. you will get rained on during your walk. The four possible outcomes represent the intersections of the two alternative actions and the two states of nature. The outcomes are illustrated in Exhibit 3-1 in the form of a decision matrix including the alternative actions, the states of nature and the outcomes.

The decision matrix completely summarizes the alternative actions A1 and A2, the states of nature, S1 and S2, and the resultant four outcomes. In our example the outcomes are non-quantitative verbal descriptions of the unfolding of the scenario. In most practical applications the outcomes are quantitative measures such as sales revenues, costs, profits, losses, etc. We shall illustrate such a case below.

Exhibit 3-2 shows a scenario of a capital investment decision for a large corporation. The corporation must decide what size plant to build to produce a new product for which the future demand is not known. If demand is large then a large plant will provide the largest profits while if demand is small, a smaller plant would be profitable while a large plant would result in losses. Similarly if a small plant were built and demand were high, profits would be low because of the lost opportunity to fulfill demand. For instance, note that profits of $20 million result if a small plant is built regardless of the demand. If a medium-size plant is built profits could be as high as $60 million and as low as break-even ($0 profits) depending on the demand. A large plant could produce profits as high as $120 million but if demand is low it might produce a loss of $30 million.

Actions	States of Nature	
	S1-RAIN	S2-NO RAIN
A1-Take along umbrella	You are able to remain dry when it rains	You are annoyed for having to carry the umbrella on a nice dry day
A2-Leave umbrella at home	You are annoyed because you will get wet when it rains	You are delighted because it remains dry and you have no umbrella to carry around

Exhibit 3-1: Decision Matrix for Long Walk Scenario

Actions	States of Nature			
	S1-Low Demand	S2-Moderate Demand	S3-Considerable Demand	S4-Large Demand
A1-Build Small Plant	20	20	20	20
A2-Build Medium-Size Plant	0	40	60	60
A3-Build Large Plant	-30	30	60	120

Exhibit 3-2: Decision Matrix for Plant Size Problem

Note: Outcomes (cell entries) are millions of dollars of profit.

To further complicate the situation the decision maker (management) feels that any one of the four states of nature could occur. Clearly if one knew beforehand that low demand (S1) would occur, then the small plant should be built. Similarly if moderate demand (S2) were to occur a medium size plant should be built. If considerable demand (S3) were to occur either a medium-size or a large plant could be built and if large demand (S4) were sure to occur, management would opt for the large plant.

To solve the dilemma, we shall find a solution under several criteria. This problem is called the decision making under "uncertainty" because no probabilistic data on the states of nature is available. The four criteria are: 1. Equal likelihood; 2. Pessimistic, also called conservative or maximin; 3. Optimistic, also called gambler's or maximax; and 4. the minimax regret for opportunity loss. Each one of the four criteria will be described below.

EQUAL LIKELIHOOD CRITERION

Under the equal likelihood criterion we assume that each one of the four states of nature is equally likely. Alternatively, one could say that the probability of each state of nature is 0.25 (or 1/4). Then we apply the average profit maximization method to the decision problem and we find that alternative action A4, to build a large plant, will provide the largest average profit as shown in Exhibit 3-3. Alternative action A1, to build a small plant, will produce an average profit of $20 million, alternative action A2, the medium size plant, will produce an average profit of $40 million and alternative action A3, the large plant, will produce the maximum average profit of $45 million.

Note that the equal likelihood criterion does not consider the risk of incurring big losses. Although alternative action A3 produces the highest average profit, it also leaves open a strong possibility of incurring a loss of $30 million. For many small firms this may be too high a risk to take.

PESSIMISTIC, CONSERVATIVE OR MAXIMIN CRITERION

Under the conservative criterion there is again an assumption that there is no knowledge about the respective probabilities of the four states of nature. The objective of the criterion is to avoid the worst outcomes. Hence, it is a pessimistic or conservative criterion.

The conservative or maximin criterion is applied as follows. For each alternative action the minimum profit is identified. Then the maximum of the three minimum profits selected and the alternative action that produces that maximum profit is chosen.

For the plant size decision problem we find that the minimum profits for each alternative action are a $20 million profit for A1, break-even for A2, and a $30 million loss for A3. The maximum of these three minimum payoffs is $20 million for A1, build a small plant. A1 is therefore selected under the conservative or maximin criterion.

OPTIMISTIC, GAMBLER'S OR MAXIMAX CRITERION

Under the gambler's criterion there is again an assumption of no knowledge about the respective probabilities of the four states of nature. The objective of the criterion is to ensure that the highest possible profit is obtained if the associated state of nature occurs. Since this criterion could also produce high losses it is called a speculator's or gambler's criterion.

	States of Nature				
Alternative Actions	S1	S2	S3	S4	Average Profit
A1	20	20	20	20	20
A2	0	40	60	60	40
A3	-30	30	60	120	45

Exhibit 3-3: Solution with Equal Likelihood Criterion

Note: Outcomes (cell entries) are profits in millions of dollars

76

The maximax criterion is applied as follows. For each alternative action the maximum profit is identified. Then the maximum of the three maximum profits is selected and the alternative action that produces that maximum profit is the chosen alternative action.

For the plant size decision problem we find that the maximum profits for each alternative action are a $20 million profit for A1, a $60 million profit for A2 and a $120 million profit for A3. The maximum of these three profits or payoffs is $120 million for A3, to build a large plant. A3 is therefore selected under the gambler's optimistic or maximax criterion.

MINIMAX REGRET FOR OPPORTUNITY LOSS CRITERION

Under the minimax regret for opportunity loss criterion there is again an assumption of no knowledge about the respective probabilities of the four states of nature. The objective of the criterion is to ensure that the larger opportunity losses are avoided.

To apply the regret criterion we must first convert the decision matrix for the plant size decision problem from a profit matrix to an opportunity loss matrix. The results are shown in Exhibit 3-4.

For each state of nature we select the largest profit. For that outcome cell, we assign a zero opportunity loss. The other outcome cells for the same state of nature are then assigned opportunity losses equal to the difference between the largest profit and their respective profits.

To illustrate this we shall apply it to the plant size decision problem. For state of nature S1 the profit outcomes are, respectively, $20 million for A1, $0 for A2 and $-30 million for A3. Hence, the opportunity loss for A1 is 0 because it is the largest profit of the three outcomes. The opportunity loss for A2 is $20 million - the difference between $20 million for A1 and zero for A2 and the opportunity loss for A3 is $50 million - the difference between $20 million for A1 and -$30 million for A3.

We shall repeat this opportunity loss determination for state of nature S2. For S2 the profit outcomes are, respectively, $20 million for A1, $40 million for A2 and $30 million for A3. Hence, the opportunity loss for A2 is zero because it is the largest profit of the three outcomes. The opportunity loss for A1 is $20 million - the difference between $40 million for A2 and $20 million for A1 - and the opportunity loss for A3 is $10 million - the difference between $40 million for A2 and $30 million for A3.

After we have completed the opportunity loss matrix for all the four states of nature we can apply the minimax regret for opportunity loss criterion. Under this criterion there is again an assumption that there is no knowledge about the respective probabilities of the four states of nature. The objective of the criterion is to ensure that the largest opportunity losses are avoided.

The minimax regret criterion is applied as follows. For each alternative action the maximum opportunity loss is identified. Then the minimum of the three maximum opportunity losses is selected and the alternative action that produces that minimum opportunity loss is the chosen alternative action.

Alternative Actions	States of Nature			
	S1	S2	S3	S4
A1	0	20	40	100
A2	20	0	0	60
A3	50	10	0	0

Exhibit 3-4: Opportunity Loss Matrix for Regret Problem

Note: Opportunity losses (cell entries) are shown in millions of dollars.
Based on the minimax regret criterion, we select alternative A3.

For the plant size decision problem we find that the maximum opportunity losses, from Exhibit 3-4, for each alternative action are a $100 million opportunity loss for A1, a $60 million opportunity loss for A2 and a $50 million opportunity loss for A3. The minimum of these three opportunity losses is $50 million for A3, or, build the large plant. A3 is therefore selected under the minimax opportunity loss regret criterion.

Based on the above application of the four decision criteria we find that alternative action A3 is selected for the equal likelihood criterion, alternative action A1 is selected for the pessimistic (conservative) criterion, alternative action A3 is selected for the optimistic (gambler's) criterion, and alternative action A3 is also selected for the minimax opportunity loss regret criterion. The results of the above are summarized in Exhibit 3-5.

THE MAXIMUM EXPECTED PROFIT CRITERION

The four decision criteria applied above all assumed that there was no explicit probabilistic information available. There are, however, situations where that assumption is not necessary. That kind of situation will be discussed below and applied to the plant size decision problem.

Suppose that the demand probabilities for the plant size decision problem are the following. The probability of low demand, S1, is 0.40, the probability of moderate demand, S2, is 0.30, the probability of considerable demand, S3, is 0.20 and the probability of large demand, S4, is 0.10.

Applying these demand probabilities to the plant size decision problem we find, as displayed in Exhibit 3-6, that alternative action A2, to build a medium-size plant, is the most desirable because it produces the largest expected profit of $30 million. Alternative action A1, to build a small plant produces an expected profit of $20 million and alternative action A3, to build a large plant produces an expected profit of $21 million. Hence, based on the maximum expected profit criterion alternative A2, to build a medium-size plant, is selected. The expected profit of $30 million for alternative A2 is also called the expected value under risk.

EXPECTED VALUE OF PERFECT INFORMATION

When probabilistic data is available for the states of nature we are able to determine the expected value of perfect information. The expected value of perfect information is a useful value because it specifies the maximum amount management should pay to obtain perfect information on the outcomes of the four states of nature. Perfect information is really never available in our uncertain world, but, through market research considerable additional information can often be obtained. The expected value of perfect information is then the absolute maximum one would want to pay for that additional market research information about the probabilities of the states of nature.

To find the expected value of perfect information (EVPI) we must first find the expected value under certainty (EVUC). We then subtract the maximum expected value under risk (EVUR) which we calculated in the previous section from the EVUC to obtain the EVPI. To show it arithmetically we thus have,

$$EVPI = EVUC - EVUR$$

Criteria	Alternative Action Selected
Equal Likelihood	A3
Maximin-Conservative	A1
Maximax-Gambler's	A3
Minimax Opportunity Loss Regret	A3

Exhibit 3-5:   Summary of Decision Criteria Selections for Plant Size Decision Problem

Alternative Actions	States of Nature				Expected Profit
	S1 P(S1)=.40	S2 P(S2)=.30	S3 P(S3)=.20	S4 P(S4)=.10	
A1	20	20	20	20	20
A2	0	40	60	60	30
A3	-30	30	60	120	21

Exhibit 3-6:   The Maximum Expected Profit Criterion - Plant Size Problem

Note: Outcomes are profits in millions of dollars
P(S1) stands for probability of S1, etc.

The maximum expected value under risk (EVUR) amounts to 30 monetary units for alternative A2.

To find the EVUC for the example problem we take the maximum profit for each state of nature and multiply it by the respective probability for that state of nature. We then sum the resultant expected values for the four states of nature to obtain the EVUC with the formula shown below,

$$EVUC = S1*P(S1) + S2*P(S2) + S3*P(S3) + S4*P(S4)$$

where S1 is the maximum profit for S1, etc. and P(S1) is the probability that S1 will take place. Hence,

$$EVUC = 20(.40) + 40(.30) + 60(.20) + 120(.10) = 44$$

which translates into $44 million.

We can now find the EVPI which is

$$EVPI = EVUC - EVUR = 44 - 30 = 14$$

Hence, the expected value of perfect information amounts to $14 million.

COSTS OR LOSSES VERSUS PROFITS OR PAYOFFS

In the preceding analysis we used profits for the outcomes except in the case of the minimax opportunity loss regret criterion. Frequently, decision problems arise where the outcomes are not profits or payoffs which one would like to maximize, but costs or losses which one would like to minimize.

In order to apply the same model and procedures one can always convert costs or losses to profits or payoffs by multiplying each cost or loss outcome by (-1). Although there are other ways of dealing with costs or losses the (-1) multiplication method is the easiest and most straightforward. Similarly if the outcomes are costs or losses the expected value criterion becomes a minimize expected cost criterion instead of a maximize expected profit criterion.

DECISION TREES

Decision trees are useful graphical tools to represent sequential decision problems. A decision tree consists of chance events (nodes) and decision events (nodes). It is customary to use squares for decision nodes and circles for chance nodes. Branches emanating from decision nodes represent decision alternatives and those emanating from chance nodes represent the possible states of nature. The decision branches have associated costs or profits and chance branches or states of nature have associated probabilities. For a terminal chance branch there is both an associated cost or profit and probability. The method is best illustrated by an example.

An investor can invest his money in one of three different investment plans over an 18-month period. At the end of the 18-month period, he will determine the value of his initial investment plus (minus) the return (the loss). The return on his investment depends on the type of investment plan purchased and the future state of the economy. The three investment plans consist of buying convertible bonds (CB), purchasing government bonds (GB), or investing in money market funds (MMF). In particular, he can buy CB for $10,000, invest $8,000 in MMF, or buy $15,000 worth of GB. The returns on the three investment plans depend on the state of the economy within the next 18 months. That is, the economy may be gloomy with a probability of 0.30, stable with a probability of 0.45, or rosy with a probability of 0.25. The total amount collected, including his initial investment, for the GB is $16,000 for rosy economy, $15,900 for stable economy, and $14,500 for gloomy economy. The amount collected for the MMF investment is $9,000 for rosy economy and $8,900 for stable economy. However, when the economy is gloomy, the investor can pay a fee of $350 and sell his MMF prematurely (before the end of 18 months) in which case he collects $8,950. Otherwise, he may wish to do nothing and collect $8,700. The CB investment will result in collecting $11,000 in rosy economy. Under a stable economy, the investor can sell the CB prior to maturity for a fee of $200 and collect $11,100, or wait until the end of the 18 months and collect $10,500. When the economy is gloomy, he can sell the CB prematurely and invest in real state bonds at a cost of $500 in which case he will collect $10,500, or he can do nothing and collect $9,800. We wish to determine the optimal investment plan which will maximize his expected profit.

This problem can be represented by a decision tree as in Figure 3-1, in which the square nodes represent the decision events and the circle nodes are chance events. In order to solve the problem, we utilize a backward procedure in which we successively determine the expected payoffs and subtract the associated cost. For example, consider the expected payoff (EP) associated with buying government bonds (GB). The expected payoff is given as:

$$EP(GB) = \$16,000(0.25) + \$15,900(0.45) + \$14,500(0.30)$$

$$= \$15,505.$$

To determine the expected profit we subtract the cost (initial investment) from the expected payoff. That is:

$$Expected\ Profit\ (GB) = \$15,505 - \$15,000 = \$505.$$

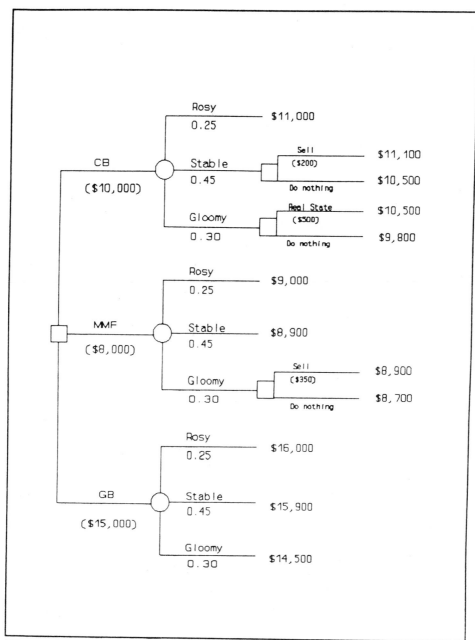

Figure 3-1:   Decision Tree for the Investment Problem

To determine the expected payoff for MMF, we note that when economy is gloomy and he decides to sell, the payoff is $8,550 ($8,900 - $350). Compared with doing nothing which pays $8,700, the sell option should not be selected.

Therefore, the expected payoff for the MMF option is:

$$EP(MMF) \quad = \$9,000(0.25) + \$8,900(0.45) + \$8,700(0.30)$$

$$= \$8,865.$$

83

Accordingly, the expected profit is $8,865 - $8,000 = $865. The computation for the expected payoff associated with CB is analogous and results in an expected profit of $655. Clearly, among the three investment plans, the MMF investment has the highest expected profit of $865. The investor, therefore should buy MMF and if the economy happens to be gloomy he should keep the MMF and do nothing. Later in this chapter, we will illustrate the use of the computer to solve the problem.

EXAMPLE 1 - DECISION MAKING UNDER UNCERTAINTY

This example problem involves decision making under uncertainty. The decision table presented in Exhibit 3-2 will be used for this solved example. To solve the problem, select the "Decision Analysis" program from the Main Menu. Once the decision analysis program is loaded, move the pointer to the INPUT option. The INPUT option includes two sub-options: 1-Decision Tables; and 2-Decision Trees. Pull the pointer down to the first option and press the <ENTER> key. The data input screens are shown below.

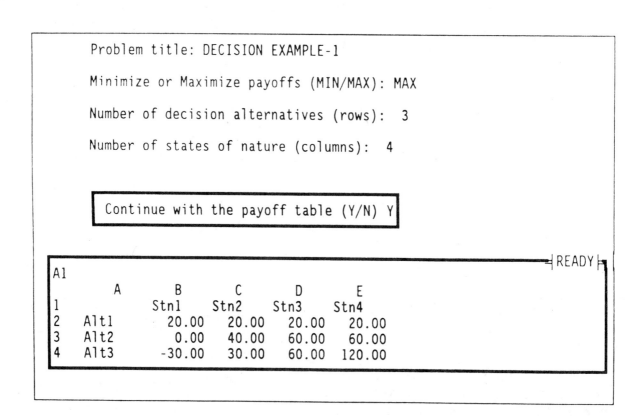

After completing the data entry process, press the <F10> key to exit the spread sheet entry program and keep the data. At this point, you may proceed to select the PRINT option to obtain a hard copy printout of the input data. Examine your data carefully to ensure it is correct.

Since the data for this example will be used for the next solved example, proceed to save the problem on disk. To save the model on disk, move the pointer to the FILE option. Several options will be presented under the file management option. Pull the pointer down two levels to highlight the "Save current file" option and press the <ENTER> key. The file save display screen is presented below.

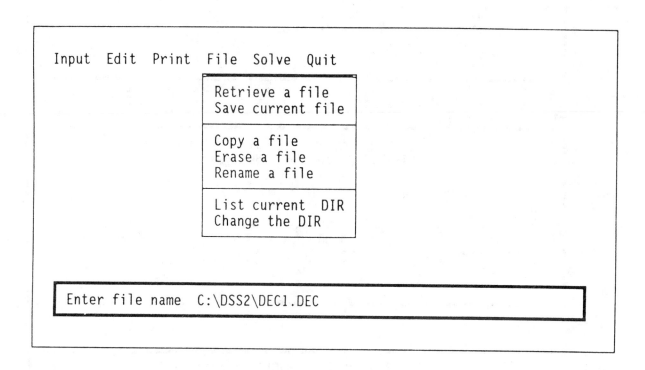

```
Input   Edit   Print   File   Solve   Quit

                     Retrieve a file
                     Save current file

                     Copy a file
                     Erase a file
                     Rename a file

                     List current  DIR
                     Change the DIR



 Enter file name   C:\DSS2\DEC1.DEC
```

Note that when the save file option is selected, the program will display the current sub-directory and ask you to enter a file name. In this solved example, the current sub-directory is \DSS2 on drive C:. Press the <END> key to move the cursor to the end of the input field. Type "DEC1.DEC" and press the <ENTER> key. The use of the three letters "DEC" as file suffix will identify this file as one containing a decision analysis problem data. This will greatly simplify the file retrieve process later.

You are now ready to solve the example problem. Move the pointer to the SOLVE option and pull the pointer down one level to highlight DISPLAY OUTPUT. Press the <ENTER> key to select it. The program will begin to solve the decision table problem and reports outcomes from several solution criteria.

```
+--------------------------------------------------------------+
|                Problem Title: DECISION EXAMPLE-1             |
|                 Decision Making:  Under Uncertainty          |
|                                                              |
|        Alternative      Expected Payoff                      |
|        -----------      ---------------                      |
|        Alt1             20.00                                |
|        Alt2             40.00                                |
|        Alt3             45.00   <=== Maximum                 |
|                                                              |
+--------------------------------------------------------------+


+--------------------------------------------------------------+
|                Problem Title: DECISION EXAMPLE-1             |
|                 MaxiMin Criterion (Pessimistic)             |
|                                                              |
|        Alternative      Worst (Minimum)                      |
|        -----------      ---------------                      |
|        Alt1              20.00   <=== MaxiMin                |
|        Alt2               0.00                               |
|        Alt3             -30.00                               |
|                                                              |
+--------------------------------------------------------------+


+--------------------------------------------------------------+
|                Problem Title: DECISION EXAMPLE-1             |
|                 MaxiMax Criterion (Optimistic)              |
|                                                              |
|        Alternative      Best (Maximum)                       |
|        -----------      ---------------                      |
|        Alt1              20.00                               |
|        Alt2              60.00                               |
|        Alt3             120.00   <=== MaxiMax               |
|                                                              |
+--------------------------------------------------------------+
```

After reporting the optimal decision alternative under the Equally Likely, Optimistic (or MaxiMax), and Pessimistic (or MaxiMin) criteria, the program will ask if you wish to see the regret table for this problem. Press <Y> to see the regret table as shown below.

```
┌──────────────────────────────────────────────────────────────────┐
│                Problem Title: DECISION EXAMPLE-1                    │
│                                                                    │
│        ┌─────────────────────────────────────────────┐            │
│        │ Display the Opportunity Loss Table (Y/N) Y  │            │
│        └─────────────────────────────────────────────┘            │
│                                                                    │
└──────────────────────────────────────────────────────────────────┘
```

```
                                                        ╢READY╟
┌──────────────────────────────────────────────────────────────┐
│A1                                                              │
│          A         B         C         D         E             │
│1                  Stn1      Stn2      Stn3      Stn4            │
│2    Alt1          0.00     20.00     40.00    100.00           │
│3    Alt2         20.00      0.00      0.00     60.00           │
│4    Alt3         50.00     10.00      0.00      0.00           │
└──────────────────────────────────────────────────────────────┘
```

Press the <ESC> key to continue with the solution process. The program will then display the optimal decision alternative under the Minimax Regret Criterion as show below.

```
┌──────────────────────────────────────────────────────────────────┐
│               Problem Title: DECISION EXAMPLE-1                    │
│                    Minimax Regret Criterion                        │
│                                                                    │
│          Alternative        Maximum Regret                         │
│          -----------        --------------                         │
│          Alt1               100.00                                 │
│          Alt2                60.00                                 │
│          Alt3                50.00   <=== MiniMax                   │
│                                                                    │
│                                                                    │
└──────────────────────────────────────────────────────────────────┘
```

EXAMPLE 2 - DECISION MAKING UNDER RISK

This solved example involves decision making under risk. Decision making under risk consists of a decision table problem in which the underlying probability distribution associated with the states of nature is known. The problem data for this example is the same as those of Solved Example 1 above. The probabilities of the states of nature are those presented in Exhibit 3-6.

To begin the data entry process, recall that you saved Solved Example 1 using the file name "DEC1.DEC". Move the pointer to the "FILE" option the pull the bar one level down to the "Retrieve a file" option and press the <ENTER> key. The program will ask if it should erase the current model and begin a new one. Note that we could have edited the current model and added the probabilities of states of nature. (The use of the file retrieve option at this point is for demonstration purposes only.) The file retrieve process is shown below.

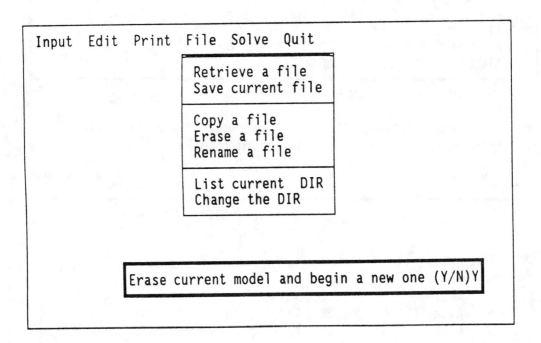

Next, you will be asked to enter a file specification. Press the <END> key to move the cursor to the end of the edit field. Now press the <BACKSPACE> key once to erase the "*" and type "DEC" as shown below.

```
Enter file spec. C:\DSS2\*.DEC
```

The program will display a vertical menu bar containing all file names with the three letter suffix "DEC" as shown below. In this case, there are three file names with suffix "DEC". Move the pointer to the proper file name and press the <ENTER> key.

```
                    DEC1.DEC
                    DEC2.DEC
                    DEC3.DEC



    Use || to highlight, ENTER to select, ESC to Exit.
```

After loading the decision problem presented in Solved Example 1, proceed to edit the data to add the probabilities of the states of nature and convert the decision model to one of decision making under risk. Move the pointer to the EDIT option and select the Input Data option. Change the problem title to "DECISION EXAMPLE-2" and press the <ENTER> key. Press the <ENTER> key three more times to accept the current values of the other three parameters. The program will ask if it should continue with the payoff table. Press <N> to bypass editing the payoff table.

To convert the current model to decision making under risk, move the pointer to the EDIT option again. This time pull the bar down to the "Change Model Type" and press the <ENTER> key as show below.

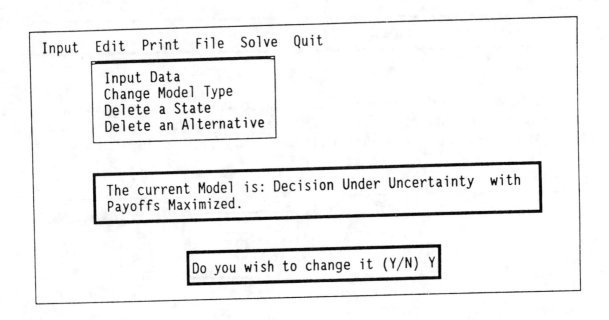

Press <Y> to proceed with changing the model. A vertical menu bar will be displayed, presenting various decision models. The pointer is on the first entry which is called "Decision Under Risk, Maximize the Payoff". Select this choice be pressing the <ENTER> key as shown below.

```
Decision under Risk , Maximize the Payoff
Decision under Risk , Minimize the Payoff
Uncertainty Model   , Maximize the Payoff
Uncertainty Model   , Minimize the Payoff
```

The program will proceed by displaying the spread sheet data entry process for entering probabilities for the various states of nature. Enter the probabilities into their appropriate cells, as shown below.

```
┌─────────────────────────────────────────────────────────────┤READY├─┐
│ E2   .1                                                              │
│         A       B      C      D      E                               │
│ 1             Stn1   Stn2   Stn3   Stn4                              │
│ 2       Prob.  0.400  0.300  0.200  0.100                           │
│                                                                      │
└──────────────────────────────────────────────────────────────────────┘
```

Press the <F10> key to exit the spread sheet and keep the values as entered. At this point, proceed to solve the model as before. The output screens are presented below.

```
┌────────────────────────────────────────────────────────────┐
│                Problem Title: DECISION EXAMPLE-2            │
│                Decision Making:  Under Risk                 │
│                                                            │
│           Alternative      Expected Payoff                 │
│           -----------      ---------------                 │
│           Alt1             20.00                           │
│           Alt2             30.00   <=== Maximum            │
│           Alt3             21.00                           │
│                                                            │
│                                                            │
└────────────────────────────────────────────────────────────┘
```

```
┌────────────────────────────────────────────────────────────┐
│                Problem Title: DECISION EXAMPLE-2           │
│                                                            │
│  Expected value of perfect information is:    14.00        │
│                                                            │
└────────────────────────────────────────────────────────────┘
```

The program reports the optimal decision alternative having the maximum expected payoff as well as the expected value of perfect information.

EXAMPLE 3 - DECISION TREE PROBLEM

This solved example involves the use of decision tree analysis to solve the problem presented in Figure 3-1. The problem involves an investor who must decide which of the three investment alternatives to choose from so that his expected profit is maximized. In order to solve the problem , you must first make sure that all of the branches in the decision tree have numbered end-nodes. As seen from Figure 3-1, several of the terminal branches do not end in numbered nodes. Therefore, the decision tree is revised so that all of these branches have end-nodes. Figure 3-2 presents the completed decision tree. Also note that for several terminal branches (e.g. (5,9), (6,11), and (7,4)) the net payoff has been computed by subtracting the associated costs from the payoffs. The tree is now ready for input into the decision analysis program.

Load the DSSPOM software and select the "Decision Analysis" option from the Main Menu. Move the pointer to INPUT option and pull the bar down to the second level to highlight "Decision Tree" sub-option and press the <ENTER> key. Proceed to enter the initial problem parameters as shown below.

```
Problem title: DECISION TREE

Minimize or Maximize payoffs (MIN/MAX): MAX

Number of branches: 18




    Continue with the decision tree (Y/N) Y
```

Press <Y> to continue with entering the decision tree structure as shown below.

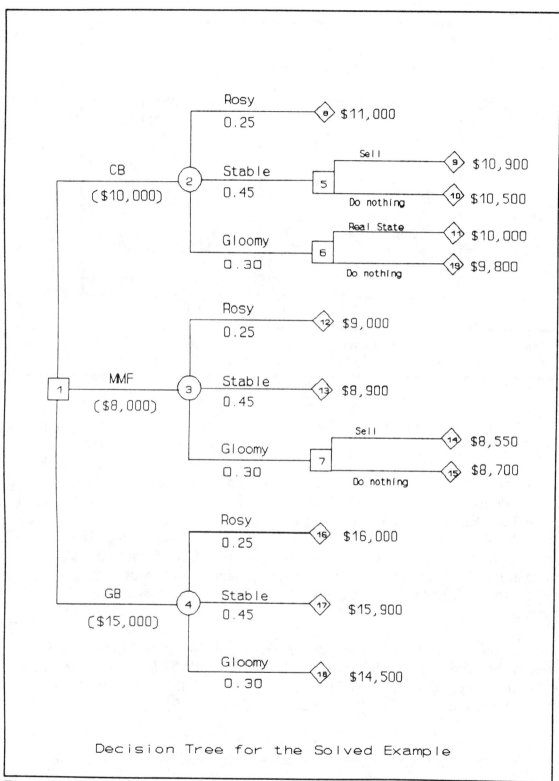

Decision Tree for the Solved Example

Figure 3-2: Revised Decision Tree

93

```
                                                    ┤READY├

A1  'BRANCH
           A        B       C       D          E
1      BRANCH    BEGIN    END    PROB-
2      LABEL     NODE     NODE   ABILITY   PAYOFF
3      CB          1        2    1.000    -10000.00
4      MMF         1        3    1.000     -8000.00
5      GB          1        4    1.000    -15000.00
6      ROSY        2        8    0.250     11000.00
7      STABLE      2        5    0.450         0.00
8      GLOOMY      2        6    0.300         0.00
9      ROSY        3       12    0.250      9000.00
10     STABLE      3       13    0.450      8900.00
11     GLOOMY      3        7    0.300         0.00
12     ROSY        4       16    0.250     16000.00
13     STABLE      4       17    0.450     15900.00
14     GLOOMY      4       18    0.300     14500.00
```

The probabilities for a Chance Node should sum to 1. The probability of a Decision Node is 1. If the Payoff is not available, enter a 0 or "Oh".

To enter the tree structure, first enter the branch labels by moving the pointer to cell A3 and type "CB". Press the <ENTER> key to accept and then the down arrow key to move the pointer to cell A4. Type "MMF" and press the <ENTER> key. Repeat this process for all of the 18 branches. Now, move the pointer to cell B3 and enter a "1" as the initial node for branch 1. Press the <ENTER> key followed by the right arrow to move to cell C3. Enter "2" for the end node of branch 1. Proceed as above to enter the end-nodes of all of the 18 branches. Next, enter the probability associated with each branch. Note that for a decision branch, the probability is 1.0 and for chance nodes, the sum of the probabilities of the branches emanating from it should be 1.0. After completing the data entry for the decision tree problem, press <F10> to keep the data and exit the spread sheet program.

If you wish to save the data, move the pointer to the "FILE" option, pull the bar down to the "Save current file" option and press the <ENTER> key. The program will display the current drive and sub-directory and ask for a file name. Enter an appropriate file name and press <ENTER> to save the model on disk.

You are now ready to solve the decision tree example problem. Move the pointer to the "SOLVE" option and select the display output. The program continues by solving the decision tree problem and presenting the optimal solution as presented below.

```
                  Problem Title: DECISION TREE
                    Decision Tree Analysis
  Branch      Branch                                 Conditional
  Number       Name        Nodes      Probability      Payoff

    1         CB         1  --> 2      Decision        655.000
    2         MMF        1  --> 3      Decision        865.000 <==
    3         GB         1  --> 4      Decision        505.000
    4         ROSY       2  --> 8      0.250          2750.000
    5         STABLE     2  --> 5      0.450          4905.000
    6         GLOOMY     2  --> 6      0.300          3000.000
    7         ROSY       3  --> 12     0.250          2250.000 *
    8         STABLE     3  --> 13     0.450          4005.000 *
    9         GLOOMY     3  --> 7      0.300          2610.000 *
   10         ROSY       4  --> 16     0.250          4000.000
   11         STABLE     4  --> 17     0.450          7155.000
   12         GLOOMY     4  --> 18     0.300          4350.000
```

```
                  Problem Title: DECISION TREE
                    Decision Tree Analysis
  Branch      Branch                                 Conditional
  Number       Name        Nodes      Probability      Payoff

   13         SELL       5  --> 9      Decision       10900.000
   14         NOTHING    5  --> 10     Decision       10500.000
   15         REAL EST   6  --> 11     Decision       10000.000
   16         NOTHING    6  --> 19     Decision        9800.000
   17         SELL       7  --> 14     Decision        8550.000
   18         NOTHING    7  --> 15     Decision        8700.000 <==


        Conditional Payoff of the Solution is:      865.000
```

As seen from the above results, the conditional expected payoff (or expected profit) is $865. The left arrows in the solution output point to the optimal decision alternatives. For example, the first arrow points to branch (1,3), labeled "MMF", which corresponds to the alternative associated with buying money market funds. The expected payoff in this case is $865. Therefore the best alternative (investment plan) is to buy MMF and earn an expected profit of $865. Clearly, if the economy is rosy, the investor will profit $1,000. When economy is stable, the profit is $900. But what should the investor do if the economy is gloomy? The second left arrow in the output points to branch (7,15) which is labeled "NOTHING". This corresponds to the best alternative when the economy is gloomy. That is, the investor should do nothing and collect a profit of $700. The three "*" in the output report represent the chance branches and their expected payoffs associated with the best decision alternative.

PROBLEMS

1. For the decision matrix with profits shown below, find the best solution under the following criteria under uncertainty and under risk, using the indicated probabilities for each state of nature. Also show what the value of each solution is. The cell entries are payoffs.

a. Pessimistic criterion
b. Optimistic criterion
c. Equal likelihood criterion
d. Opportunity loss regret criterion
e. Assume that the probabilities of states of nature are 0.20, 0.25, 0.15, and 0.40. What is the best alternative? What is the expected value of perfect information?

Alternative Actions	States of Nature			
	S1	S2	S3	S4
A1	90	80	-15	-40
A2	75	70	10	-20
A3	0	65	80	55
A4	-30	0	35	60
A5	-30	-10	75	110

2. A corporation is planning to launch a new consumer product. It is very uncertain how the public will react to the product. The three alternatives it decides to explore are: 1. distribute the product locally, 2. distribute the product regionally, or 3. distribute the product nationally. The profits that the product will produce depend on either good, fair or poor public acceptance of the product. If acceptance is poor the profits will be, respectively, 0, -6 and -18 for local, regional and national distribution. If acceptance is fair profits will be 4, 9, and 8, respectively, and if acceptance is good profits will be 10, 14, and 52, respectively, for local, regional, and national distribution. All profits are in millions of dollars.

a. Develop the decision matrix.
b. Use decision analysis program to find best solutions under pessimistic criterion, optimistic criterion, equal likelihood criterion, and opportunity loss regret criterion.
c. If probabilities are 0.5 for poor, 0.2 for fair and 0.3 for good public acceptance, determine the best solution for the expected profit maximization criterion.
d. What is the expected value of perfect information?
e. Does the distribution method change if the probabilities for public acceptance are 0.2, 0.1 and 0.7 for poor, fair, and good public acceptance, respectively?

3. Central Airlines is considering adding several routes because of aircraft availability. Five different configurations are being considered and three states of nature are anticipated. The states of nature are stated in terms of percentage seats filled on each route configuration. The outcomes are measured in terms of profits in units of $10,000 and are listed below in the decision matrix. Apply both decision analysis models under uncertainty and under risk. Also, find expected value of perfect information.

	Percentage of Seats Filled		
	50%	60%	75%
Route Configurations	S1	S2	S3
A1	15	45	95
A2	10	40	100
A3	-10	15	90
A4	0	65	85
A5	-50	20	120
Probability	.30	.60	.10

4. Idaho Oil Company has the opportunity to drill on a certain property with three levels of outside participation. The first level is no outside participation at all, the second level is partial participation and the third level is significant participation by outside investors. The profits for each outcome are shown in the decision matrix. Solve the problem for the case under uncertainty and under risk using the indicated probabilities for each state of nature.

	States of Nature			
Level of Participation	Dry Well	Partial Flow	Good Flow	Excellent Flow
None	-85	-15	450	750
Partial	35	50	250	450
Significant	65	145	200	275
Probability	.40	.30	.20	.10

Note: Outcomes are payoffs in thousands of dollars.

5. The Bloomfield Company produces special items for the Halloween season. Revenue amounts to $10 per item. From previous years' sales experience, probability estimates of sales levels have been derived. Production cost data in the form of variable and nonvariable costs are also available. These data are shown below.

Demand in Units	Estimated Probability	Nonvariable Cost	Variable Cost	Total Cost
100	0.1	$650	$ 50	$700
150	0.3	650	75	725
200	0.3	650	100	750
250	0.2	650	125	775
300	0.1	650	150	800

Excess production can be disposed off at $1.00 per unit up to 100 items. Remaining items have no value. Production can be done only in blocks of 50 units.

a. Prepare a profit table for Bloomfield showing revenue and cost for each of the five demand levels.

b. What is expected profit for Bloomfield at the full price $10 per unit?

c. How many units should Bloomfield produce under the optimal production level?

6. Using the data in the problem 5, what is the expected value of perfect information for Bloomfield Company? How much could Bloomfield afford to spend to acquire the information?

7. Cytonic Research Associates is considering submitting a proposal to the Federal government to develop a unique system for transporting the aged and poor in an urban community between their respective residences and places where they must appear at regular or irregular intervals such as health clinics, etc. Management of Cytonic estimates that it would cost $40,000 to prepare the proposal; the chance of being awarded the contract were estimated at about 0.40.

Cytonic systems personnel had three alternative systems were they to be awarded the contract. Approach A would cost $500,000 with an estimated probability of success of 0.50; approach B would cost $800,000 with probability of success of 0.75; and approach C would cost $1,000,000 but would be successful with near certainty. Management therefore attached a probability of success of 0.95 to the latter approach.

The contract, if awarded, would provide for payments of $1,200,000, if successful and payments of only $750,000 if not successful.

a.   Prepare a decision tree analysis for Cytonic Research Associates to provide them with information in making their decision.

b.   Make your recommendation to Cytonic in the form of a memo.

8. MURGEON CHEMICAL CORPORATION

In early January 1988, Murgeon Chemical Corporation received an order for 10,000 gallons of its new product, Murgo. Murgo is an ingredient used to manufacture a new variety of drugs. This was by far the largest order ever received for Murgo - total production in 1987 had been only 1,200 gallons. The order called for 5,000 gallons to be delivered in June and the remainder in November.

The process now used to synthesize Murgo is a long one which involves processing small batches of raw material through several stages. The company would need to invest $400,000 in new equipment to bring the production capacity up to the 1,000 gallons per month level to meet the order. (It would take the month of January to order and set up the equipment.) The variable manufacturing cost per gallon using this process was known to be $25.

One of the research chemists at Murgeon had just discovered a new process for synthesizing Murgo. If the process could be made to work on a large scale, it would greatly simplify the production process, with potentially great savings in cost. Ordinarily, a discovery of this sort would be tested thoroughly in the laboratory as well as a small pilot plant to be sure it worked and to estimate production costs. This would take about a year. However, because of the potential savings, management wondered if it should shorten this test period. The engineering department suggested a crash testing program lasting five months. At the end of this period, it would be known whether or not the process would work, and estimated production costs would be determined. This test would cost $80,000 more than the more extended test.

It was estimated that there was a probability of 0.9 the new process would work. Further, given that the new process worked, the probability was 0.4 that the production cost would be $4 per gallon, 0.4 that it would be $20 per gallon, and 0.2 that it would be $36 per gallon.

If a decision was made at this stage to use the new process, the month of June would be used to set up the new manufacturing process. Thus, if this testing program were utilized, the company would have to set up and run the first 5,000 gallons using the old process.

Note that only the incremental testing costs associated with crashing the test program need to be charged against that alternative. Since Murgeon Chemical would test and buy the equipment for the new process, if the tests were successful independent of this decision, the costs associated with these activities need not be considered at this point.

a. Draw a decision tree for Murgeon Chemical Corporation so that management can analyze this problem.

b. What decisions do you recommend? What is the expected cost of filling this order?

c. What would be the worst decision alternative to select?

CHAPTER 4

LINEAR PROGRAMMING

INTRODUCTION

Linear programming is a widely utilized technique to allocate scarce resources to competing activities. Its use is best illustrated with a profit maximization or cost minimization problem. The decision variables are usually measures of the level of the activities.

In a profit maximization problem the profit generated by the aggregate of all activities represented by the decision variables are then maximized subject to availability of the constrained resources that are required to supply and support the activities.

In a cost minimization problem the cost incurred by the aggregate of all activities represented by the decision variables are then minimized subject to the requirements of the demands of the system for which the activities are performed.

Below we shall first give an example of a profit maximization problem. Suppose a manufacturer of trucks assembles two types of trucks, a five-ton model and a ten-ton model. The manufacturer has only one assembly line with a weekly capacity of 200 trucks. The engines supplied for the ten-ton truck cannot exceed 60 per week. Profits on each truck produced amount to $200 on each five- ton truck and $600 on each ten-ton truck. How can you formulate the above problem in a linear programming framework?

There are two decision variables in the profit maximization problem. They represent the number of five-ton trucks to produce and the number of ten-ton trucks to produce. There are two constraints, the assembly line capacity constraint and the engine supply constraint for the ten-ton truck. You can now formulate the problem. It will appear as,

Maximize $P = 200X_1 + 600X_2$

subject to

$$X_1 + X_2 \leq 200 \quad \text{assy. line constraint}$$
$$X_2 \leq 60 \quad \text{engine constraint}$$
$$X_1 \geq 0$$
$$X_2 \geq 0$$

In the above formulation the two decision variables are represented by X1 and X2 which respectively stand for the number of five-ton and for the number of ten-ton trucks. The two coefficients of 200 and 600 stand respectively for profit per unit for five and ten ton trucks. The upper equation is called the objective function and the lower relations are the constraint equations. You can ignore the last two constraint equations because all linear programming solution methods assume that the decision variables are larger than or equal to zero.

The solution to the above problem is rather simple. Since you want to maximize profit (P) you should attempt to manufacture as many ten-ton trucks (X2) as possible since the profit per unit is three times as high on ten-ton trucks as it is on five-ton trucks. However, you only have sufficient engines for 60 ten-ton trucks, which thus puts an upper limit on the ten-ton truck production. If you manufacture 60 ten-ton trucks then you can only manufacture 140 five-ton trucks per assembly line constraint. Hence, the solution to the profit maximization problem is to manufacture 140 five-ton trucks (X1 = 140) and 60 ten-ton trucks (X2 = 60) for a total profit of $64,000 per week. We were able to solve the simple problem by inspection because it was only a two variable problem with two constraints. Most realistic linear programming problems are not so simple and need the computer for obtaining the solution.

A typical cost minimization problem is the spaghetti and meatball meal planning problem. The three decision variables consist of how many ounces of uncooked meatballs (X1), how many ounces of uncooked spaghetti (X2), and how many ounces of spaghetti sauce (X3) to use in each meal. The total meal must weigh at least 15 ounces before it is cooked. Also, each meal must contain at least four ounces of meatballs, six ounces of spaghetti, and three ounces of spaghetti sauce.

The formulation of this problem is straightforward and the solution is simple. The objective is cost minimization. The formulated problem will appear as,

$$\text{Minimize} \quad C = \quad 12X1 + 4X2 + 9X3$$

subject to

$$
\begin{array}{llll}
X1 + X2 + X3 & \geq 15 & \text{meal weight constraint} \\
X1 & \geq 4 & \text{meatball constraint} \\
X2 & \geq 6 & \text{spaghetti constraint} \\
X3 & \geq 3 & \text{sauce constraint}
\end{array}
$$

In the above formulation the three decision variables are represented by X1, X2, and X3 which respectively stand for ounces of meatballs, ounces of spaghetti, and ounces of spaghetti sauce. The upper equation is now a cost minimization objective function and the constraints are all larger than or equal to constraints. The cost per ounce of uncooked meatball is 12 cents, the cost per ounce of uncooked spaghetti is 4 cents, and the cost of spaghetti sauce is 9 cents per ounce.

The solution to the above problem is rather trivial. Since you must minimize cost (C), you should try to minimize the cost of the more expensive ingredients. That is, you should use as few meatballs as possible and as little spaghetti sauce as possible in each meal. However, you must use at least four ounces of meatballs and at least three ounces of spaghetti sauce. If you use four ounces of meatballs in each meal and three ounces of spaghetti sauce, then you must use also at least eight ounces of spaghetti to satisfy the constraint which specifies that the meal must weigh at least fifteen ounces. Hence, the solution to the cost minimization problem is to make up a meal consisting of four ounces of meatballs $(X1 = 4)$, eight ounces of spaghetti $(X2 = 8)$, and three ounces of spaghetti sauce $(X3 = 3)$. The total cost of the meal will then amount to:

$$C = 12(4) + 4(8) + 9(3) = 107$$

SENSITIVITY ANALYSIS

It is frequently desirable to evaluate to what extent the objective function coefficients and the values on the right hand side of the constraint equations can be varied. For example, in the spaghetti and meatball problem presented earlier, we may wish to know the range of spaghetti price for which the optimal mix remains the same (i.e., $X_1 = 4$, $X_2 = 8$, and $X_3 = 3$). Similarly, in the truck assembly problem, we may wish to know the range of assembly line capacity for which the optimal solution remains the same.

For the coefficients of the objective function and for the right hand sides of the constraint equations the maximum increase and maximum decrease are shown. This information is useful for evaluating changes in the linear programming formulation.

EXAMPLE 1 - THE SPAGHETTI PROBLEM

In this example you will use the Linear Programming module to solve the spaghetti and meatball problem presented earlier. To solve the problem load the DSSPOM program into the computer and select the Linear Programming module from the Main Menu. The computer will pause for a few seconds and then will display the Linear Program Menu. Move the pointer to the INPUT option and press the <ENTER> key to begin the data entry process as described below.

The computer will begin the input process by placing the pointer in the title field. Enter a title such as "SPAGHETTI+MEATBALL" and press <ENTER>. The program continues by requesting the type of objective. This problem is a cost minimization problem, hence enter "MIN" and press <ENTER>. The program will continue by requesting the number of constraints and the number of variables. For this problem, there are four constraints and three decision variables. Enter these numbers as shown below.

```
  Problem title: SPAGHETTI+MEATBALL

  Minimize or Maximize objective (MIN/MAX): MIN

  Enter number of constraints:  4

  Enter number of variables:  3

 ┌─────────────────────────────────────────────────────────┐
 │ Enter problem parameters as requested.  Press RETURN to accept, │
 │ or ESC to exit.   Maximum problem size is 30 constraints and 50 │
 │ variables.  Constraint coefficients should be within -9999 and  │
 │ 9999.  Right-hand side values should be within -99999 and 99999.│
 └─────────────────────────────────────────────────────────┘
```

The computer will proceed the data input process by asking you if it should continue with the constraints and objective coefficients as shown below.

```
 ┌──────────────────────────────────────────┐
 │ Continue with coefficients (Y/N) Y        │
 └──────────────────────────────────────────┘
```

Press <Y> to proceed. The computer will then display the spread sheet data editor. The spread sheet is initialized with three variables labeled VAR1, VAR2, and VAR3. The variable names appear in the first row of the spread sheet. The second row (row 2) is used for the objective function and has been labeled OBJECTIVE. The objective function coefficients should be entered in this row. There are also three constraints (rows), labeled ROW1, ROW2, and ROW3. These rows correspond to the three structural constraints. The constraints' directions are all set to "<" and placed in column E. Note that the width of this column is one character and should hold "<", ">", or "=", depending on the constraint type. The last column of the spread sheet contains the right-hand side values, all initialized to zero. Note that the constraints are $\leq$, $\geq$, or =. However, for ease of data entry and presentation we use the symbols <, >, and =.

Entering Variable Names and Row Labels

You are now ready to begin the spread sheet data entry process. To begin, change the variable names from the default labels to more meaningful labels as shown below.

Move the pointer to cell B1   type   MEAT <ENTER>
Move the pointer to cell C1   type   SPAGHETT <ENTER>
Move the pointer to cell D1   type   SAUCE <ENTER>
Move the pointer to cell A2   type   COST <ENTER>   (label for the objective)

Now proceed to change the row labels as shown below.

Move the pointer to cell A3	type	WEIGHT <ENTER>
Move the pointer to cell A4	type	REQ MEAT <ENTER>
Move the pointer to cell A5	type	REQ SPAG <ENTER>
Move the pointer to cell A6	type	REQ SAUCE <ENTER>

Entering the Objective Function

Proceed with the data entry to enter the objective function coefficients as shown below.

Move the pointer to cell B2	type	12.0 <ENTER>
Move the pointer to cell C2	type	4.0 <ENTER>
Move the pointer to cell D2	type	9.0 <ENTER>

Entering the Constraints

The last stage of the data entry involves entering the structural constraints. This process involves entering the constraint coefficients, relational operator (<, >, or =), and the right-hand side value for each constraint. The following is the illustration of the process for the first constraint.

Move the pointer to cell B3	type	1.0 <ENTER>
Move the pointer to cell C3	type	1.0 <ENTER>
Move the pointer to cell D3	type	1.0 <ENTER>
Move the pointer to cell E3	type	> <ENTER>
Move the pointer to cell F3	type	15 <ENTER>

The data entry for the remaining three constraints is analogous. The completed spread sheet is presented below. Note that the zero coefficients do not need to be entered. However, the implied coefficient 1 must be entered as shown above.

```
                                                    READY
F3    15
            A         B         C         D     E     F
1                     MEAT      SPAGHETT  SAUCE        RHS Val.
2         COST        12.00     4.00      9.00
3         WEIGHT      1.00      1.00      1.00  >      15.00
4         REQ MEAT    1.00      0.00      0.00  >      4.00
5         REQ SPAG    0.00      1.00      0.00  >      6.00
6         REQ SAUCE   0.00      0.00      1.00  >      3.00
```

After completing the data entry process, press <F10> to keep the data in memory and exit from the spread sheet editor.

You may now obtain a hard copy printout of the problem by moving the pointer to the PRINT option and press <ENTER>. You may also save the problem on disk for future use. Move the pointer to the FILE option and select the "Save current file" sub-option. The computer will display the current drive and sub-directory and will ask you to enter a file name. Enter an appropriate name and use the suffix "LP" to identify the file as one containing a linear programming problem. Press <ENTER> to save the file.

You are now ready to solve the Spaghetti and Meatball linear programming problem. Move the pointer to the SOLVE option and select the Display output sub-option. The computer will begin the solution process by asking if you wish to see the intermediate solutions as shown below.

```
Show intermediate solutions (Y/N) N
```

The intermediate solutions are the extreme point solutions that the simplex method generates to achieve the optimal solution. For this example, you do not need to examine the intermediate solutions. Press <ENTER> to continue the solution process. The computer will pause for a few seconds and then will display the optimal solution as shown below.

```
                 Problem Title: SPAGHETTI+MEATBALL
                 ***** Optimal Solution *****
     No. of iterations =  4        COST =      107.000

                 Decision Variables Section
     Variable        Status         Value       Reduced Cost
     ---------       ---------      --------     ------------
     MEAT            Basic            4.000          0.000
     SPAGHETT        Basic            8.000          0.000
     SAUCE           Basic            3.000          0.000
```

As seen from the above report, the optimal solution consists of using 4 ounces of meatballs, 8 ounces of spaghetti, and 3 ounces of sauce. The cost of the optimal solution is 107 cents. Note that the total weight of the optimal mix is 15 ounces as required by the weight constraint.

The program will also report the status of the constraints. Press <ENTER> to proceed as shown below.

```
                    Problem Title: SPAGHETTI+MEATBALL
                    ***** Optimal Solution *****
    No. of iterations =  4        COST =      107.000

                    Slack Variables Section
        Variable       Status        Value        Shadow Price
        ----------    ----------    -----------    ------------
    WEIGHT           Nonbasic        0.000           -4.000
    REQ MEAT         Nonbasic        0.000           -8.000
    REQ SPAG         Basic           2.000            0.000
    REQ SAUC         Nonbasic        0.000           -5.000
```

The above report shows the status of the constraints (slack variables). It indicates that the slack of the weight constraint is 0 which implies that this constraint has been satisfied as an equality (i.e., if you substitute the values of the decision variables in this constraint, the left hand sid will equal the right hand side). Constraints which are satisfied as equalities are referred to as "binding" or "tight". The slack variables for the meat requirement and sauce requirement constraints are also equal 0. These constraints are also binding. However, the spaghetti requirement constraint has a slack of 2. The reason is that the number of ounces of spaghetti in the optimal solution is 8 which is 2 ounces more than its minimum requirement.

SHADOW PRICES

Every constraint in a linear programming problem has an associated entity referred to as the "shadow price" for that constraint. In short, a shadow price represents the per unit change in the objective value due to a unit change in the right-hand side of that constraint. For example, in a profit maximization linear program, the shadow price associated with a less than or equal to constraint represents the increase in profit due to one additional unit of the right-had side for that constraint. Therefore, the shadow price can also be interpreted as the marginal value of the resource as represented by the slack of that constraint. Shadow prices are of special interest to decision makers because they represent the marginal worth of the resources at optimum.

The Slack Variable Section of the optimal solution report contains the values of the shadow prices. Consider the shadow price of the Weight constraint. This shadow price, as indicated in the output report, is -4.00 which implies that if the weight requirement is decreased (marginally) from 15 to 14, the optimal cost of the mix would decrease by 4 cents. On the other hand, the shadow price for the Required Spaghetti constraint is 0 which implies that if the minimum requirement is decreased from 6 to 5, the optimal cost of the mix would not decrease. This is quite logical because the minimum requirement of this constraint has been over-satisfied by 2 units.

Note that the interpretation of the shadow prices should be done with special care because shadow prices only apply in the marginal and not absolute sense. That is, there is no guarantee for example, that the decrease in the weight requirement of the above example from 15 to 14 would not change the optimal mix and consequently the shadow prices. In the next section, addressing sensitivity analysis, the range of right-hand side for which a solution remains optimal will be discussed. This in turn will delineate the range for which the associated shadow price remains valid.

SENSITIVITY ANALYSIS

Continue the solution process by pressing the <ENTER> key. The computer will ask if you wish to examine the sensitivity analysis report as shown below.

```
Do sensitivity analysis (Y/N) Y
```

Press <Y> to see the sensitivity analysis report.

```
                    Problem Title: SPAGHETTI+MEATBALL

            Objective Function Coefficients Ranges
                    Original      Maximum            Maximum
        Variable    Coefficient   Increase           Decrease
        --------    -----------   ----------         ----------
        MEAT          12.000      Infinity              8.000
        SPAGHETT       4.000         5.000              4.000
        SAUCE          9.000      Infinity              5.000
```

The first part of the sensitivity analysis involves the objective function coefficients. As seen from the above report, for each variable, the maximum increase and maximum decrease are reported. For example, the maximum increase in the coefficient of MEAT is Infinity and the maximum decrease is 8 cents. This implies that the current mix in the optimal solution remains valid for as long as the cost coefficient of the MEAT variable remains in the range of 12 - 8 = 4 and above (to infinity). Outside of this range, the current optimal solution is no longer the minimum cost (optimal) solution. The range for the SPAGHETT variable is much tighter and is equal 0-9. This indicates that the optimal mix is quite sensitive to the price of spaghetti.

Press <ENTER> to continue with the sensitivity analysis report for the right-hand side values as shown below.

111

```
                  Problem Title: SPAGHETTI+MEATBALL

                   Right-Hand Side Ranges
                    Original      Maximum           Maximum
                     RHS          Increase          Decrease
      Row
      --------      ----------    ----------        ----------
      WEIGHT         15.000       Infinity           2.000
      REQ MEAT        4.000        2.000             4.000
      REQ SPAG        6.000        2.000            Infinity
      REQ SAUC        3.000        2.000             3.000
```

As seen from the above output, the sensitivity analysis report contains the maximum increase and maximum decrease values for the right-hand sides. For example, the maximum increase, for the REQ MEAT constraint is 2.00 and the maximum decrease is 4.00. This implies that the current solution remains optimal for as long as the requirement for the ounces of meat remains in the range of 0 to 6. Outside of this range the optimal solution will change and the current mix is no longer the best one.

EXAMPLE 2 - PROFIT MAXIMIZATION

In this example, you will use the linear programming module to solve a profit maximization problem. Consider the following three variable, three constraint problem.

```
Maximize Profit = $8X1 - $4X2 + $4X3
Subject to:        3X1 +   X2 +   X3 < 360
                    X1 -   X2 +  2X3 < 60
                    X1 +   X2 -   X3 < 120
```

Load the DSSPOM program and select the Linear Programming module. After a few seconds the computer will display the Linear Program Menu. Move the pointer to the INPUT option and press <ENTER>. (If you are continuing Example 1, the computer will ask if it should erase the current problem, press <Y> and continue). The computer will begin the data entry process by asking the problem title and other relevant parameters as shown below.

```
Problem title: MAXIMIZING PROFIT

Minimize or Maximize objective (MIN/MAX): MAX

Enter number of constraints:  3

Enter number of variables:  3

        ┌─────────────────────────────────────────┐
        │ Continue with coefficients (Y/N) Y       │
        └─────────────────────────────────────────┘
```

Next press <Y> and continue with the spread sheet data entry process.

```
A2 'PROFIT                                              ─┤READY├
        A        B        C        D    E    F
1                X1       X2       X3        RHS Val.
2      PROFIT    8.00    -4.00     4.00
3      Row1      3.00     1.00     1.00  <   360.00
4      Row2      1.00    -1.00     2.00  <    60.00
5      Row3      1.00     1.00    -1.00  <   120.00
```

Press <F10> to complete the data entry process. You are now ready to solve this profit maximization problem. Move the pointer to the SOLVE option and select the Display Output sub-option. Press <N> to avoid the intermediate solutions. The computer will pause a few seconds and then report the optimal solution as shown below.

```
                Problem Title: MAXIMIZING PROFIT
                ***** Optimal Solution *****
        No. of iterations = 2        PROFIT =      600.000

                Decision Variables Section
        Variable      Status       Value       Reduced Cost
        ---------     ---------    ---------    ------------
        X1            Basic         90.000         0.000
        X2            Basic         30.000         0.000
        X3            Nonbasic       0.000         6.000
```

113

The above solution report indicates that the optimal solution has a profit of $600.00. The value of the first decision variable X1 is 90 and the value of X2 is 30. X3 is non-basic and is equal 0. Press <ENTER> to proceed as shown below.

```
Problem Title: MAXIMIZING PROFIT
***** Optimal Solution *****
No. of iterations = 2        PROFIT =       600.000

                 Slack Variables Section
    Variable      Status         Value        Shadow Price
    ----------    ----------   ------------   ------------
    Row1          Basic          60.000          0.000
    Row2          Nonbasic        0.000          6.000
    Row3          Nonbasic        0.000          2.000
```

As seen from the above report, constraint 1 (Row1) is non-binding and its slack variable is equal to 60. The other two constraints have been satisfied in the form of equality and their associated slack variables are equal to zero.

The shadow prices in the slack variables section indicate by how much the objective function value will change for each unit of change in the resources available (the right-hand side of the constraint equations). For instance, the shadow price of the 3rd row is 2 implying that if we increase the right-hand side of the third constraint from 120 to 121 profit will increase by 2.

Similarly, the reduced cost for a decision variable indicates the minimum increase (for a maximization problem), in the per unit profit, needed for that variable to make it attractive. For example, in the above problem, the reduced cost of X3 is 6. This implies that X3 would become an attractive activity (one that would enter the basis and take a positive value at optimum) if it had a profit coefficient of 10 or more (6 units more than its original value of 4).

Press the <ENTER> key to continue the solution process and then press <Y> to obtain the sensitivity analysis report as shown below.

```
                    Problem Title: MAXIMIZING PROFIT

              Objective Function Coefficients Ranges
                    Original       Maximum            Maximum
        Variable    Coefficient    Increase           Decrease
        --------    -----------    ----------         ----------
        X1              8.000      Infinity              4.000
        X2             -4.000         4.000              4.000
        X3              4.000         6.000           Infinity
```

```
                    Problem Title: MAXIMIZING PROFIT

                       Right-Hand Side Ranges
                    Original       Maximum            Maximum
        Row         RHS            Increase           Decrease
        --------    ---------      ----------         ----------
        Row1        360.000        Infinity             60.000
        Row2         60.000          60.000            180.000
        Row3        120.000          30.000             60.000
```

The objective function coefficient ranges and right-hand side ranges in the Sensitivity Analysis shows the maximum increase and decrease of those values without changing the status of the decision variables (i.e. from basic to nonbasic or vice versa). For example, the original objective function coefficient of X3 which is 4.0 may be increased by 6.0 units to 10.0 without changing the optimal solution. This coefficient may also be decreased by an infinite amount without changing the optimal solution. Note that X3 is nonbasic and therefore has a value of 0 at the optimum solution.

As another example, consider the right-hand side of the third constraint which has an original value of 120. This value may be increased by 30 to 150 or may be decreased by 60 to 60 without changing the set of basic variables forming the optimal solution.

EXAMPLE 3 - "WHAT IF" ANALYSIS ON RESOURCE AVAILABILITY

The relevance of shadow prices was explained in the previous section. Suppose that the second (constraint) resource is increased from 60 to 65 units and the third resource from 120 to 130 units. Based on the shadow prices, the value of profit will increase by 50

(5 times 6 plus 10 times 2), from the previous value of 600. Furthermore, the status of the decision variables will not be changed (X1, X2 are basic and X3 is nonbasic) according to the sensitivity analysis.

Make the above changes to the original data by using the editor. Move the pointer to the EDIT option and select the first sub-option "Input Data". Press <ENTER> several times to accept the current values of the title, type of objective, number of constraints, and number of variables. Then press <Y> to continue with the spread sheet editor. Change the right-hand sides of the second and third constraints as stated above. The completed spread sheet is presented below.

```
                                                                  ⊣READY⊢
 F5   130
             A        B          C        D     E     F
 1            X1       X2         X3             RHS Val.
 2    PROFIT   8.00    -4.00      4.00
 3    Row1     3.00     1.00      1.00  <     360.00
 4    Row2     1.00    -1.00      2.00  <      65.00
 5    Row3     1.00     1.00     -1.00  <     130.00
```

After the change is made, press the <F10> key to return to the Linear Program Menu. Now move the pointer to the SOLVE option and select the Display Output sub-option. Press <N> to bypass the intermediate solutions. The optimal solution is then displayed as shown below.

```
               Problem Title: MAXIMIZING PROFIT
               ***** Optimal Solution *****
      No. of iterations =  2        PROFIT =      650.000

                  Decision Variables Section
        Variable       Status        Value       Reduced Cost
        ---------      ----------    ----------   ------------
        X1             Basic          97.500         0.000
        X2             Basic          32.500         0.000
        X3             Nonbasic        0.000         6.000
```

The optimum value of the objective function (PROFIT) is 650 with X1 = 97.5, X2 = 32.5, and X3 = 0. The value of Profit went up by 50 as explained by the shadow prices. Note that the value of X3 is still zero. You can only vary the right hand side values of constraints and explain the resulting increase in Profit using shadow prices so long as the status of the decision variables remains unaltered. Continued changes in resources available

116

will, at some point, change the status of the decision variables (e.g., X3 becoming a basic variable) and the resulting optimum solution can no longer be explained by the shadow prices as given in the original solution.

EXAMPLE 4 - SCALING LARGE NUMBERS TO REASONABLE SIZE

A digital computer such as IBM-PC performs arithmetic operations with limited accuracy. This accuracy is directly related to the word size of the computer. In most personal computers, real numbers can include up to five decimal places. Therefore, problems that are solved through many arithmetic operations can suffer from round-off errors which either generate an infeasible solution or at best a solution which is not accurate or incorrect.

For the above reason it is therefore necessary to scale large numbers in problem formulations down to smaller numbers. For instance a number such as 10,000 can be inserted in the formula as 10, which then means 10 units of 1000 each. Reducing large numbers in a problem formulation such as the one above is called scaling down. In scaling we redefine the amount of each constraint that is available. Hence, each constraint can be scaled back by varying amounts.

Scaling therefore refers to the relative magnitude of the numbers that comprise the problem data. An easy way to check the proper scaling of a linear programming problem is to determine the ratio of the largest number (in absolute value) to the smallest non-zero number (in absolute value) among all of the constraint coefficients. If this ratio is larger than say 10,000, then the computer solution may include round-off errors and produce the wrong solution. Such problems need proper scaling before they are entered into the computer. We illustrate this phenomenon through the following linear programming problem.

```
Min Z =    4 X1 -      3 X2 +   6 X3 -        X4

s.t.
  1 )   .0001 X1 +  .0001 X2                        < 10
  2 )                          X3 +       X4  < 20000
  3 )        X1 +               X3            < 40000
  4 )               .0001 X2 +       .0001 X4  < 6
  5 )        X1 -     10 X2                         < 0
  6 )                      6000 X3 -  5000 X4  < 0
  7 )      2 X1 -      8 X2                         < 0
  8 )                         2 X3 -     8 X4  < 0
  9 )     10 X1 +     10 X2                         > 500000
 10 )                       100 X3 +   100 X4  > 500000
```

Note that, in the above problem, the ratio of the largest (6000) to the smallest (.0001) nonzero number is 60,000,000 which is larger than 1000. Solving this problem with the linear programming module will give the results as shown below (the data entry process has not been shown).

```
Warning: This problem is poorly scaled.  The results may
include round-off errors and not represent the actual
solution to the problem.
```

```
                    Problem Title: SCALING EFFECTS
                    ***** Optimal Solution *****
        No. of iterations = 9        OBJECTIV = -176818.187

                      Decision Variables Section
            Variable      Status         Value      Reduced Cost
            --------      --------       ---------   ------------

            Var1        Nonbasic          0.000         4.000
            Var2        Basic         57272.729         0.000
            Var3        Nonbasic          0.000         5.364
            Var4        Basic          5000.000         0.000
```

In order to scale this problem properly, we multiply both sides of constraints 1 and 4 by 1000, divide both sides of constraints 9 by 100, and divide both sides of constraints 6 and 10 by 1000. The scaled problem is shown below.

Min Z =   4 X1-3 X2+ 6 X3-X4

s.t.

```
 1 )    .1 X1 + .1 X2                        < 10000
 2 )                        X3+      X4       < 20000
 3 )       X1 +             X3                < 40000
 4 )            .1 X2 +          .1 X4        < 6000
 5 )       X1 - 10 X2                         < 0
 6 )                      6 X3 - 5 X4         < 0
 7 )     2 X1 -  8 X2                         < 0
 8 )                      2 X3 - 8 X4         < 0
 9 )    .1 X1 + .1 X2                         > 5000
10 )    .1 X3 +                  .1 X4        > 500
```

The ratio of the largest coefficient (in absolute value) to the smallest coefficient (among the constraint equations) is now 10/0.1 or 100. Solving this problem with the linear programming module will give the results as shown below.

```
         Problem Title: SCALING EFFECTS
         ***** Optimal Solution *****
 No. of iterations =  9        OBJECTIV =  -170000.000

                Decision Variables Section
    Variable      Status        Value       Reduced Cost
   ----------   ----------    ----------    ------------
   Var1         Nonbasic          0.000           4.000
   Var2         Basic         54999.999           0.000
   Var3         Nonbasic          0.000           4.000
   Var4         Basic          5000.000           0.000
```

Note that the round-off error, in the objective function value, due to inadequate scaling amounts to about 4.01% (6,818.187 in 170000). Further, the value of the decision variable X2 is off by 2,272.

PROBLEMS

For each of the following two problems:
- a - Solve the problem,
- b - identify the objective function value at optimum,
- c - identify the values of the decision and slack variables at optimum, and
- d - identify the shadow prices and reduced costs.

1. Maximize $P = X_1 + 5X_2$

   subject to

   $$5X_1 + 6X_2 \leq 30$$

   $$3X_1 + 2X_2 \leq 12$$

   $$X_1 \geq 0 \quad X_2 \geq 0$$

2. Minimize $C = 3X_1 + 4X_2$

   subject to

   $$X_1 + X_2 \geq 6$$

   $$2X_1 + 4X_2 \geq 21$$

   $$X_1 \geq 0 \quad X_2 \geq 0$$

For each of the following two problems:
- a - Solve the problem,
- b - identify which variables are Basic/Nonbasic,
- c - identify the range of objective function coefficients for which each variable remains Basic, and
- d - identify the range of right-hand side values for each row such that the current solution remains optimal.

3. Maximize $P = 50X_1 + 60X_2 + 120X_3$

   subject to

   $$2X_1 + 4X_2 + 6X_3 \leq 160$$

   $$3X_1 + 2X_2 + 4X_3 \leq 120$$

   $$X_1 \geq 0 \quad X_2 \geq 0 \quad X_3 \geq 0$$

4. Maximize P = 32X1 + 15X2 + 12X3

   subject to   1X1 + 2X2 + 3X3 ≤ 10

                       2X1 + 1X2 + 2X3 ≤ 15

                       X1 ≥ 0 X2 ≥ 0 X3 ≥ 0

5. Consider the following linear programming problem:

   Maximize R = 6X1 + 4X2

   subject to   8X1 + X2 ≤ 180

                       2X1 + X2 ≤ 50

                       3X1 + X2 ≤ 300

                       X1 + 4X2 ≤ 50

                       X1 ≥ 0   X2 ≥ 0

   a -   Solve the problem and identify the optimal solution,
   b -   determine which of the four constraints are satisfied as equality (binding),
   c -   determine the value of the objective function if the second right-hand
          side is changed from 50 to 53, and
   d -   determine the value of the objective function if the objective coefficient of X1
          is changed from 6 to 9.

6. Consider the following linear programming problem:

   Maximize R = 2X1 + 3X2 - 1X3 + 1X4

   subject to   3X1 + 4X2 - X3 + 2X4 ≤ 10000

                       8X1 + 1X2 - 5X3 - X4 ≤ 3000

                       2X1 + X2 + X3 - 3X4 ≤ 9000

                       X1 ≥ 0 X2 ≥ 0 X3 ≥ 0 X4 ≥ 0

   a -   Solve the problem.

b - Add the constraint X2 < 2000 and solve the problem. How has the optimal objective value changed? Why?

c - Delete the added constraint (in Part b) and variable X2 and solve the problem. How has the optimal objective value changed? Why?

7. Consider the following linear programming problem:

Minimize $C = 5X1 + 14X2 + 20X3$

subject to

$$3X1 + X2 \geq 16$$

$$X1 + X2 + X3 \geq 24$$

$$X1 \leq 10$$

$$X1 \geq 0 \quad X2 \geq 0 \quad X3 \geq 0$$

a - Solve the problem.

b - Assume that X3 is unrestricted in sign, make the appropriate changes to the problem and solve (Hint: X3 must be replaced by the difference between two nonnegative variables). What has happened to the optimal solution? Why?

c - Add the constraint X2 ≤ 50 to the problem in Part b and solve. Compare the new problem to that obtained in Part a. What is the value of X3?

8. Two products, A and B, during the manufacturing process must pass through four machine operations I, II, III and IV. The machine times (in hours per unit produced) and machine time availabilities are listed below.

	I	II	III	IV
Product A	2	4	3	1
Product B	1/4	2	1	4
Total Machine Time Available	45	100	300	50

Product A sells for $6 per unit and Product B sells for $4 per unit. What combination of A and B should be manufactured in order to maximize profits? Suppose 22 units of A are required as a minimum.

9. Superior Steel has 10,000 tons of ore B_1, 30,000 tons of ore B_2, and 9,000 tons of ore B_3. Four steel products can be extracted from the three ores:

Product x_1 requires 3 tons of B_1, 8 tons of B_2, and 2 tons of B_3.
Product x_2 requires 4 tons of B_1, 2 tons of B_2 and 1 ton of B_3.
Product x_3 produces 1 ton of B_1, but requires 5 tons of B_2, and 1 ton of B_3.
Product x_4 requires 2 tons of B_1, and produces 1 ton of B_2 and 3 tons of B_3.

Profits are: $2 per ton on product x_1,
               $3 per ton on product x_2, and
               $1 per ton on product x_4.

Product x_3 has to be disposed of and the cost of disposal is $1 per ton.

Formulate the above problem as a linear programming problem and solve.

10. INTERNATIONAL MOTORS

The Machine Shop Division of International Motors was faced with the problem of having to decide whether to machine several products themselves or to subcontract. The products were to be used by the assembly division. The machine shop would be credited with a specified transfer price and management was anxious to supply the product or products in the quantities that would be most profitable.

Each of the products required casting, machining, and assembly and packaging. Casting operations for products A and B could be subcontracted, but the castings for product C required special equipment which precluded the use of subcontractors. Direct costs of the three operations, the transfer of prices for the products, and the respective contributions to overhead and profits are shown below.

Each unit of product A required nine minutes of casting time, nine minutes of machining time, and five minutes for assembly and packaging. For product B, the times were fifteen minutes, five minutes, and three minutes, respectively. A unit of product C took twelve minutes for casting, twelve minutes for machining, and three minutes for assembly and packaging.

The Machine Shop Division had capacities of 12,000 minutes of casting time, 18,000 minutes of machining time, and 15,000 minutes of assembly and packaging time per week.

Direct costs, transfer prices, and contributions to overhead and profits

Item	Product A	Product B	Product C
Subcontract cost	$0.65	$0.80	-
Cost of Machining	0.25	0.15	$0.35
Cost of assembly and packaging	0.40	0.25	0.25
Cost of casting (in house)	0.20	0.25	0.30
Price	2.25	2.35	2.35

Solve the problem. Give economic interpretations for all of the shadow prices. Give a detailed explanation for the right hand side ranges (reported in the sensitivity analysis).

11. Grabo Company has two plants that produce white wine and red wine. Because of the different process required and a different set-up at each plant, there are differences in the yields and costs of producing each wine. Each plant has 100,000 pounds of grapes available. A minimum of 400 bottles of white wine and 600 bottles of red wine must be produced. The yields and costs are shown in the table below.

Formulate and solve an LP to minimize Grabo's costs.

	PLANT 1	PLANT 2
Grapes/bottle red wine	80 lbs.	100 lbs.
Cost/bottle red wine	$10	$8
Grapes/bottle white wine	50 lbs.	70 lbs.
Cost/bottle white wine	$8	$7

12. Streetsmart Investment Company must determine its investment strategy for the next three years. Streetsmart has four investments to choose from -- A, B, C, and D. In year 1, there is $40,000 available to invest. In year 2, there will be $20,000 to invest and in year 3 there will be $10,000. The cash outflows and NPV of each investment are shown in the table below.

Formulate and solve the LP to maximize Streetsmart's profits. Assume fractional investments can be made.

	INVESTMENTS ($000)			
	A	B	C	D
Year 1 Outflow	10.0	50.0	7.0	15.0
Year 2 Outflow	3.5	8.0	6.5	18.0
Year 3 Outflow	15.0	7.0	4.0	13.0
NPV	18.0	24.0	10.0	15.0

13. BBB Deodorant Company manufactures two types of deodorant---scented and unscented. These two deodorants are produced by blending 2 raw materials together in varying proportions. The scented deodorant must contain at least 60% raw material A, and the unscented deodorant must contain at least 50% raw material A. The scented deodorant sells for $3/oz and the unscented deodorant sells for $2/oz. Raw materials A and B can be processed in one of two ways. Running process 1 for one hour requires 4 ounces of chemicals and 3 hours of labor, and yields 4 ounces of each raw material. Running process 2 for one hour requires 3 ounces of chemicals and 4 hours of labor, and yields 3 ounces of raw material A and 1 ounce of raw material B. A total of 140 hours of labor and 112 ounces of chemicals are available.

Formulate and solve an LP that will maximize profits for BBB Deodorant Company.

14. U.S.A. Lemonade Company sells bags of lemons and cartons of lemonade. U.S.A. Lemonade grades the lemons on a scale of 1 (poor) to 10 (excellent). Currently, U.S.A. Lemonade has 50,000 pounds of grade 8 lemons and 60,000 pounds of grade 5 lemons. The average quality of lemons sold by the bag must be 6 and an average grade of 7 must be in the lemonade. Each pound of lemons sold in juice form yields $1.90 in revenue and incurs costs of $0.80. Likewise, each pound of lemons sold by the bag yields $1.05 in revenue and incurs costs of $0.45.

Formulate and solve an LP to maximize U.S.A. Lemonade's profits.

15. A grocery store requires a different number of full time workers depending on the day of the week. The number of full time workers needed each day is shown below. Store practice is that each full time employee works 5 consecutive days and has 2 days off each week. For example, a full time employee working Monday through Friday receives Saturday and Sunday off.

Formulate and solve and LP that minimizes the number of full time workers needed, while meeting the staffing requirements (fractional number of workers are allowed).

NUMBER OF WORKERS

Day 1 - Monday		15
Day 2 - Tuesday		13
Day 3 - Wednesday		13
Day 4 - Thursday		15
Day 5 - Friday		19
Day 6 - Saturday		14
Day 7 - Sunday		9

CHAPTER 5

TRANSPORTATION METHOD

INTRODUCTION

The transportation method or distribution method is a technique which provides an optimal allocation of inventories from multiple sources, such as supplier plants, to multiple destinations, such as distribution warehouses. The measure of effectiveness used is usually the cost of transportation which is therefore minimized. However, in certain formulations, the problem may be stated so that the measure of effectiveness is profit or utility. In that case, the measure of effectiveness, profit or utility, is maximized.

This can best be illustrated with an example. Suppose we have four distribution warehouses and three supplier plants. The distribution or transportation costs between each of the three supplier plants (sources) and the four distribution warehouses (destinations) can be readily estimated. Suppose the transportation or distribution costs are as shown in Table 5-1. For example, note that the cost to move one unit of inventory from plant 2 to warehouse 3 amounts to $15.

In Table 5-2 we provide a listing of the plant supply capacities in units per month and the warehouse demands in units per month. Note that the plant supply capacities and warehouse demands are exactly equal. This is a rather unusual situation and in most cases the two will not be equal. When the two are not equal we add a "dummy" plant or a "dummy" warehouse. For the "dummy" plant or "dummy" warehouse we then insert transportation costs of $0. Before we explore this alternative let us first set up the above problem.

The transportation cost data and the plant supply capacity and warehouse demands data are combined in Table 5-3. Note that the warehouse demands are shown at the bottom margin of the matrix. The plant supply capacities are shown in the right-hand margin of the matrix. The transportation cost values are shown in each respective matrix cell. Each cell intersects with one plant (source) and one warehouse (destination).

The goal of the transportation method is to find the lowest cost transportation arrangement between plants and warehouses. The computer program is designed to achieve this objective.

Suppose we have a solution to the above problem as shown in Table 5-4. Note that the cost of that solution can be determined by multiplying the units shipped between plants (sources) and warehouses (destinations) by the respective transportation costs. The above allocation solution directs that plant 1 ship 75 units per month to warehouse 3 and 100 units to warehouse 4. Similarly, plant 2 ships 10 units per month to warehouse 1 and 75 units to warehouse 4. Finally, plant 3 ships 115 units per month to warehouse 1 and 100 units to warehouse 2. The total cost per month of the above arrangement will amount to 75(8) + 100(7) + 10(21) + 75(16) + 115(18) + 100(5) = \$5280. Whether this solution is the lowest cost solution we do not know. With the computer solution method we will be assured that we will arrive at the lowest cost solution.

		Warehouses (Destinations)			
		1	2	3	4
	1	14	21	8	7
Plants	2	21	19	15	16
(Sources)	3	18	5	17	23

Table 5-1: Unit Transportation or Distribution Cost Matrix

Note: The cell entries are the transportation or distribution costs per unit.

Plants (Sources)	Plant Supply Capacities (Units/Month)	Warehouses (Destinations)	Warehouse Demands (Units/Month)
1	175	1	125
2	85	2	100
3	215	3	75
		4	175
Total	475		
		Total	475

Table 5-2: Plant Capacities and Warehouse Requirements

		Warehouses (Destinations)				
		1	2	3	4	Supplies
Plants	1	14	21	8	7	175
	2	21	19	15	16	85
(Sources)	3	18	5	17	23	215
Warehouse Demands		125	100	75	175	475

Table 5-3: Transportation Method Cost Matrix

		Warehouses (Destinations)				
		1	2	3	4	Supplies
Plants	1	14	21	8 75	7 100	175
	2	21 10	19	15	16 75	85
(Sources)	3	18 115	5 100	17	23	215
Warehouse Demands		125	100	75	175	475

Table 5-4: Solution to Transportation Problem

Note: The entries in the lower parts of the cells are the transportation or distribution allocations.

The transportation problem can also be formulated as a linear programming problem and solved by using the linear programming solution method. However, it is more efficient and easier to solve this type of problem with the transportation solution method.

APPLICATION TO THE PRODUCTION PLANNING PROBLEM

The transportation model can be used to solve aggregate production planning problems. The aggregate planning problem involves the development of a production schedule, over a fixed number of time periods, to satisfy occasional demands called "lumpy" demands. The production amount in each period is subject to limitations of available production capacity. The production capacity may consist of regular time capacity, overtime capacity, and subcontracting. In addition, excess production in one period may be carried forward as inventory to satisfy the demand of a later period. Consider the numerical example presented in Table 5-5. The problem is to determine the production schedule to satisfy the demands of 500, 650, and 700 for months 1, 2, and 3, respectively. The general formulation of the aggregate planning problem as a transportation model is shown in Table 5-6.

	Period (Month)		
	1	2	3
Demand	500	650	700 *
Capacity			
Regular	450	450	450
Overtime	50	50	50
Subcontract	100	100	100
Beginning inventory	100		
Costs			
Regular time	$30 per unit		
Overtime	$40 per unit		
Subcontract	$45 per unit		
Inventory holding	$0.50 per unit per month		

Table 5-5: Aggregate Production Planning Example

* No backorder is allowed

130

Period		Period 1	Period 2	Period 3	...	Ending invent.	Capacity
Period	Beginning inventory	0	h	$2h$	...	nh	I
1	Reg. time	p	$p+h$	$p+2h$	...	$p+nh$	R_1
	Overtime	q	$q+h$	$q+2h$	...	$q+nh$	O_1
	Subcont.	s	$s+h$	$s+2h$	...	$s+nh$	S_1
2	Reg. time	M	p	$p+h$	...	$p+(n-1)h$	R_2
	Overtime	M	q	$q+h$	...	$q+(n-1)h$	O_2
	Subcont.	M	s	$s+h$	...	$s+(n-1)h$	S_2
3	Reg. time	M	M	p	...	$p+(n-2)h$	R_3
	Overtime	M	M	q	...	$q+(n-2)h$	O_3
	Subcont.	M	M	s	...	$s+(n-2)h$	S_3
	Demand	D_1	D_2	D_3		E	

Table 5-6: Transportation Model for Aggregate Planning Problem*

*Legend: I = initial inventory n = number of periods
p = regular time production cost per unit
q = overtime production cost per unit
s = subcontracting cost per unit
h = holding cost per unit per period
R_i = regular time capacity for period i
O_i = overtime capacity for period i
S_i = subcontracting capacity for period i
D_i = demand in period i
E = required ending inventory
M = a large positive number used to avoid backorders

Using this approach, the transportation model for our numerical example is presented in Table 5-7. As we will show, we can solve this problem using the transportation program.

		Period 1	Period 2	Period 3	Capacity
Period	Beginning inventory	0	.5	1.0	100
1	Reg. time	30	30.5	31.0	450
	Overtime	40	40.5	41.0	50
	Subcont.	45	45.5	46.0	100
2	Reg. time	M	30	30.5	450
	Overtime	M	40	40.5	50
	Subcont.	M	45	45.5	100
3	Reg. time	M	M	30	450
	Overtime	M	M	40	50
	Subcont.	M	M	45	100
	Demand	500	650	700	

Table 5-7 Transportation Model for the Numerical Example

EXAMPLE 1 - BALANCED TRANSPORTATION PROBLEM

This example involves solving the balanced transportation problem presented in Table 5-3. To solve the problem, select the Transportation Method from the Main Menu. The computer will then load the transportation method and display the Transportation Menu. Move the pointer to the INPUT option and press the <ENTER> key. Use "BALANCED PROBLEM" for the title. The problem has 3 sources and 4 destinations. The initial data entry screen for this problem is shown below.

```
Problem title: BALANCED PROBLEM

Number of sources:  3

Number of destinations:   4

┌─────────────────────────────────────────────────────────┐
│ Continue with the cost and requirements table (Y/N) Y   │
└─────────────────────────────────────────────────────────┘
```

Press <Y> to continue with the spread sheet data entry process to enter the cost and requirements table. The initial spread sheet for this problem will have three sources labeled SOR1, SOR2, and SOR3, and four destinations labeled as DTN1, DTN2, DTN3, and DTN4. You may keep the default labels for the sources and destinations or change them to more meaningful labels (such as BFLO, NYC, ATHENS, etc.). To change the labels, move the pointer to cell A2 and type "PLANT-1." Press the down arrow key to move to cell A3 and type "PLANT-2." Repeat this process for the other source and destinations to change their labels to "PLANT-3" for source 3 and WH-1, WH-2, WH-3, and WH-4 for destinations one to four, respectively. The completed spread sheet data entry screen is displayed below.

```
A1                                                      ═╡READY╞
        A       B       C       D       E       F
1              WH-1    WH-2    WH-3    WH-4    Supply
2      PLANT-1  14.00   21.00    8.00    7.00   175.0
3      PLANT-2  21.00   19.00   15.00   16.00    85.0
4      PLANT-3  18.00    5.00   17.00   23.00   215.0
5      Demand   125.0   100.0    75.0   175.0
```

Once all of the data has been entered, press <F10> to exit the spread sheet data entry mode and keep the data.

You may now continue and obtain a hard copy printout of the input data by moving the pointer to the print option and press <ENTER>. Be sure that your printer is "ON" and ready before continuing at this point. The program will display this message and ask you to verify the status of the printer. Examine the printout of the data carefully and make sure the input data is correct. If the data contains any errors, move the pointer to the EDIT option and select the sub-option "Input Data". Correct the input data if necessary and proceed to solve the problem as described below.

To solve the problem, move the pointer to the SOLVE option and select the sub-option Display Output, and press <ENTER>. The program will continue and solve the problem using the transportation simplex method. It will then report the optimal solution as shown below.

```
              Problem Title: BALANCED PROBLEM
       Optimal Solution: Total Shipping Cost =      5130.00


Ship       115.00 units from source PLANT-3  to dest. WH-1
Ship       100.00 units from source PLANT-3  to dest. WH-2
Ship        10.00 units from source PLANT-2  to dest. WH-1
Ship       175.00 units from source PLANT-1  to dest. WH-4
Ship        75.00 units from source PLANT-2  to dest. WH-3
Ship         0.00 units from source PLANT-2  to dest. WH-4
```

As seen from the above output report, the optimal solution has a total shipping cost of $5,130.00. The solution consists of shipping 115 units from plant 3 to warehouse 1, 100 units from plant 3 to warehouse 2, 10 units from plant 2 to warehouse 1, 175 units from plant 1 to warehouse 4, 75 units from plant 2 to warehouse 3, and nothing (zero units) from plant 2 to warehouse 4.

EXAMPLE 2 - PRODUCTION PLANNING PROBLEM

In this example, you will solve the aggregate production planning problem presented earlier in this chapter. The data for this example is shown in Table 5-7. To enter the problem data, select the INPUT option and proceed as requested. The number or sources for this problem is 10, including the nine production sources and one source for the initial inventory. The number of destinations is three, corresponding to the three production periods. The initial data entry screen is shown below.

```
Problem title: PRODUCTION PLANNING

Number of sources: 10

Number of destinations:   3


    ┌──────────────────────────────────────────────────────────┐
    │ Continue with the cost and requirements table (Y/N) Y     │
    └──────────────────────────────────────────────────────────┘
```

Press <Y> to continue with spread sheet data entry of the cost and requirements table. The completed spread sheet screen is shown below.

```
                                                          ─┤READY├─
A1
            A         B        C        D        E
  1                  P-1      P-2      P-3      Supply
  2   BI            0.00     0.50     1.00     100.0
  3   RT-1         30.00    30.50    31.00     450.0
  4   OT-1         40.00    40.50    41.00      50.0
  5   SB-1         45.00    45.50    46.00     100.0
  6   RT-2       1000.00    30.00    30.50     450.0
  7   OT-2       1000.00    40.00    40.50      50.0
  8   SB-2       1000.00    45.00    45.50     100.0
  9   RT-3       1000.00  1000.00    30.00     450.0
 10   OT-3       1000.00  1000.00    40.00      50.0
 11   SB-3       1000.00  1000.00    45.00     100.0
 12   Demand      500.0    650.0    700.0
```

As seen from the display screen, the three destinations, representing the three periods have been labeled P-1, P-2, and P-3, respectively. The source corresponding to the initial inventory has been labeled BI and the three production sources in the first period have been labeled RT-1 (for regular time), OT-1 (for overtime) and SB-1 (for sub-contracting). The labels for the other six sources are analogous. The demands are set at 500, 650, and 700 for periods one, two, and three, respectively. The supply of the first source is 100 units corresponding to the initial inventory. The supplies for the other sources are the available capacities. Note that for the cells corresponding to backlogs, a shipping cost of $1000 per unit is used to prevent allocation of real supplies to these cells.

You are now ready to proceed with solving the problem. Select the SOLVE option and pull the pointer down to the Display Output sub-option. Press the <ENTER> key to solve the problem and display the results on the screen. In this problem the total demand is less than the total supplies. The program will display a message informing you that a "Dummy" column will be added with shipping costs equal to zero and demand equal to the extra supply amount as shown below.

```
Total demand is less than total supply, a dummy column  will
be added with shipping costs equal to 0.
```

```
                   Problem Title: PRODUCTION PLANNING
            Optimal Solution: Total Shipping Cost =    57875.00


    Ship      100.00 units from source BI      to dest. P-1
    Ship      400.00 units from source RT-1    to dest. P-1
    Ship       50.00 units from source RT-1    to dest. P-2
    Ship       50.00 units from source OT-1    to dest. P-2
    Ship       50.00 units from source SB-1    to dest. P-2
    Ship      450.00 units from source RT-2    to dest. P-2
    Ship       50.00 units from source OT-2    to dest. P-2
    Ship        0.00 units from source OT-2    to dest. P-3
    Ship      100.00 units from source SB-2    to dest. P-3
    Ship      450.00 units from source RT-3    to dest. P-3
    Ship       50.00 units from source OT-3    to dest. P-3
    Ship      100.00 units from source SB-3    to dest. P-3
    Ship       50.00 units from source SB-1    to dest. WH-4
```

As seen from the above results, the 500 units demand of the first period is satisfied from the initial inventory of 100 units (source BI to dest. P-1) and 400 units regular time production during the first period (source RT-1 to dest. P-1). The 650 units demand of the second period is satisfied from 50 units of regular time production in period 1 (source RT-1 to dest. P-2), 50 units of overtime in period 1 (source OT-1 to P-2), 50 units of sub-contracting in period 1 (source SB-1 to dest. P-2), 450 units of regular time in period 2 (source RT-2 to dest. P-2), and 50 units of overtime in period 2 (source OT-2 to dest. P-2). The 700 units demand in period 3 is satisfied from 100 units of sub-contracting in period 2 (source SB-2 to dest. P-3), 450 units of regular time production in period 3 (source RT-3 to dest. P-3), 50 units of overtime production in period 3 (source OT-3 to dest. P-3), and 100 units of sub-contracting in period 3 (source SB-3 to dest. P-3). The extra unused capacity is 50 units (total capacity minus total demand) which in this case corresponds to the remaining 50 units of sub-contracting in period 1 (source SB-1 to dest. WH-4 which is dummy). The total cost of optimal production plan is $57,875.

PROBLEMS

1. Find the minimum cost solution for the transportation problem shown below.

Warehouse

		1	2	3	4	5	6	Plant Capacities
Plants	1	14	24	18	28	22	19	450
	2	17	18	25	16	23	21	250
	3	30	16	22	30	25	18	500
Warehouse Requirements		350	250	150	175	200	75	

2. Suppose a new plant is added to problem 1 with a capacity of 300 units. The unit shipping costs from the new plant to warehouses 1, 2, 3, 4, 5, and 6 amount to $25, $14, $17, $24, $19, and $16, respectively. What is the minimum cost solution?

3. Suppose two new warehouses are added to problem 1 with requirements of 75 and 125 units, respectively. The unit shipping costs from the plants to the first new warehouse amount to $25, $29, and $15, respectively, and to the other warehouse the shipping costs amount to $27, $19, and $23, respectively. What is the minimum cost solution?

4. Find the minimum cost solution for the transportation problem below.

Warehouse

		1	2	3	4	5	Plant Capacities
Plants	1	9	8	6	8	12	860
	2	12	7	11	9	13	350
	3	11	1	14	3	5	420
	4	13	10	8	15	4	280
Warehouse Requirements		180	350	400	470	250	

138

5. Suppose a new plant, plant 5, is added to problem 4 with capacity of 380 units and shipping costs of 3, 9, 8, 4 and 2 to warehouses 1, 2, 3, 4 and 5, respectively. Find minimum cost solution.

6. Suppose a new warehouse is added to problem 5 with requirements of 160 units and shipping costs of 4, 9, 12, 8 and 4 to plants 1, 2, 3, 4 and 5, respectively. Find the minimum cost solution.

7. Find the minimum cost solution for the following transportation problem.

		Destinations							Source Capacities
		1	2	3	4	5	6	7	
	1	5	6	5	10	9	7	11	350
	2	11	3	7	4	11	10	15	270
Sources	3	10	12	9	8	13	11	20	400
	4	7	15	11	9	10	13	22	330
	5	9	8	13	6	7	9	16	150
	6	8	9	15	10	12	7	14	350
Requirements		250	200	200	150	400	300	350	1850

8. Suppose a new source 7 is added to problem 7 with capacity of 200 units and shipping costs of 10, 9, 8, 11, 6, 7 and 13 to destinations 1, 2, 3, 4, 5, 6 and 7, respectively. Find the minimum cost solution.

9. Determine the optimum shipping plan for the transportation matrix below.

Warehouse

		1	2	3	4	5	Plant Capacities
	1	20	22	26	18	11	500
	2	33	17	14	21	9	100
Plants	3	10	16	23	20	16	200
	4	16	14	13	18	18	300
	5	14	12	18	21	26	150
	6	17	9	17	11	19	250
Warehouse Requirements		150	150	300	400	500	1500

10. Suppose a new warehouse is added to problem 9 with requirements of 200 units. The unit shipping costs from the plants to the new warehouse are 9, 15, 17, 22, 19 and 11, respectively. What is the optimum cost solution?

140

11. Solve the following aggregate production planning problem using the transportation model. Assume that backorders are not allowed.

	Period (Month)		
	1	2	3
Demand	550	600	750
Capacity			
Regular	450	450	450
Overtime	75	85	50
Subcontract	120	90	100
Beginning inventory	100		

Costs
  Regular time $20 per unit
  Overtime $25 per unit
  Subcontract $30 per unit
  Inventory
    holding $2.00 per unit per month

12. Solve problem 11, assuming that backorders are permitted at a cost of $5 per unit per month.

13. Solve problem 11, assuming that there is no initial inventory but the regular time production capacity of the first period is 500 units.

14. Solve problem 11, assuming that the regular time production capacity for the first period is 550 and you will need an ending inventory of 75 units. Note that an ending inventory is not unused capacity but units that are produced and carried to the next planning horizon.

15. CORDOBA FOODS

Cordoba Foods is a national producer and marketer of packaged dried foods which it sells nationally under the Cordoba brand name. Cordoba operates three plants from which it ships to regional warehouses or directly to warehouse depots of large customers. Demand for Cordoba products amounted to 48,000,000 pounds in 1990, distributed over six sales regions.

Sales Region	Demand in Million of Pounds
New York	7
Atlanta	4
Chicago	14
Denver	7
Los Angeles	12
Seattle	4
Total Demand	48

Each of the six regional warehouses were under direct supervision of a regional sales manager. Transfer prices were $0.40 per pound from each plant but regional managers had to pay for shipping from the supplying plant to their respective warehouses. A schedule of shipping rates (in cents) and plant capacities are shown below.

Shipping Costs in Center per Pound and Plant Capacities - Cordoba

Warehouse	Boston Plant	Desmoines Plant	Dallas Plant
New York	12	26	25
Atlanta	17	20	16
Chicago	15	10	21
Denver	22	14	11
Los Angeles	34	30	18
Seattle	32	25	24
Plant Capacity in Millions of Pounds	16	17	19

142

Since each plant had a limited production capacity and regional managers attempted to obtain their supplies at the lowest transportation cost, there were frequent conflicts between regional managers and plant managers about shipping schedules. As a result, considerable dissatisfaction resulted and some regional managers felt their region's profits were adversely affected by the haphazard shipping schedules.

Suppose you are called in as a consultant to analyze the complaints and, if possible, to arrive at a minimum cost shipping schedule. How would you go about it? How much could Cordoba Foods save by utilizing the optimal schedule? Which regional managers would be satisfied with the new schedule if the current schedule is as shown below? How could you overcome the regional managers' resistance to the new schedule?

Current Shipping Schedule in Millions of Pounds - Cordoba

Warehouse	Boston Plant	Desmoines Plant	Dallas Plant
New York	7		
Atlanta			4
Chicago	9	5	
Denver		7	
Los Angeles			12
Seattle		4	
Excess Capacity		1	3
Total Capacity	16	17	19

16. The Knicknak Company produces 3 types of statues at 3 different plants. The time required to produce one statue, regardless of type, and the costs at each plant are shown below. Each week 100 statues of each type must be produced. Each plant is open 40 hours a week.

Formulate and solve a balanced transportation problem to minimize the cost of Knicknak's requirements.

COST

	Statue 1	Statue 2	Statue 3	Time (min)
Plant 1	$20	$15	$9	30
Plant 2	$16	$10	$10	20
Plant 3	$14	$7	$7	12

17. There are 3 school districts in the town of Mexicana, a large town on the California - Mexico border. The number of whites and Mexicans in each school district are shown below. The town would like to balance the schools racially in order to provide the best possible education for all of the students. Each school must have 300 students and an equal number of Mexicans at each school. The distance between school districts is shown below.

Formulate and solve a balanced transportation problem to minimize the distance that students must be bussed. Assume that if the student attends school in his own district, there is no bussing.

	STUDENTS		DISTANCE TO (MILES)	
	American	Mexican	District 1	District 2
District 1	95	150	-	-
District 2	150	105	5	-
District 3	250	150	3	7

18. Textco Corporation is trying to determine how many books to manufacture over the summer to meet the demand for the Fall start of classes. Assume students can begin purchasing text books in May. They can purchase books throughout the summer (June, July, August), but all students must have their books by September 1. Textco has an initial inventory of 100 books. Because it takes time to set-up manufacturing and train workers, only 100 books can be produced in May. As efficiency improves and more skilled labor is added, Textco can increase production by 10% per month (assume integers). These production levels are met by running the plant at full capacity. Therefore, no overtime can occur. However, Textco may subcontract some books to another manufacturer for $5, place their own label on them for $2, and sell them to the students. The number of books that Textco can subcontract for resale is limited to 30 a month. The books may be backlogged, but a fee of $3 per book per month is incurred. Conversely, if there are books left over at the end of the month, the holding cost is $2 per book per month. The demand is as follows: May 200, June 100, July 100, and August 250. Each book Textco manufactures incurs a cost of $4.50.

Formulate and solve a balanced transportation problem to minimize Textco's costs. State your answer in sentence form.

CHAPTER 6

ASSIGNMENT METHOD

INTRODUCTION

The assignment method is able to provide an optimal matching of jobs to candidates for the jobs. Specific examples are assignments of jobs to machines, jobs to work centers, jobs to individuals, etc. Optimal matching is attained by maximizing or minimizing some measure of effectiveness of the assignment such as profit, utility or cost. Each potential job assignment is evaluated and an effectiveness measure is determined for that job assignment. If the effectiveness measure is profit or utility, it is, of course, maximized and, if the effectiveness measure is cost, it is minimized.

For example, suppose we have four jobs that need to be assigned to four candidates, who in this case are four contractors. Only one job can be assigned to each contractor. Note that the number of jobs equals the number of contractors. We shall develop a table or matrix to show all possible relationships between the four jobs and the four contractors. The contractors are represented by the rows of the matrix and the jobs are represented by the columns of the matrix as shown in Table 6-1. The sixteen cells of the matrix contain the costs associated with each possible job- contractor combination. For instance, job 2 assigned to contractor 2 will cost as much as $19. The entries in the matrix cells are, therefore, the measures of effectiveness that will be minimized because they are costs. If the entries were profits or utilities, then we would, of course, maximize them.

One possible solution to the above problem is the following:

        Assign job 1 to contractor 2 - cost: $ 7
        Assign job 2 to contractor 3 - cost: $ 6
        Assign job 3 to contractor 1 - cost: $14
        Assign job 4 to contractor 4 - cost: $ 4

The total cost for the above assignment of four jobs to four contractors amounts to $31. Is that the lowest possible cost? It may be or it may not be. The procedure used in the computer model will, however, determine the lowest aggregate cost assignment. The above problem can also be formulated as a linear programming problem and solved using the linear programming solution module. However, it is more efficient and easier to use the assignment method to solve this type of problem.

		Jobs			
		1	2	3	4
Candidates (Contractors)	1	16	9	14	17
	2	7	19	8	14
	3	15	6	9	10
	4	19	17	11	4

Table 6-1: Assignment Matrix - Jobs to Contractors

Note: Cell Entries Are Costs Associated with the Respective Job-Contractor Combinations.

The solution technique for the assignment problem requires that the number of jobs and candidates be equal. If they are not, the computer will expand the matrix so that the matrix is square. For instance, if there were 5 contractors but only four jobs, then the computer will expand the matrix to a 5 x 5 matrix by adding a dummy job. All cost values of the dummy job would be set equal to zero as shown on Table 6-2. Note that the cost assignments for contractor 5 must, of course, be determined and inserted in the appropriate matrix cells.

In the case of having more jobs than contractors (candidates) the computer would again expand the matrix so that it becomes square. For instance, suppose we have six jobs and only four contractors (candidates). The computer will then expand the matrix to a 6 x 6 matrix as shown on Table 6-3. Note that contractors 5 and 6 are dummy contractors and the cost values for the dummy contractors are set equal to zero.

Candidates (Contractors)	Jobs				
	1	2	3	4	5
1	16	9	14	17	0
2	7	19	8	14	0
3	15	6	9	10	0
4	19	17	11	4	0
5	14	11	18	16	0

Table 6-2: Expanded Assignment Matrix - Four Jobs to Five Candidates

Note: Cell Entries are Assignment Costs.

Candidates (Contractors)	Jobs					
	1	2	3	4	5	6
1	16	9	14	17	8	11
2	7	19	8	14	13	18
3	15	6	9	10	17	6
4	19	17	11	4	9	14
5	0	0	0	0	0	0
6	0	0	0	0	0	0

Table 6-3: Expanded Assignment Matrix - Six Jobs to Four Candidates

Note: Cell Entries are Assignment Costs.

EXAMPLE 1 - JOBS TO CONTRACTORS PROBLEM

In this example you will use the Assignment Program to solve the "Job to Contractor" problem presented earlier. The objective is to assign the four jobs to the four contractors so as to minimize the total cost of assignments. The assignment costs for this problem are presented in Table 6-1.

Load the DSSPOM program into the computer and select the Assignment Method from the Main Menu. After a few seconds, the computer will load the assignment program and display the Assignment Menu. Move the pointer to the INPUT option and press <ENTER>. The program will begin the data entry process by asking you to enter a title. Choose a title that you find appropriate and enter it into the title field. Press <ENTER> to continue with the next parameter.

The next item to enter is the type of objective. Since the problem involves assigning jobs to candidates and therefore incurring a cost, the objective is to minimize the cost. Type "MIN" and press the <ENTER> key to continue. Note that for this field, the program only accepts either "MIN" or "MAX". Any other value is not acceptable and therefore the program will not proceed. Also, note that during the data entry process, you can press the up arrow key to backtrack to a previous field to revise its value.

Now continue the data entry process by pressing the right arrow once and type "4" for the number of candidates. Press <ENTER> to continue with the number of jobs. Again, press the right arrow key once and type "4" then press <ENTER>. The completed initial data entry screen is presented below.

```
Problem title: JOB CONTRACT

Objective type (MIN/MAX): MIN

Number of candidates (rows):  4

Number of jobs (columns):  4


┌─────────────────────────────────────────────────┐
│ Enter problem parameters as requested.  Press RETURN to │
│ accept, or ESC to exit.   Maximum problem size is 30 by 30, │
│ assignment costs should be within 0 and 9999. │
└─────────────────────────────────────────────────┘
```

After the initial data entry process, the program will resume by asking if you wish to continue by entering the assignment costs as shown below.

```
┌─────────────────────────────────────────────────────┐
│ Continue with assignment costs (Y/N) Y              │
└─────────────────────────────────────────────────────┘
```

Press <Y> to continue with the spread sheet data entry for the assignment costs. The completed spread sheet data entry screen is shown below.

```
                                              ─┤READY├─
B1  'Job1
            A       B      C      D      E
1                  Job1   Job2   Job3   Job4
2   Candid1         16      9     14     17
3   Candid2          7     19      8     14
4   Candid3         15      6      9     10
5   Candid4         19     17     11      4
```

If you wish to use other more meaningful names for the contractors (other than Candid1, Candid2, ...,etc.), move the pointer to column A of the spread sheet and make changes as appropriate. You can also move the pointer to the first row and change the job names. After completing the data entry process, press <F10> to keep the data and exit from the spread sheet editor.

You may now obtain a hard copy printout of the input data by moving the pointer to the PRINT option and press <ENTER>. Be sure that the printer is on and ready before you proceed. You may also save the problem on the disk for future references. If so, move the pointer to the FILE option and select the "Save current file" sub-option by pulling the bar down one level. Press the <ENTER> key to select. The program will display the current drive and sub-directory and ask you to enter a file name. Enter an appropriate DOS file name.

You are now ready to proceed and solve the problem. Move the pointer to the SOLVE option and select the "Display output" sub-option. The program will pause for a few seconds and then report the optimal assignment as shown below.

```
┌─────────────────────────────────────────────────────┐
│              Problem Title: JOB CONTRACT            │
│           Optimal Solution: Objective value = 29    │
│                                                     │
│     Candid1       assigned to     Job2              │
│     Candid2       assigned to     Job1              │
│     Candid3       assigned to     Job3              │
│     Candid4       assigned to     Job4              │
│                                                     │
└─────────────────────────────────────────────────────┘
```

As seen from the above output report, the optimal (minimum cost) assignment is to assign Contractor 1 to Job 2, Contractor 2 to Job 1, Contractor 3 to Job 3, and Contractor 4 to Job 4. The total cost of this assignment is $29.

EXAMPLE 2 - JOBS TO CONTRACTORS PROBLEM (UNBALANCED)

In this example, you will solve a revised version of Example 1. Suppose that there is an additional contractor available but there are still four jobs. The assignment costs are presented in Table 6-2.

As indicated in the introduction, this type of assignment problem is called "unbalanced". To solve an unbalanced problem, the computer adds additional dummy jobs (or candidates if necessary) to make the assignment matrix square. The assignment costs for the dummy jobs (or candidates) are set to zero.

To solve the problem, move the pointer to the EDIT option and press the <ENTER> key to modify the problem. The program will begin the edit process by placing the pointer in the title field. Change the title to "EXAMPLE 2" and press <ENTER>. Press the <ENTER> key again to accept the objective type. Change the number of candidates to 5 by moving the cursor one position and type "5" and press <ENTER>. Press <ENTER> to accept the current value for the number of jobs. The completed initial data entry screen is shown below.

```
Problem title: EXAMPLE 2

Objective type (MIN/MAX): MIN

Number of candidates (rows):  5

Number of jobs (columns):  4



┌─────────────────────────────────────────┐
│ Continue with assignment costs (Y/N) Y   │
└─────────────────────────────────────────┘
```

Press <ENTER> to continue with revising the assignment costs. Note that the new spread sheet contains an extra candidate with assignment costs set to zero. Move the pointer to the last row (Candid5) and enter the assignment costs in columns B through E. The completed spread sheet is shown below.

```
                                                                    ┤READY├
E6   16
               A        B      C      D      E
1                       Job1   Job2   Job3   Job4
2          Candid1      16      9     14     17
3          Candid2       7     19      8     14
4          Candid3      15      6      9     10
5          Candid4      19     17     11      4
6          Candid5      14     11     18     16
```

After completing the data entry for the new candidate, press <F10> to keep the input data and exit from the spread sheet editor.

You are now ready to solve the revised problem. Move the pointer to the SOLVE option and select the Display output sub-option. After a few seconds, the program will display a message reporting that the problem is unbalanced and that additional dummy columns will be added as shown below.

```
┌──────────────────────────────────────────────────────────────┐
│  Since there are fewer columns than rows, additional dummy     │
│  columns will be added with zero value in each cell.           │
└──────────────────────────────────────────────────────────────┘
```

Press the <ENTER> key to continue with the solution process. The optimal solution will be reported as shown below.

```
┌─────────────────────────────────────────────────────────┐
│                                                         │
│              Problem Title: EXAMPLE 2                    │
│         Optimal Solution: Objective value = 29          │
│                                                         │
│    Candid1      assigned to     Job2                     │
│    Candid2      assigned to     Job1                     │
│    Candid3      assigned to     Job3                     │
│    Candid4      assigned to     Job4                     │
│    Candid5      assigned to     Dummy5                   │
│                                                         │
│                                                         │
│                                                         │
└─────────────────────────────────────────────────────────┘
```

As seen from the above output report, the optimal assignment has a cost of $29 (as in Example 1) and the optimal assignment as the same as that of Example 1. The only difference is that the new contractor has been assigned to the fifth and Dummy job. This implies that the new contractor cannot out-perform any of the existing four contractors.

EXAMPLE 3 - JOBS TO CONTRACTORS: A NEW CONSTRAINT

Now suppose that for some reason, the additional (fifth) contractor *must* be assigned an actual and not a dummy job. How should you solve this problem? One alternative is to introduce a new dummy job explicitly and make the cost of assigning the fifth contractor to it quite large. The cost of assigning the other four contractors to this dummy job can be set to zero.

To solve the problem, move the pointer to the EDIT option and press the <ENTER> key. The program will begin the edit process by placing the pointer in the title field again. Change the title to "EXAMPLE 3" and press <ENTER>. Press the <ENTER> key two more times to advance to the number of jobs. Change the value to "5" to add an additional job and press the <ENTER> key to accept the new value. The completed screen is shown below.

```
      Problem title: EXAMPLE 3

      Objective type (MIN/MAX): MIN

      Number of candidates (rows):  5

      Number of jobs (columns):  5




                  ┌─────────────────────────────────────────┐
                  │ Continue with assignment costs (Y/N) Y   │
                  └─────────────────────────────────────────┘
```

Press <Y> to continue with the assignment costs. Note that a new "Dummy" job (number 5) has been added to the problem with assignment costs equal to 0. Move the pointer to the cell F6, which represents the cost of assigning Contractor 5 to the dummy job and change its value to 1000. This large assignment cost will prevent the fifth contractor from being assigned to the dummy job. The completed spread sheet is shown below.

```
                                                        ─┤READY├─
F6    1000
          A       B      C      D      E      F
1               Job1   Job2   Job3   Job4   Dummy5
2     Candid1     16      9     14     17      0
3     Candid2      7     19      8     14      0
4     Candid3     15      6      9     10      0
5     Candid4     19     17     11      4      0
6     Candid5     14     11     18     16    1000
```

Press <F10> to keep the changes and exit from the spread sheet editor.

You are now ready to solve this constrained assignment problem. Move the pointer to the SOLVE option and press <ENTER>, select the display output sub-option to solve the problem and display the output on the screen as shown below.

```
              Problem Title: EXAMPLE 3
          Optimal Solution: Objective value = 31

Candid1      assigned to    Dummy
Candid2      assigned to    Job1
Candid3      assigned to    Job3
Candid4      assigned to    Job4
Candid5      assigned to    Job2
```

As seen from the above output report, this solution is different from the one in Solved Example 2. Contractor 1 (or Candidate 1) is assigned to the dummy job, Candidate 2 is assigned to job 1, Contractor 3 is assigned to job 3, Contractor 4 is assigned to job 4, and Contractor 5 is assigned to job 2. The total cost of this new solution is $31 which is slightly larger than the earlier on (at $29).

PROBLEMS

1. The RMC Corporation needs to assign five jobs to five contractors. Find the optimal assignment on the basis of the cost matrix shown below.

		Jobs			
	1	2	3	4	5
Contractors 1	115	158	174	75	96
2	160	148	165	127	142
3	90	139	95	118	198
4	127	85	170	185	135
5	146	90	119	140	112

2. Assign five workers to five jobs on the basis of the cost matrix shown below.

		Jobs			
	1	2	3	4	5
Workers 1	14	15	19	18	17
2	16	14	18	13	15
3	17	13	20	18	16
4	15	12	15	16	18
5	12	17	13	14	19

3. The BKW Corporation is a multi-division general contracting firm that bids on jobs. The profitability of the five jobs for its five divisions is as shown below. Develop an optimal bidding strategy.

		Jobs				
		1	2	3	4	5
Division	1	75	55	50	65	70
	2	35	30	95	110	100
	3	30	15	25	65	125
	4	55	60	65	95	85
	5	45	95	75	85	110

4. Assign the four jobs to the five machines shown below so that cost is minimized.

		Jobs			
		1	2	3	4
Machines	1	19	18	25	42
	2	13	11	35	14
	3	41	32	16	19
	4	14	39	19	26
	5	33	21	40	32

5. Assign four of the five jobs to the four contractors in such a way that profit is maximized.

		Jobs				
		1	2	3	4	5
Contractors	1	1	9	8	19	21
	2	17	4	17	11	26
	3	16	19	7	10	4
	4	8	22	12	23	17

6. Assume costs in problem 4 are profits and maximize.

7. Assume profits in problem 5 are costs and minimize.

8. In problem 1, assume that job 1 must be given to the second contractor. Find the optimal solution.

9. In problem 2, assume that worker 2 cannot be assigned to either job 4 or 5. Find the optimal solution.

10. In problem 3, assume that there is an additional division (number 6) with profitabilities 20, 60, 30, 300 and 40. Find the optimal solution. Which division would not get a job? Why?

11. In problem 5, assume that job 4 must be performed at any cost. Find the optimal solution.

12. In problem 5, assume that there is an additional contractor which can perform jobs 1, 3 and 5 with profits 50, 20 and 100, respectively. This contractor however, is not capable of performing jobs 2 and 4. Find the optimal solution.

13. Find the minimum and the maximum solution to the assignment problem shown below.

Work Center	Job				
	1	2	3	4	5
A	9	2	9	8	1
B	8	9	1	5	4
C	3	4	7	4	9
D	4	7	6	6	8
E	2	5	7	2	5

14. Six applicants are interviewing for five jobs. The value of each applicant and the cost of each applicant in the respective jobs on a monthly basis is shown below in two separate matrices. Find the job allocation on the basis of value and, separately, on the basis of cost. How much will it cost the organization (per month) to have the best allocation in terms of maximizing value instead of minimizing cost. The figures in the value table are not necessarily in terms of dollars or other money units.

Value per Month

Jobs

Applicants	1	2	3	4	5
1	13	18	19	21	18
2	14	15	17	18	19
3	12	17	25	24	20
4	19	21	16	17	25
5	24	25	21	19	14
6	16	17	24	23	19

Cost per Month

Jobs

Applicants	1	2	3	4	5
1	800	850	775	750	700
2	1100	1000	1050	950	1000
3	600	550	700	750	650
4	900	950	1100	850	1000
5	600	700	600	800	900
6	850	900	750	800	750

15. In a job shop operation, 6 machinists were uniquely qualified to operate certain machines in the shop. However, they were all able to operate any one of the five machines in the shop. The job shop had considerable backlog and all five machines were kept busy at all times. The one machinist not operating a machine was usually occupied doing clerical or routine maintenance work. Given the value schedule below for each machinist on each of the five machines, develop an optimal assignment.

	Machine				
Machinist	1	2	3	4	5
A	65	50	60	55	80
B	30	75	125	50	40
C	75	35	85	95	45
D	60	40	115	130	110
E	90	85	40	80	95
F	145	60	55	45	85

16. The Vincal Yacht has been marooned on an island off the coast of South America. Aboard the ship were 10 people - 4 men and 6 women. Below is a matrix of compatibility measures of the men and women. Based on this information, determine which 4 couples will end up together before they are rescued by the Coast Guard.

		WOMEN					
		Sue	Lynne	Mary	Sandy	Shery	Lisa
M	Bob	7	1	6	2	7	2
E	Frank	5	5	7	3	8	7
N	Joe	9	4	3	6	5	6
	Glen	10	8	5	4	3	9

17. Davis Auction has 4 cars up for sale. Based on the bids from 4 potential buyers given below, decide who should get which car in order to maximize Davis' profit.

	Chevy	Ford	Dodge	Pontiac
Carol	5,000	4,000	3,200	4,900
John	3,500	3,500	3,100	5,000
Harry	4,200	3,700	2,950	4,750
Paul	3,800	4,100	3,000	4,600

18. Assume you and your partners are the bidders in question 17. Resolve this problem in order to minimize the cash outlay of you and your partners.

19. The Hot Rocks Fire Company has just received 4 fire calls and 2 paramedic calls. It can dispatch any 4 of the 5 fire trucks that are available and any 2 of the 3 paramedic units available. Based on how close each unit is from the call, dispatch the fire trucks and paramedic units to minimize response time. Use only one assignment matrix to solve the problem.

		DISTANCE TO FIRE				DISTANCE TO PARAMEDIC	
		1	2	3	4	A	B
A V A I L	1	4	3	2	5	-	-
A V A I L	2	3	5	4	2	-	-
A V A I L	3	2	6	6	1	-	-
A V A I L	4	3	6	4	7	-	-
A V A I L	5	7	3	5	8	-	-
A B L E	A	-	-	-	-	10	8
A B L E	B	-	-	-	-	9	6
A B L E	C	-	-	-	-	7	9

CHAPTER 7

LOCATIONAL LAYOUT ANALYSIS

INTRODUCTION

The locational layout analysis program assigns or locates departments, facilities or plants to certain locations such that the transportation cost between the several departments, facilities or plants is minimized. Up to thirty facilities and locations can be accommodated in the program.

This concept is based illustrated by a simple example. Suppose there are six facilities and six locations. We can locate each facility therefore in six different locations, but the number of different configurations is much larger. As the number of facilities and locations increases so does the size of the problem.

Two alternative configurations are shown in Figure 7-1. Note that the locations as indicated by the numbers 1 to 6 are fixed. However, the departments, facilities or plants can be moved to any one of the six locations.

Between each location is a given or known distance or cost per unit moved or transported. These costs can be summarized in a cost matrix as shown in Table 7-1. The locations shown are not necessarily located to scale. Also, the distance between locations 1 and 2 is assumed to be the same as between locations 2 and 1. Hence, the upper triangular part of the matrix is a mirror image of the bottom triangular part of the matrix. This type of a distance matrix is called "symmetric." This is, however, not always true and actual distances between locations should be used.

The next piece of information that is required is the volume of material flow between the departments, facilities or plants. This volume of material flow can be measured in tons of material, truck loads of products, gallons of oil or by whatever measure is common in the respective industry. We shall assume that it is measured in tons of product per day. The product flow can then be summarized in the flow matrix shown in Table 7-2. Note that the flow is measured between facilities or departments and the matrix is _not_ symmetric.

For any configuration of facilities onto the locations we can now develop a single cost value by multiplying the distances or costs between locations with the product flow between the facilities assigned to the respective locations. For instance, for configuration 1 on the above figure we find that the total transportation cost amounts to $219200 as calculated in Table 7-3. We can, of course, repeat the same calculation for any other configuration.

162

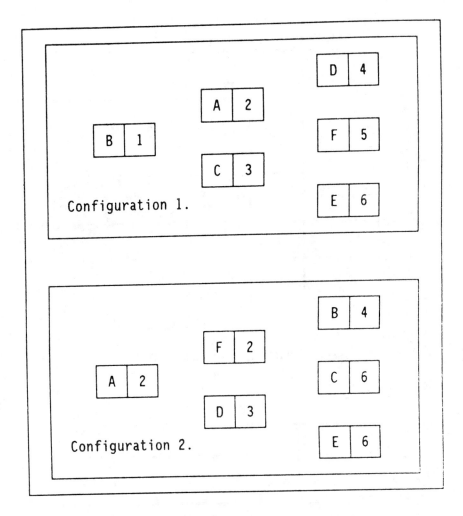

Figure 7-1: Two Facility Configurations

Note: Numbers 1 to 6 indicate locations; letters A to F indicate facilities.

TO

Location	1	2	3	4	5	6
1	0	55	75	195	175	120
2	55	0	90	165	140	140
3	75	90	0	130	115	105
4	195	165	130	0	70	220
5	175	140	115	70	0	145
6	120	140	105	220	145	0

FROM

Table 7-1: Costs or Distances Between the Six Locations

TO

Facilities	A	B	C	D	E	F
A	0	50	30	65	15	90
B	60	0	25	70	75	80
C	30	35	0	60	5	85
D	65	90	60	0	40	35
E	75	95	15	40	0	10
F	90	90	85	35	10	0

FROM

Table 7-2: Product Flow Between the Six Facilities

164

Movement Between Facility and Location			Product Flow	Cost or Distance	Flow X Cost
B1	–	A2	60	55	3300
B1	–	C3	25	75	1875
B1	–	D4	70	195	13650
B1	–	E6	75	120	9000
B1	–	F5	80	175	14000
A2	–	B1	50	55	2750
A2	–	C3	30	90	2700
A2	–	D4	65	165	10725
A2	–	E6	15	140	2100
A2	–	F5	90	140	12600
C3	–	A2	30	90	2700
C3	–	B1	35	75	2625
C3	–	D4	60	130	7800
C3	–	E6	5	105	525
C3	–	F5	85	115	9775
D4	–	A2	65	165	10725
D4	–	B1	90	195	17550
D4	–	C3	60	130	7800
D4	–	E6	40	220	8800
D4	–	F5	35	70	2450
F5	–	A2	90	140	12600
F5	–	B1	90	175	15750
F5	–	C3	85	115	9775
F5	–	D4	35	70	2450
F5	–	E6	10	145	1450
E6	–	A2	75	140	10500
E6	–	B1	95	120	11400
E6	–	C3	15	105	1575
E6	–	D4	40	220	8800
E6	–	F5	10	145	1450
		Total Flow Times Cost			219200

Table 7-3: Flow-Cost Calculation for Configuration 1

SOLUTION METHOD

The solution methods available for solving the Location Analysis problem consist of (1) Random Assignments, (2) Pairwise Exchange, and (3) User Exchange. We now describe the underlying procedures in each of the above options.

Random Assignments

The first approach, Random Assignments, consists of assigning the departments to locations at random, excluding departments having fixed locations or sites. If a problem has six departments to be assigned to six locations, first the six department numbers are ordered at random. In absence of forced assignments, the first department (in the sequence) is then assigned to the first location, the second department is assigned to the second location and so on. The assignment continues until all of the departments have been assigned. For example, consider a problem with four departments. Let 4, 2, 3, 1, be a random ordering of the numbers 1 through 4. These numbers are then used as department numbers and are assigned to locations. The resulting solution is

Location	Department
1	4
2	2
3	3
4	1

The next step is to compute the total transportation cost. This is done by adding the products of the flow between each department pair and their respective distance. When the requested number of trials are completed, the assignment with the lowest transportation cost is presented as the best solution.

Pairwise Exchange

The second approach, Pairwise Exchange consists of starting with an initial assignment and trying to improve its aggregate transportation cost. The initial assignment is either entered by the user, generated at random, or obtained from a previous run. A trial of the pairwise exchange consists of selecting a department at random and comparing it with other departments (starting at 1 and continuing sequentially, skipping departments with fixed locations) for possible exchange. A trial ends as soon as an exchange is found which results in a decrease in the total transportation cost. Note, however, that a trial may end without the occurrence of any improvement (any exchange) in the aggregate value. In either case, the next trial begins by using the layout from the previous trial and examining it for a possible pairwise exchange. As with the random assignments, when the requested number

166

of trials are performed, the solution with the lowest transportation cost is presented as the best solution.

User Exchange

This solution option consists of allowing the user to selectively perform pairwise exchanges of department pairs and observe the impact on the overall solution. The option involves asking the user to highlight a department to be selected for exchange. It then presents the list of locations, with the current location of the selected department marked by an "*". The user then selects a new location for the selected department. If any of the two departments have fixed locations, the program will warn the user that one or both departments have fixed locations. Note that allowing the user to change the location of departments with fixed sites (in this option) has been intentional. The reason is that for certain situations the decision maker (or user) may wish to explore the possibility of moving a department with fixed site.

Fixed Locations

In certain situations, it may be desirable and probably necessary to pre-assign one or more departments to fixed locations or sites. For example, in industrial applications, the shipping and receiving department is often placed at the entrance to the plant or department.

The Location Analysis program provides for pre-assigning one or more department to fixed locations (or sites). This is done by entering the location numbers of departments with pre-assigned locations in row two (this row has been labeled "Fixed Site") of the spread-sheet data editor. The program will scan row two for non-zero entries and utilizes the information if present. Note that locations should be numbered sequentially starting with location 1. In the spread sheet editor's Distance Matrix section, the first location is considered location number 1.

During the solution process, any departments with pre-assigned locations are first assigned to their permanent sites and then the remaining departments are assigned as appropriate.

EXAMPLE 1 - THE SIX DEPARTMENT PROBLEM

In this example you will use the Location Analysis program to solve the six-department location problem presented earlier. Load DSSPOM into the computer and select the Location Analysis program. The computer will pause for a few seconds and then display the Location Menu.

Move the pointer to the INPUT option and press <ENTER>. The computer will begin the data entry process by asking you to enter the title. Type "LOCATION EXAMPLE" and press <ENTER>. The computer will then ask you to enter the number of departments. Type 06 and press <ENTER>. The next question relates to the flow matrix. The flow matrix for this example is not symmetric therefore press <N> followed by <ENTER>. The distance matrix however is symmetric, press <ENTER> to request a symmetric distance matrix. The initial data entry process is shown below.

```
Problem title: LOCATION EXAMPLE

Number of Departments:    6

Flow Matrix Symmetric (Y/N):  N

Distance Matrix Symmetric (Y/N): Y




  ┌──────────────────────────────────────────────────┐
  │ Enter problem parameters as requested.  Press RETURN to │
  │ accept, or ESC to exit.   Maximum problem size is 30 │
  │ departments, distance values and flow values should be │
  │ within 0 and 999.                                  │
  └──────────────────────────────────────────────────┘
```

After the initial data entry process, the computer will ask if you are ready to enter the distance and flow matrix as shown below.

```
┌──────────────────────────────────────────────────┐
│ Continue with distance/flow matrix (Y/N) Y        │
└──────────────────────────────────────────────────┘
```

Press <ENTER> to continue with the spread sheet data entry process. The computer will then display the spread sheet data entry with all distances and flows initialized to 0 as shown below.

```
A1 'Dept. Flow
            A        B       C        D        E        F        G
1    Dept. Flow DEP1     DEP2     DEP3     DEP4     DEP5     DEP6
2    Fixed Site  .        .        .        .        .        .
3    DEP1         .       0.00     0.00     0.00     0.00     0.00
4    DEP2        0.00      .       0.00     0.00     0.00     0.00
5    DEP3        0.00     0.00      .       0.00     0.00     0.00
6    DEP4        0.00     0.00     0.00      .       0.00     0.00
7    DEP5        0.00     0.00     0.00     0.00      .       0.00
8    DEP6        0.00     0.00     0.00     0.00     0.00      .
9
10   Distance   LOC1     LOC2     LOC3     LOC4     LOC5     LOC6
11   LOC1         .       0.00     0.00     0.00     0.00     0.00
12   LOC2         .        .       0.00     0.00     0.00     0.00
13   LOC3         .        .        .       0.00     0.00     0.00
14   LOC4         .        .        .        .       0.00     0.00
15   LOC5         .        .        .        .        .       0.00
16   LOC6         .        .        .        .        .        .
```

Description of the Initial Spread Sheet

The first row of the spread sheet (row 1) contains the department default labels. For example the label for the department 1 is DEP1, for department 2 is DEP2, etc. Row 2 of the spread sheet is labeled "Fixed Site" and is initialized with periods. This row is used for problems in which one or more departments are pre-assigned to fixed locations. In this example, you will not use this row. Rows 3 through 8 are used for the flow matrix with all diagonal entries initialized by periods. The use of the period (.) in the spread sheet indicates that no data is needed for that cell. Since the flow matrix is not symmetric, all of the entries below the diagonal have also been initialized to 0.

Row 10 of the spread sheet is labeled "Distance" and contains the default labels for the six locations. If you prefer to use more meaningfull labels for the locations or departments you may move the pointer to these cells and change them as appropriate. Rows 11 through 16 are reserved for the distance matrix. The diagonal as well as below diagonal elements of this matrix have been initialized with periods to indicate that no data is needed for these cells. Note that any data placed in these cells will not be used.

Entering the Flow Matrix

You are now ready to enter the flow and distance matrixes. Move the pointer to cell C3 to enter the flow from department 1 to department 2. Enter 50 and press the

<ENTER> key. Now move the pointer one cell to the right, to cell D3 to enter the flow from department 1 to department 3. Enter 30 and press <ENTER>. Move the pointer to the right again and proceed by entering the flows from department 1 to departments 4, 5, and 6. Next move the pointer to cell B4 to enter the flow from department 2 to 1. Enter 60 and press <ENTER>. Repeat the process to complete the flows for all of the departments.

Entering the Distance Matrix

The distance matrix is symmetric and therefore you only need to enter the elements of the upper triangular matrix. Move the pointer to cell C11 to enter the distance between locations 1 and 2. Enter 55 and press <ENTER>. Next move the pointer to cell D11 to enter the distance between locations 1 and 3. Enter 75 and press <ENTER>. Enter the remaining distances as appropriate. The completed spread sheet is shown below.

```
                                                                  ┤READY├
G15    145
           A         B         C         D         E         F         G
1   Dept. Flow    DEP1      DEP2      DEP3      DEP4      DEP5      DEP6
2   Fixed Site    .         .         .         .         .         .
3   DEP1          .         50.00     30.00     65.00     15.00     90.00
4   DEP2          60.00     .         25.00     70.00     75.00     80.00
5   DEP3          30.00     35.00     .         60.00     5.00      85.00
6   DEP4          65.00     90.00     60.00     .         40.00     35.00
7   DEP5          75.00     95.00     15.00     40.00     .         10.00
8   DEP6          90.00     90.00     85.00     35.00     10.00     .
9
10  Distance   LOC1      LOC2      LOC3      LOC4      LOC5      LOC6
11  LOC1          .         55.00     75.00     195.00    175.00    120.00
12  LOC2          .         .         90.00     165.00    140.00    140.00
13  LOC3          .         .         .         130.00    115.00    105.00
14  LOC4          .         .         .         .         70.00     220.00
15  LOC5          .         .         .         .         .         145.00
16  LOC6          .         .         .         .         .         .
```

After completing the spread sheet data entry process, press <F10> to keep the data in memory and exit the spread sheet editor.

You may wish to save this problem for future use. To save the problem, move the pointer to the FILE option and select the Save Current File sub-option and press <ENTER>. The computer will show the current drive and sub-directory and will ask you to enter a file name. Use an appropriate name and a sufixx such as "LOC" to indicate that this file contains a Location Analysis problem. You may also obtain a hard copy printout of the problem by selecting the PRINT option. Be sure that the printer is On and Ready. Press <ENTER> to print os <ESC> to abort print and exit.

Solving the Problem - Random Assignments

You are now ready to solve the problem. Move the pointer to the SOLVE option and select the Display Output sub-option. The computer will pause a few seconds and then ask if you have an initial assignment as shown below.

```
┌─────────────────────────────────────────────┐
│ Wish to enter an initial assignment (Y/N) N │
└─────────────────────────────────────────────┘
```

Since there is no initial assignment available, press <ENTER> to proceed. The computer will then display the solution option menu as shown below.

```
┌─────────────────────────────────────────────────┐
│                                                 │
│            *** SOLUTION METHOD ***              │
│        ┌─────────────────────────────┐          │
│        │ Random Assignments          │          │
│        │ Pairwise Exchange           │          │
│        │ User Exchange               │          │
│        └─────────────────────────────┘          │
│                                                 │
│    ┌───────────────────────────────────────┐    │
│    │ Use the arrow keys to highlight a     │    │
│    │ method.  Press ENTER to select or ESC to │  │
│    │ exit.                                 │    │
│    └───────────────────────────────────────┘    │
│                                                 │
└─────────────────────────────────────────────────┘
```

As seen from the above exhibit, three solution methods are available. The first method involves random assignment of the departments to the locations and storing the solutions with lower transportation cost. This solution option is much faster than the next option which involves pairwise exchanges.

Select the Random Assignment option by pressing the <ENTER> key. The computer will ask you to enter the number of trials. It suggests a default value of 10. Press <ENTER> to accept 10 and perform 10 trials of random layouts as shown below.

```
+--------------------------------------------------+
|              *** SOLUTION METHOD ***             |
|                                                  |
|            Number of trials:    10               |
+--------------------------------------------------+
```

The computer will pause for a few seconds and then report the results as shown below.

```
+------------------------------------------------------------------+
|              Problem Title: LOCATION EXAMPLE                     |
|                                                                  |
|   Number of Trials:  10          No. of Successful Trials:  1    |
|   Best Assignment Found on Trial:  10                            |
|   Transportation Cost:   195600                                 |
|                                                                  |
|            Department        Location                            |
|            ----------        --------                            |
|            DEP1              LOC1                                |
|            DEP6              LOC2                                |
|            DEP4              LOC3                                |
|            DEP2              LOC4                                |
|            DEP5              LOC5                                |
|            DEP3              LOC6                                |
|                                                                  |
+------------------------------------------------------------------+
```

As seen from the above report, the suggested solution indicates that deparment 1 should be assigned to location 1, department 6 to location 2, 4 to 3, 2 to 4, 5 to 5, and department 3 to location 6. The total cost of transportation 195600. The report indicates that, as requested, 10 random layouts were generated of which 1 had a lower transportaion cost than the initial solution (also generated at random).

Improving the Solution - Pairwise Exchange

The random assignment solution method is heuristic and there is no guarantee that the above solution is the least cost one. To explore the possibility of improving the above solution, you may use several iterations (trials) of pairwise exchanges. Move the pointer to the SOLVE option again and select the Display Output as sub-option. The computer will ask if you wish to use the results of the last run as an initial solution. Press "Y" to use the previous solution as an initial one as shown below.

172

```
┌─────────────────────────────────────────────────────────────┐
│ Use the result of last run as initial assignment (Y/N) Y     │
└─────────────────────────────────────────────────────────────┘
```

The computer will then display the solution option menu. Move the bar to "Pairwise Exchange" and press <ENTER>. When asked to enter the number of trials, press <ENTER> to select 10 which is the default number as shown below.

```
┌─────────────────────────────────────────────┐
│                                             │
│            *** SOLUTION METHOD ***          │
│                                             │
│         Number of trials:    10             │
│                                             │
└─────────────────────────────────────────────┘
```

The computer will pause for a few seconds and then display the solution report as shown below.

```
┌─────────────────────────────────────────────────────────────┐
│                Problem Title: LOCATION EXAMPLE              │
│                                                             │
│   Number of Trials:  10        No. of Successful Trials:  3 │
│   Best Assignment Found on Trial:  3                        │
│   Transportation Cost:   184750                             │
│                                                             │
│           Department      Location                          │
│           ----------      --------                          │
│           DEP6            LOC1                               │
│           DEP1            LOC2                               │
│           DEP2            LOC3                               │
│           DEP5            LOC4                               │
│           DEP4            LOC5                               │
│           DEP3            LOC6                               │
│                                                             │
└─────────────────────────────────────────────────────────────┘
```

As seen from the above report, the initial solution from the previous run has been improved. The total cost of the new solution is 184750 which was obtained during the third trial. There were also three successfull trials. The above layout is more efficient than the previous one but there is no guarantee that it is the best possible layout. You may continue to solve the problem over and over again using either the random assignments or pairwise exchanges. When no further improvement can be found, you may select the suggested solution as a reasonably good solution.

<u>"What If" Analysis - User Exchanges</u>

In practical application of location analysis, one is often faced with inquiries regarding the consequences of making changes to a layout. For example, you may wish to determine what will be the total transportation cost for the above solution, if you re-assign department 2 to location 5 instead of its current location 3.

To solve the above problem, move the pointer to the SOLVE option again and select the Display Output sub-option. Next press enter to keep the results of the last run as initial solution. When presented with the menu of solution methods, move the bar down to "User Exchange" and press <ENTER>. The computer will display the following screen.

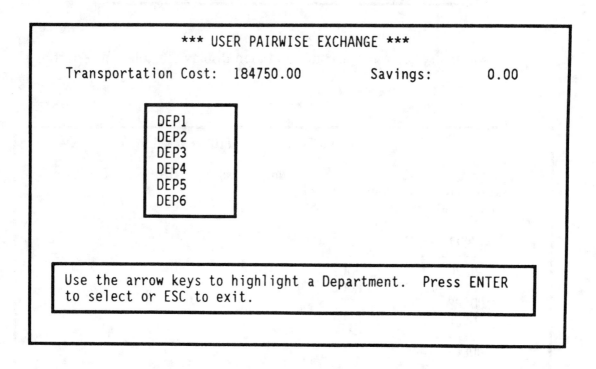

The above display indicates that the total cost of the current solution is 184750, and the savings is 0 (since no exchange has been made there is no saving). Move the bar down to department 2 (e.g., DEP2) and press <ENTER>. The computer will then display the following screen.

```
*** USER PAIRWISE EXCHANGE ***

Transportation Cost:  184750.00          Savings:          0.00

        ┌──────────┐
        │ LOC1     │
        │ LOC2     │
        │ LOC3*    │
        │ LOC4     │
        │ LOC5     │
        │ LOC6     │
        └──────────┘


  ┌─────────────────────────────────────────────────────────────┐
  │ Use the arrow keys to highlight a Location.  Press ENTER to   │
  │ select or ESC to exit.  Current location has been marked      │
  │ with (*).                                                     │
  └─────────────────────────────────────────────────────────────┘
```

The above screen indicates that department 2 is currently assigned to location 3 (marked by an "*"). Move the bar down to location 5 (LOC5) and press <ENTER>. The computer will pause for a few seconds and then displays the following screen.

```
*** USER PAIRWISE EXCHANGE ***

Transportation Cost:  185950.00          Savings:      -1200.00




              ┌───────────────────────┐
              │ More  Exchanges (Y/N) N│
              └───────────────────────┘
```

The above report indicates that moving department 2 to location 5 will increase the total transportation cost by 1200 to 185950. You may keep this new layout by pressing <ENTER> to indicate no more user exchanges are needed. Alternatively, you can restore the solution back to its original one by asking for another exchange. In this case you will select department 2 again and assign it to location 3 (this process is not shown here). Press <N> to keep this new solution and continue with the next report as shown below.

```
                    Problem Title: LOCATION EXAMPLE

Number of Trials:  40          No. of Successful Trials:  0
Best Assignment Found on Trial:  0
Transportation Cost:   185950

        Department      Location
        ----------      --------
        DEP6            LOC1
        DEP1            LOC2
        DEP4            LOC3
        DEP5            LOC4
        DEP2            LOC5
        DEP3            LOC6
```

As seen from the above solution, department 2 has been assigned to location 5 and department 4 has been assigned to location 3.

EXAMPLE 2 - DEPARTMENTS WITH FIXED LOCATIONS

In this example you will solve the above problem, this time requiring that departments A (DEP1) and F (DEP6) have fixed or permanent locations. In particular, suppose that department DEP1 is pre-assigned to location 3 (LOC3) and department DEP6 is pre-assigned at location 5.

To solve the above problem, move the pointer to the EDIT option and press <ENTER>. The computer will begin the data edit process by placing the pointer in the title field. Press <ENTER> five times to accept the current values of the initial parameters and invoke the spread sheet editor. When presented with the spread sheet containing the flow matrix and distance matrix, move the pointer to cell B2 to enter the fixed location for department DEP1. Enter a 3 in this cell and press <ENTER>. Next move the pointer to cell G2 and enter a 5, then press <ENTER>. The completed spread sheet is presented below.

G2 5

	A	B	C	D	E	F	G
1	Dept. Flow	DEP1	DEP2	DEP3	DEP4	DEP5	DEP6
2	Fixed Site	3	.	.	.	.	5
3	DEP1	.	50.00	30.00	65.00	15.00	90.00
4	DEP2	60.00	.	25.00	70.00	75.00	80.00
5	DEP3	30.00	35.00	.	60.00	5.00	85.00
6	DEP4	65.00	90.00	60.00	.	40.00	35.00
7	DEP5	75.00	95.00	15.00	40.00	.	10.00
8	DEP6	90.00	90.00	85.00	35.00	10.00	.
9							
10	Distance	LOC1	LOC2	LOC3	LOC4	LOC5	LOC6
11	LOC1	.	55.00	75.00	195.00	175.00	120.00
12	LOC2	.	.	90.00	165.00	140.00	140.00
13	LOC3	.	.	.	130.00	115.00	105.00
14	LOC4	.	.	.	.	70.00	220.00
15	LOC5	.	.	.	.	.	145.00
16	LOC6	.	.	.	.	.	.

As seen from the above display, the fixed site for DEP1 is location 3 and that of DEP6 is location 5. Press <F10> to keep the data and proceed with the solution process as described below.

Move the pointer to the SOLVE option and select the Display output sub-option. The computer will pause for a few seconds and then ask if you wish to enter an initial solution. Press <ENTER> to indicate that there is no initial solution available. The computer will then display the menu of solution options. Select the random assignment solution method and request 30 trials as shown below.

```
          *** SOLUTION METHOD ***


          Number of trials:   30
```

The computer will pause a few seconds and then report the following solution.

```
+-----------------------------------------------------------------+
|                                                                 |
|                   Problem Title: LOCATION EXAMPLE               |
|                                                                 |
|   Number of Trials: 30        No. of Successful Trials:  3      |
|   Best Assignment Found on Trial:  8                            |
|   Transportation Cost:  188550                                  |
|                                                                 |
|           Department      Location                              |
|           ----------      --------                              |
|           DEP2            LOC1                                   |
|           DEP4            LOC2                                   |
|           DEP1            LOC3                                   |
|           DEP3            LOC4                                   |
|           DEP6            LOC5                                   |
|           DEP5            LOC6                                   |
|                                                                 |
+-----------------------------------------------------------------+
```

As seen from the above solution report, department A (DEP1) has been assigned to location 3 and department F (DEP6) has been assigned to location 5 as requested. The total transportation cost however is 3800 units higher that the cost of the best solution in Example 2. This is due to the additional cost incurred by requiring departments A and F with relatively high inter-departmental work flow (90x2 = 180 units) to be located relatively far from each other (115 distance units).

PROBLEMS

1. Based on the distance matrix and the material flow matrix below, find the best possible facilities layout.

Locations	1	2	3
1	0	75	30
2	75	0	95
3	30	95	0

Distance Matrix

Facilities	A	B	C
A	0	565	410
B	565	0	395
C	410	395	0

Material Flow Matrix

2. Based on the distance matrix and the material flow matrix below, find the best possible facilities layout.

Locations	1	2	3	4
1	0	195	265	125
2	195	0	430	85
3	265	430	0	315
4	125	85	315	0

Distance Matrix

Facilities	A	B	C	D
A	0	5	15	25
B	5	0	30	20
C	15	30	0	10
D	25	20	10	0

Material Flow Matrix

3. Ace Manufacturing plans to open a new warehouse for distribution of its recently launched new product. The new warehouse will be supplied from two plants (A,B) to be located at locations 1 and 2. The distance and cost matrices below represent the problem. Find the locations of the new plants.

Locations	1	2	3	4	5
1	0	0	75	125	95
2	0	0	90	110	105
3	75	90	0	60	75
4	125	110	60	0	135
5	95	105	75	135	0

Distance Matrix

Facilities	A	B	C	D	E
A	0	0	560	560	560
B	0	0	390	390	390
C	560	390	0	60	95
D	560	390	60	0	110
E	560	390	95	110	0

Material Flow Matrix

4. The distances between the nine departments in the plant layout shown below consist of one distance unit for adjacent departments, two distance units for diagonally adjacent departments, and four distance units for all other departments. The material flow matrix for the nine departments is also listed below. Find a low cost plant layout.

1	4	7
2	5	8
3	6	9

Location Layout

Facilities	A	B	C	D	E	F	G	H	I
A	0	150	740	630	310	120	950	840	130
B	150	0	160	710	210	790	890	150	180
C	740	160	0	900	350	480	760	730	350
D	630	710	900	0	510	220	240	510	760
E	310	210	350	510	0	980	560	590	410
F	120	790	480	220	980	0	120	270	910
G	950	890	760	240	560	120	0	840	240
H	840	150	730	510	590	270	840	0	360
I	130	180	350	760	410	910	240	360	0

Material Flow Matrix

5. The West Valley Machine Shop was moving to a new building. The three locations, identified as 1, 2 and 3 in the building were separated as shown in the distance matrix below. The material flow per week between the three departments, identified as A, B and C, amounted to the number of loads shown in the material flow matrix below. Develop an appropriate layout which minimizes loads x distance travelled.

Locations	1	2	3
1	0	75	30
2	75	0	95
3	30	95	0

Distance Matrix

Facilities	A	B	C
A	0	565	410
B	565	0	395
C	410	395	0

Material Flow Matrix

6. The Dryden Cereals Corporation is opening a new four department plant. The distances between the four departmental locations are shown on the distance matrix below. The four departments identified as A, B, C and D are projected to have material flow (loads) per day as shown in the material flow matrix below. Develop an appropriate layout which minimize loads x distance travelled.

Locations	1	2	3	4
1	0	195	265	125
2	195	0	430	85
3	265	430	0	315
4	125	85	315	0

Distance Matrix

Facilities	A	B	C	D
A	0	5	15	25
B	5	0	30	20
C	15	30	0	10
D	25	20	10	0

Material Flow Matrix

7. The Lockport Machine Shop is in the process of moving to a new building where its six equally-sized departments will be located in a 3x2 grid building as shown below with the six building locations numbered from 1 to 6. Each location measures 100 ft by 100 ft.

1	2	3
4	5	6

The distances between departmental locations are measured from the center of each department to the center of each other department. Travel routes in the building are parallel to outside walls and pass through the center of each departmental location. Develop the distance matrix for the six departmental locations.

8. The loads to be transported daily between departments of the Lockport Machine (see problem 7) are shown below. The cost of moving each load between each department is equal per unit distance. Develop a layout which minimizes total departmental loads x distance travelled. Departments are identified as A, B, C, D, E and F.

Loads Matrix						
	A	B	C	D	E	F
A	-	50	75	40	30	85
B	85	-	145	10	10	35
C	95	30	-	25	95	60
D	15	40	25	-	40	115
E	75	40	35	40	-	45
F	55	50	45	10	85	-

9. In problem 8, suppose that department A must be situated at location 6. Find a minimum cost layout.

10. Upon re-examination of the Lockport Machine Shop problem it became clear that the cost of moving each load per unit distance was not equal because of the different means of transportation used. To respond to that variation a matrix was developed which showed the relative cost of moving a load per unit distance between departments. The matrix is shown below. Develop a layout for the Lockport Machine Shop.

Relative Unit Cost per Distance Matrix						
	A	B	C	D	E	F
A	-	1	1	2	3	1
B		-	3	4	1	2
C			-	3	4	2
D				-	3	1
E					-	3
F						-

11. The Wheatport Clinic was in the process of moving to the second floor of a hexagonal tower. The eight office locations on the second floor were on the periphery of the building with the elevator shaft located at the center of the building as shown below. The eight office locations were about equal size and each office location was about 50 feet from the adjacent office.

Develop distance matrices for the eight office locations on the basis of:

    a.   One-way traffic only (e.g., clockwise movements)
    b.   Two-way traffic.

12. The number of trips per day between the Wheatport Clinic's six offices and two laboratories are as shown below in the number of trips matrix. Develop an appropriate location for the Clinic's six offices and laboratories identified as A and B for laboratories and C, D, E, F, G and H for offices.

	A	B	C	D	E	F	G	H
A	-	55	70	95	40	30	85	15
B	30	-	15	25	35	65	40	65
C	10	20	-	5	15	90	25	20
D	5	55	65	-	10	60	45	35
E	25	90	80	45	-	20	15	15
F	40	50	15	75	10	-	10	10
G	75	10	40	10	70	10	-	85
H	70	50	55	25	75	85	15	-

13. Snyder Packing was in the process of designing a new plant layout for a nine-department packing plant. The departments are all about equal size and measure about 6400 square feet. The plant will be a square building measuring 240 ft by 240 ft. The department locations are numbered 1 through 9. The routes through the plants run parallel to the outside walls of the building and through the center of each departmental location. Develop a distance matrix for the nine square departmental locations. Show the locations on a 3x3 grid.

14. The material flow in loads per week for the Snyder Packing Plant discussed above is shown below. Develop a minimum cost plant layout.

Facilities	A	B	C	D	E	F	G	H	I
A	0	150	740	630	310	120	950	840	130
B	150	0	160	710	210	790	890	150	180
C	740	160	0	900	350	480	760	730	350
D	630	710	900	0	510	220	240	510	760
E	310	210	350	510	0	980	560	590	410
F	120	790	480	220	980	0	120	270	910
G	950	890	760	240	560	120	0	840	240
H	840	150	730	510	590	270	840	0	360
I	230	180	350	760	410	910	240	360	0

Material Flow Matrix

15. As design and development for the Snyder Packing Plant proceeded it was decided to use different methods of material handling. As a result the cost of material building was not equal. A matrix was developed which shows the relative cost of moving a load per unit distance between departments. The matrix is shown below. Develop a revised layout for the Snyder Packing Plant.

	A	B	C	D	E	F	G	H	I
A	-	2	1	2	3	1	3	1	3
B		-	3	2	3	3	2	3	1
C			-	1	2	1	1	3	2
D				-	1	3	3	3	2
E					-	1	3	1	3
F						-	2	2	3
G							-	2	1
H								-	2
I									-

16. You are called in to be a consultant for a major luggage company. They are calling on you to arrange the plant in order to minimize transportation costs. The number of trips between departments and the cost per unit of distance are shown in the table below.

Develop nearness priorities and give a layout design to minimize the transportation costs. The facility should be 3 x 2.

MOVEMENT		EXPECTED	COST PER
FROM	TO	NUMBER OF TRIPS	UNIT OF DISTANCE
A	B	100	.10
A	C	200	.15
A	D	300	.10
A	E	100	.10
A	F	250	.20
B	C	200	.15
B	D	300	.10
B	E	100	.20
B	F	150	.15
C	D	300	.15
C	E	275	.15
C	F	100	.20
D	E	225	.10
D	F	150	.10
E	F	185	.20

17. Zigmond Manufacturing Company is a job shop that produces many varied items. Flow within the plant is also varied. Some departments deal with heavy items that are expensive to transport. The costs to move items between departments is shown below. Also shown is an estimate of the number of items expected to flow between departments this year.

a) Develop nearness priorities for each of the departments.

b) Formulate a layout design (2 x 3) to minimize expenses.

COST PER UNIT OF DISTANCE

From To	Lathe	Mills	Drills	Casting	Finishing	Assembly
Lathe	--	.04	.05	.02	.05	.03
Mills	.02	--	.07	.03	.04	.02
Drills	.03	.02	--	.04	.07	.10
Casting	.05	.03	.10	--	.03	.07
Finishing	.07	.04	.03	.07	--	.05
Assembly	.04	.10	.04	.05	.07	--

EXPECTED NUMBER OF TRIPS BETWEEN DEPARTMENTS

From To	Lathe	Mills	Drills	Casting	Finishing	Assembly
Lathe	--	100	400	100	400	200
Mills	100	--	300	200	100	100
Drills	200	100	--	300	100	250
Casting	400	200	250	--	200	300
Finishing	300	100	200	300	--	400
Assembly	100	250	100	400	300	--

18. The Administrative Building at Weaver University contains 6 rooms that are 20 feet square in size. You are called in to help the University decide where each department should reside within the Administrative Building, which is 40 feet long and 60 feet wide. The two way flows between departments are shown below. Besides minimizing the distance that must be traveled, the following considerations must be taken into account; student accounts and scheduling must be close together because they share a computer; the Dean and the Vice President, who resides in the advisement department, must be close because they share a secretary; and the career counseling people aren't real happy with some of the Dean's decisions and there is animosity between them.

Develop nearness priorities and formulate a layout design.

	S.A.	SCHED.	PAYROLL	DEAN	CAREER	ADVISEMENT
Student Acct.	--	400	100	200	50	100
Scheduling		--	50	300	300	250
Payroll			--	25	75	50
Dean				--	100	100
Career Counsel.					--	300
Advisement						--

19. As the facility layout engineer of your company, you have been given the task of assigning 6 work centers to a 90 foot long by 60 foot wide area. Each work center is 30 feet wide by 30 feet long. Below are the distances in feet between locations and the number of trips between locations each day. Assume work center 6 must be in spot A.

a) Assign the work centers to minimize the total distance traveled.

b) Compute the cost of this plan if transportation costs per load per foot is $3.00.

DISTANCE BETWEEN LOCATIONS (FEET)

To/From	A	B	C	D	E	F
A	-	35	85	35	65	115
B		--	35	75	25	55
C			--	125	45	35
D				--	35	105
E					--	35
F						--

NUMBER OF TRIPS PER DAY BETWEEN CENTERS

To/From	1	2	3	4	5	6
1	--	85	20	18	6	13
2	30	--	3	1	5	9
3	32	0	--	0	0	2
4	36	7	0	--	1	0
5	9	11	0	4	--	1
6	27	33	8	0	0	--

```
-----------------
| A | B | C |
| D | E | F |
-----------------
```

189

CHAPTER 8

FACILITIES LAYOUT ANALYSIS

INTRODUCTION

Facilities layout analysis using preference ratings has been widely adopted and is presented in nearly all text books on production and operation management. The approach is popular because it allows inclusion of a number of considerations in determining the location of facilities. As a result the approach is a general method for developing an acceptable layout of physical facilities such as manufacturing plants, inventory warehouses, department stores and service facilities.

An application of the facilities layout method will be illustrated by an example of a facility with nine relatively equal-sized departments. The departments are located in a three by three grid as shown in Figure 8-1. Also shown are a number of potential combinations of various layouts that can occur and from which the manager or layout engineer must choose. The facilities layout method attempts to find the best layout according to a number of preferences shown in Figure 8-2. The preference table shows the preferred relationships between each pair of the nine departments. Since there are nine departments there will be $(9)(8)/2 = 36$ department pairs, each with its preference rating. Preference ratings are limited to six categories: absolutely necessary (A), very important (E), important (I), ordinary importance (O), unimportant (U) and undesirable (X).

The tabular listing of the departmental pairs can be shown in a more graphical format by using an arrowlike graphical matrix device as shown in Figure 8-3. Note that each of the 36 departmental pairs are listed by preference rating as indicated in the previous figure.

With smaller facility layouts one can use the departmental pair preference ratings and arrive at a reasonable layout that satisfies most of the listed departmental pair preferences. However, with larger facilities a manual layout becomes rather cumbersome. For instance, the computer method to be discussed below is able to consider up to thirty departments. Sixteen departments generate 190 departmental pairs and to consider that many departmental pair constraints in developing a desirable facilities layout becomes rather difficult.

PAIRWISE RATINGS WEIGHTS

In order to develop a solution method for obtaining a layout design which will maximize the preference relationships, one may associate a weight structure with the pairwise preference ratings. For example, large positive weights can be assigned to more desirable ratings such as "A", "E", and "I", and a large negative weight can be assigned to "X". Then, for any given layout design, one can determine an aggregate weight or value based on the number of occurrences of "A"s, "E"s, etc. The aggregate value can be used to evaluate and compare different layouts.

The internal weight structure which is used in the computer program for the Layout Analysis consists of using a weight of 16 for "A", 8 for "E", 4 for "I", 2 for "O", 0 for "U", and -80 for "X". This weight structure has a nice property in that each more desirable rating is weighed twice the previous one. In addition, the weight assigned to "X" or undesirable adjacency is -80 which is 5 times worse than the most desirable rating "A". The choice of this particular weight structure is rather ad-hoc. For another layout engineer, absolutely important rating "A" may have a much higher degree of importance than essentially important or "E". In this case, the weight associated with "A" should be more than twice the weight of "E". The Layout Analysis program edit option enables you to edit and change the weights. If the pre-assigned weights are not appropriate for your particular application, use the editor to change the weights as appropriate.

CALCULATING THE AGGREGATE LAYOUT VALUE

With the earlier problem we only have to consider thirty-six departmental pairs. A departmental layout that satisfies most of the departmental pairs' preference ratings appears in Figure 8-4. Assuming the numerical weight preference rating used in the computer program we arrive at an aggregate weight assignment of 120. This weight assignment is based on a weight of 16 to A, of 8 to E, of 4 to I, of 2 to O, of 0 to U and of -80 to X. The layout shown is not necessarily the best layout. You may be able to develop one with a higher aggregate weighting. If you cannot improve upon it, one would expect that the computer program at least will be able to make a marginal improvement.

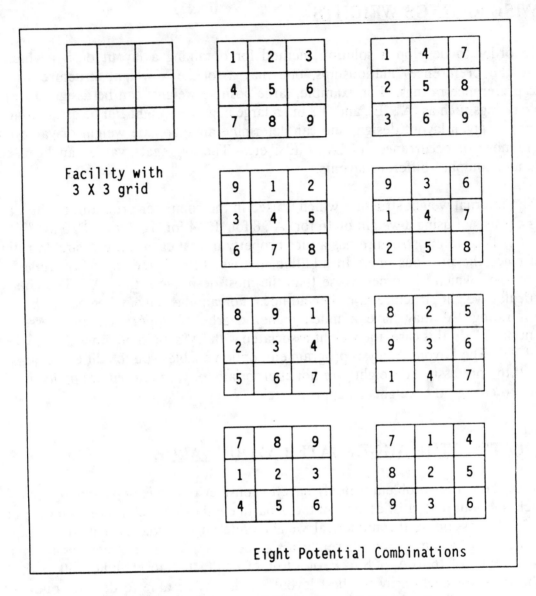

Facility with
3 X 3 grid

Eight Potential Combinations

Figure 8-1   Nine-grid Facility with Some Potential Layouts

192

Department Pair	Preference Rating	Department Pair	Preference Rating
1 - 2	U	4 - 5	U
1 - 3	A	4 - 6	I
1 - 4	I	4 - 7	U
1 - 5	I	4 - 8	X
1 - 6	E	4 - 9	U
1 - 7	U	5 - 6	I
1 - 8	U	5 - 7	A
1 - 9	X	5 - 8	A
2 - 3	I	5 - 9	X
2 - 4	E	6 - 7	U
2 - 5	U	6 - 8	A
2 - 6	A	6 - 9	I
2 - 7	I	7 - 8	U
2 - 8	E	7 - 9	X
2 - 9	U	8 - 9	I
3 - 4	X		
3 - 5	U		
3 - 6	I		
3 - 7	A		
3 - 8	U		
3 - 9	I		

Figure 8-2   Preference Rating of All Departmental Pairs

193

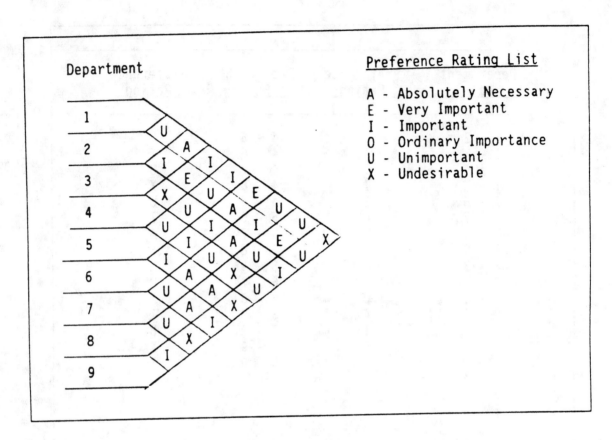

Figure 8-3 Graphical Display of Departmental Pair Preference

4	6	9
1	2	3
8	5	7

Departmental Pairs	Rating	Respective Rating Weights
1-2	U	0
1-4	I	4
1-5	I	4
1-6	E	8
1-8	U	0
2-3	I	4
2-4	E	8
2-5	U	0
2-6	A	16
2-7	I	4
2-8	E	8
2-9	U	0
3-5	U	0
3-6	I	4
3-7	A	16
3-9	I	4
4-6	I	4
5-7	A	16
5-8	A	16
6-9	I	4
Aggregate Weight		120

Figure 8-4: Layout Developed Based on Departmental Pair Rating Weight Assignments

SOLUTION METHOD

The solution methods available for solving the Facilities Layout problem consist of (1) Random Assignments, (2) Pairwise Exchange, and (3) User Exchange. We now describe the underlying procedures in each of the above options.

Random Assignments

The first approach, Random Assignments, consists of generating layout designs which are purely random. If a problem has six departments to be assigned to a 2 by 3 grid, first the six department numbers are ordered at random. In absence of forced assignments, the first department (in the sequence) is then assigned to grid (1,1), the northwest corner cell. The assignment continues horizontally until the first row is completed. It then continues with the next row and so on. For example, the sequence 6, 3, 2, 1, 5, 4 will result in the following layout:

6	3	2
1	5	4

The next step in this procedure consists of computing the aggregate preference value of the generated layout based on the adjacency ratings and the associated weights. This is done by summing the weights associated with preference ratings for department pairs which are adjacent. For instance, in the above example, department pairs (6,3), (6,5), (6,1), (3,2), (3,4), (3,5), (3,1), (2,4), (2,5), (1,5), and (5,4) are considered adjacent. Hence, the weights associated with their preference ratings will be added to give the aggregate value of that layout. Each random layout constitutes one random trial. When all random trials are completed, the layout with the largest aggregate value is presented as the best solution.

Pairwise Exchange

The second approach, Pairwise Exchange consists of starting with an initial layout and trying to improve its aggregate preference value. The initial layout is either entered by the user, generated at random, or obtained from a previous run. A trial of the pairwise exchange consists of selecting a department at random and comparing it with other departments (starting at (1,1) and moving horizontally) for possible exchange. A trial ends as soon as an exchange is found which results in an increase of the aggregate value. Note, however, that a trial may end without the occurrence of any improvement (any exchange) in the aggregate value. In either case, the next trial begins by using the layout from the previous trial and examining it for a possible pairwise exchange. As with the random layouts, when the requested number of trials are performed, the layout with the largest aggregate value is presented as the best solution.

User Exchange

This solution option consists of allowing the user to selectively perform pairwise exchanges of department pairs and observe the impact on the overall layout design. The option involves asking the user to highlight a department to be selected for exchange. It then presents the list of departments again and asks the user to select a second department to be exchanged with the first one. If any of the two departments have fixed locations, the program will warn the user that one or both departments have fixed locations. Note that allowing the user to change the location of departments with fixed sites (in this option) has been intentional. The reason is that for certain situations the decision maker (or user) may wish to explore the possibility of moving a department with fixed site.

Fixed Locations

In certain situations, it may be desirable and probably necessary to pre-assign one or more departments to fixed locations or sites. For example, in a faculty and staff office assignment, it is usually customary (and efficient) to situate the staff or secretarial office space at a corner point or the entrance. In industrial applications, the shipping and receiving department is often placed at the entrance to the plant or department.

The Layout Analysis program provides for pre-assigning one or more department to fixed locations (or sites). This is done by entering the coordinates (row and column numbers) of departments with pre-assigned locations in rows two and three of the spreadsheet data editor. The program will scan these rows for non-zero entries and utilizes the information if present.

During the solution process, any departments with pre-assigned locations are first assigned to their permanent sites and then the remaining departments are assigned as appropriate.

EXAMPLE 1 - THE NINE DEPARTMENT LAYOUT PROBLEM

In this example, you will solve the layout analysis problem presented earlier in this chapter. The preference rating chart for this problem is presented in Figure 8-3. The nine departments are to be assigned to a 3 by 3 grid so as to maximize the aggregate value of the layout (total preference value).

Load DSSPOM into the computer and select the Layout Analysis program. The computer will pause for a few seconds and then display the Layout Menu. Move the pointer to the INPUT option and press < ENTER >. The computer will begin the data entry process by placing the pointer in the title field. Enter a title such as "LAYOUT EXAMPLE" and press < ENTER >. The computer will then ask the number of rows in the grid, type "03"and press < ENTER >. The next item involves the number of columns in the grid, type "03" and press < ENTER >. The initial data entry screen is presented below.

```
Problem title: LAYOUT EXAMPLE

Number of Grid Rows:  03

Number of Grid Columns:  03




┌─────────────────────────────────────────────────────┐
│ Enter problem parameters as requested.  Press RETURN to │
│ accept, or ESC to exit.   Maximum problem size is 30    │
│ departments.                                            │
└─────────────────────────────────────────────────────┘
```

The computer will then ask if you are ready to enter the pairwise preference ratings. Press < ENTER > to invoke the spread sheet editor to enter the preference ratings as shown below.

```
Continue with rating matrix (Y/N) Y
```

The computer will then display the spread sheet of pairwise preference ratings. All of the ratings are initialized to "U" or unimportant. You only need to enter the ratings which are different than "U".

198

The first row of the spread sheet contains the department labels initialized to DEP1, DEP2, etc.. If you wish to use more meaningful labels, move the pointer to the cells in row 1 and change the labels as needed. Note that the editor only uses the labels in row one (and not column one) to identify the departments. Rows two and three of the spread sheet have been labeled as "Site Row" and "Site Column". These two rows are used to assign certain departments to permanent locations (sites). You will use these rows in the next example and not at this time.

The pairwise ratings may be entered in lower or upper case letters. The program will recognize both. However, entering the ratings in upper case letters is less confusing. To enter the ratings all in upper case, you may press the <CAPS Lock> key once and then proceed with the data entry process.

Begin with department pair (1,3). The rating for this pair is "A" for absolutely important. Move the pointer to cell D4 and type "A" then press <ENTER>. The ratings between department 4 and departments 1,2, and 3 are all different than "U". To enter these ratings, move the pointer to column E, cell E4. Enter "I" and press the down arrow key to move the pointer to cell E5. Now type "E" and press enter. Move the pointer to other cells. one at a time and enter the associated ratings. The completed spread sheet is shown below.

```
                                                                    ⌐READY⌐
 J11 'I
            A      B      C      D      E      F      G      H      I      J
 1   Department DEP1   DEP2   DEP3   DEP4   DEP5   DEP6   DEP7   DEP8   DEP9
 2   Site Row    .      .      .      .      .      .      .      .      .
 3   Site Col    .      .      .      .      .      .      .      .      .
 4   DEP1        .      U      A      I      I      E      U      U      X
 5   DEP2        .      .      I      E      U      A      I      E      U
 6   DEP3        .      .      .      X      U      I      A      U      I
 7   DEP4        .      .      .      .      U      I      U      X      U
 8   DEP5        .      .      .      .      .      I      A      A      X
 9   DEP6        .      .      .      .      .      .      U      A      I
 10  DEP7        .      .      .      .      .      .      .      U      X
 11  DEP8        .      .      .      .      .      .      .      .      I
```

After completing the data entry process, press <F10> to keep the data in memory and exit from the spread sheet editor.

If you wish to save the problem for future use, move the pointer to the FILE option and select the Save Current File sub-option. The computer will ask you to enter a file name. Enter an appropriate DOS file name and use a suffix such as "LAY" to indicate that the file contains a Layout Analysis problem. To obtain a hard copy printout of the model, move the pointer to the PRINT option and press <ENTER>. The computer will pause a few seconds and then print the model.

199

You are now ready to solve the problem. Move the pointer to the SOLVE option and select the Display Output sub-option. The computer will ask if you have an initial layout as shown below.

```
┌─────────────────────────────────────────────┐
│Wish to enter an initial assignment (Y/N) N   │
└─────────────────────────────────────────────┘
```

Press <ENTER> to indicate that there is no initial layout. The computer will then present a menu of the available solution techniques as shown below.

```
┌──────────────────────────────────────────────────────┐
│                                                      │
│                *** SOLUTION METHOD ***               │
│              ┌──────────────────────────┐            │
│              │ Random Assignments       │            │
│              │ Pairwise Exchange        │            │
│              │ User Exchange            │            │
│              └──────────────────────────┘            │
│                                                      │
│           ┌──────────────────────────────────────┐  │
│           │ Use the arrow keys to highlight a    │  │
│           │ method.  Press ENTER to select or ESC to │
│           │ exit.                                │  │
│           └──────────────────────────────────────┘  │
│                                                      │
└──────────────────────────────────────────────────────┘
```

To begin the solution process, select the Random Assignments option by pressing the <ENTER> key. The computer will ask you to enter the number of trials. Press <ENTER> to accept the default value of 10 as shown below.

```
┌──────────────────────────────────────────────┐
│                                              │
│           *** SOLUTION METHOD ***            │
│                                              │
│           Number of trials:    10            │
│                                              │
└──────────────────────────────────────────────┘
```

The computer will pause for a few seconds and then display the solution report as shown below.

```
+--------------------------------------------------------------+
|              Problem Title: LAYOUT EXAMPLE                   |
|                                                              |
| Number of Trials:  10        No. of Successful Trials:  1    |
| Best Assignment Found on Trial:  3                          |
| Aggregate Layout Value: -56                                 |
|                                                              |
|         Department      Row          Column                  |
|         ----------      ------       ------                  |
|         DEP1            2            2                        |
|         DEP2            2            3                        |
|         DEP3            3            1                        |
|         DEP4            1            1                        |
|         DEP5            1            2                        |
|         DEP6            1            3                        |
|         DEP7            2            1                        |
|         DEP8            3            3                        |
|         DEP9            3            2                        |
|                                                              |
+--------------------------------------------------------------+
```

As seen from the above report, the aggregate value of the layout is -56. The negative value indicates that the proposed layout contains at least one adjacent department pair with an "X" rating. You may proceed to improve the layout by solving the problem again. To do this, move the pointer to the SOLVE option and select the Display Output (process not shown here).

The computer will ask if you wish to use the results of the last run as an initial solution. Press <ENTER> to accept "Y" as shown below.

```
+--------------------------------------------------------------+
| Use the result of last run as initial assignment (Y/N) Y     |
+--------------------------------------------------------------+
```

The computer will then display the menu of solution techniques. This time move the bar down to select the Pairwise Exchange option (process not shown here). The computer will ask you to enter the number of trials. Press <ENTER> to accept the default value of 10. The computer will then display the solution report as shown below.

```
                    Problem Title: LAYOUT EXAMPLE

  Number of Trials:  10         No. of Successful Trials:  5
  Best Assignment Found on Trial:  10
  Aggregate Layout Value:   112

          Department        Row          Column
          ----------        ------       ------
          DEP1              1            2
          DEP2              2            2
          DEP3              3            2
          DEP4              1            1
          DEP5              3            1
          DEP6              2            3
          DEP7              2            1
          DEP8              1            3
          DEP9              3            3
```

As seen from the above report, the proposed layout has an aggregate value of 112. The best solution was obtained in trial 10 and that there were 5 successful pairwise exchange trials. This implies that 50 percent of the pairwise exchange trials resulted in improvements. When the number of trials (either random or pairwise exchange) is large and the percentage of successful trials is very low, finding an improved solution is rather unlikely. You may continue to try to improve the proposed solution by selecting the SOLVE option again and requesting additional trials of pairwise exchange.

EXAMPLE 2 - AN L-SHAPED LAYOUT

In this example you will solve a layout problem which involves assigning 13 departments to an L-shaped layout. Figure 8-5(a) represents the L-shape floor space with 13 department locations. The preference ratings for the 13 departments are shown in Table 8-1. The problem is to assign the 13 departments to the 13 locations so as to maximize the aggregate preference value of the layout.

1	2	3	4
5		6	7
8		9	10
11		12	13

(a)

	1	2	3	4
1				
2		D14		
3		D15		
4		D16		

(b)

Figure 8-5: An L-Shaped Layout Design

Dep	2	3	4	5	6	7	8	9	10	11	12	13
1	A	U	U	O	O	X	U	U	I	I	U	U
2		U	U	O	O	X	U	U	I	I	U	U
3			A	A	A	X	X	X	E	E	U	U
4				A	A	X	X	X	E	E	U	U
5					A	X	X	X	U	U	U	U
6						X	X	X	U	U	U	U
7							A	U	X	X	A	U
8								A	X	X	U	U
9									X	X	U	U
10										A	U	U
11											U	U
12												A

Table 8-1: Preference Rating for the L-Shaped Layout Example

To solve the above, you should revise the problem data slightly. In particular, since the Layout Analysis program requires that the available space be a rectangular grid, you need to introduce additional fictitious spaces and departments to convert the L-shape space into a rectangular grid. Figure 8-5(b) presents the modified floor space. Three fictitious (dummy) cells have been added to the original space to make it rectangular.

The next step is to define three fictitious departments to be assigned to the dummy cells. The preference rating between the three fictitious departments and the existing 13 departments should all be "unimportant' or "U". Recall that the weight associated with U is zero, hence the existence of the fictitious departments will not affect the aggregate layout value. Note that the revised preference rating chart is the same as the chart in Table 8-1 with three additional columns containing "U" ratings.

As a last modification to the problem, you should ensure that the fictitious departments are all assigned to dummy locations. This is done by pre-assigning the three fictitious departments to the three fictitious cells as shown in Figure 8-5(b).

You are now ready to enter the problem into the computer. Load DSSPOM and select the Layout Analysis program. Move the pointer to the INPUT option and press <ENTER>. The computer will begin the data entry process by asking you to enter a problem title. Type "IRREGULAR PLAN" and press <ENTER>. The computer will then ask the number of rows, type "4" and press <ENTER>. The next item is the number of columns, type "4" and press <ENTER> as shown below.

```
Problem title: IRREGULAR PLAN

Number of Grid Rows:    4

Number of Grid Columns:   4




  ┌────────────────────────────────────────────────────┐
  │ Enter problem parameters as requested.  Press RETURN to │
  │ accept, or ESC to exit.   Maximum problem size is 30 │
  │ departments.                                        │
  └────────────────────────────────────────────────────┘
```

The computer will then ask if you are ready to enter the preference ratings as shown below.

```
Continue with rating matrix (Y/N) Y
```

Press <ENTER> to continue with the spread sheet data entry process. The computer will then invoke the spread sheet editor for entering the preference ratings. Initially, all of the pairwise ratings are set to "U". Note that you only need to enter ratings which are different than "U". To do this, move the pointer to each cell for which the rating is other than a "U" and enter the rating. For example, the pairwise rating between departments 1 and 2 is "A". To enter this rating, move the pointer to cell C4 and type <A> and then <ENTER>. Note that you may enter the ratings in lower case such as "a" and the program will recognize them properly. If you which to enter the ratings in upper case, press the <Caps Lock> key once at this time. The completed spread sheet for the first part of the preference ratings, involving departments 1 through 9 is shown below.

```
                                                                  ┤READY├
C4  'A
             A       B     C     D     E     F     G     H     I     J
   1  Department DEP1  DEP2  DEP3  DEP4  DEP5  DEP6  DEP7  DEP8  DEP9
   2  Site Row    .     .     .     .     .     .     .     .     .
   3  Site Col    .     .     .     .     .     .     .     .     .
   4  DEP1        .     A     U     U     0     0     X     U     U
   5  DEP2        .     .     U     U     0     0     X     U     U
   6  DEP3        .     .     .     A     A     A     X     X     X
   7  DEP4        .     .     .     .     A     A     X     X     X
   8  DEP5        .     .     .     .     .     A     X     X     X
   9  DEP6        .     .     .     .     .     .     X     X     X
  10  DEP7        .     .     .     .     .     .     .     A     U
  11  DEP8        .     .     .     .     .     .     .     .     A
  12  DEP9        .     .     .     .     .     .     .     .     .
  13  DEP10       .     .     .     .     .     .     .     .     .
  14  DEP11       .     .     .     .     .     .     .     .     .
  15  DEP12       .     .     .     .     .     .     .     .     .
  16  DEP13       .     .     .     .     .     .     .     .     .
  17  DEP14       .     .     .     .     .     .     .     .     .
  18  DEP15       .     .     .     .     .     .     .     .     .
```

To enter the ratings of the remaining cells, press the <TAB> key or the right arrow key to move to the next screen. The completed spread sheet is shown below.

```
G4 '0
```

	G	H	I	J	K	L	M	N	O	P	Q
1	DEP6	DEP7	DEP8	DEP9	DEP10	DEP11	DEP12	DEP13	DEP14	DEP15	DEP16
2	.	.	.	.	.	.	.	.	2	3	4
3	.	.	.	.	.	.	.	.	2	2	2
4	0	X	U	U	I	I	U	U	U	U	U
5	0	X	U	U	I	I	U	U	U	U	U
6	A	X	X	X	E	E	U	U	U	U	U
7	A	X	X	X	E	E	U	U	U	U	U
8	A	X	X	X	U	U	U	U	U	U	U
9	.	X	X	X	U	U	U	U	U	U	U
10	.	.	A	U	X	X	A	U	U	U	U
11	.	.	.	A	X	X	U	U	U	U	U
12	.	.	.	.	X	X	U	U	U	U	U
13	.	.	.	.	.	A	U	U	U	U	U
14	.	.	.	.	.	.	U	U	U	U	U
15	.	.	.	.	.	.	.	A	U	U	U
16	.	.	.	.	.	.	.	.	U	U	U
17	.	.	.	.	.	.	.	.	.	U	U
18	.	.	.	.	.	.	.	.	.	.	U

```
                                                    READY
```

Note that the last three departments (DEP14, DEP15, and DEP16) are the three fictitious departments. They have been pre-assigned to the dummy locations (2,2), (2,3), and (2,4).

After completing the spread sheet data entry process, press <F10> to keep the data in memory and exit the spread sheet editor.

You may now save the input data on disk for future use. Move the pointer to the FILE option and select the Save Current File sub-option. The computer will display the current drive and sub-directory. Enter an appropriate file name and use the suffix "LAY" to indicate that this file contains a layout analysis problem.

You are now ready to solve the problem. Move the pointer to the SOLVE option and select the Display Output sub-option. The computer will ask if you have an initial solution as shown below.

```
Wish to enter an initial assignment (Y/N) N
```

Press <ENTER> to indicate that there is no initial solution available at this time. The computer will then display the menu of solution methods as shown below.

```
+--------------------------------------------------+
|                                                  |
|              *** SOLUTION METHOD ***             |
|                                                  |
|         +------------------------------+         |
|         | Random Assignments           |         |
|         | Pairwise Exchange            |         |
|         | User Exchange                |         |
|         +------------------------------+         |
|                                                  |
|                                                  |
|     +------------------------------------+       |
|     | Use the arrow keys to highlight a  |       |
|     | method.  Press ENTER to select or  |       |
|     | ESC to                             |       |
|     | exit.                              |       |
|     +------------------------------------+       |
|                                                  |
+--------------------------------------------------+
```

Begin the solution process by selecting the Random Assignment method with 20 trials (process not shown). The computer will pause for a few seconds and then display the following output report.

```
+----------------------------------------------------------+
|                                                          |
|          Problem Title:  IRREGULAR PLAN                  |
|                                                          |
|  Number of Trials:  20         No. of Successful Trials:  2 |
|  Best Assignment Found on Trial:  13                     |
|  Aggregate Layout Value: -218                            |
|                                                          |
|        Department       Row          Column             |
|        ----------       ------       ------             |
|        DEP1             4            3                   |
|        DEP2             2            4                   |
|        DEP3             4            1                   |
|        DEP4             1            4                   |
|        DEP5             1            2                   |
|        DEP6             2            3                   |
|        DEP7             3            3                   |
|        DEP8             3            4                   |
|        DEP9             4            4                   |
|                                                          |
+----------------------------------------------------------+
```

```
                    Problem Title: IRREGULAR PLAN

Number of Trials:  20          No. of Successful Trials:  2
Best Assignment Found on Trial:  13
Aggregate Layout Value: -218


       Department        Row          Column
       ----------        ------       ------
       DEP10             3            1
       DEP11             1            3
       DEP12             2            1
       DEP13             1            1
       DEP14             2            2
       DEP15             3            2
       DEP16             4            2
```

As seen from the above output report, the aggregate value of the proposed solution is -218.
This implies that the proposed layout contains several adjacent department pairs with
undesirable or "X" rating. You can improve the above layout by solving the problem again,
using the above layout as a starting solution and using the Pairwise Exchange solution
method. Move the pointer to the SOLVE option and press <ENTER>. You will be asked
if you wish to use the results of the last run as an initial solution. Press <ENTER> to
indicate yes as shown below.

```
Use the result of last run as initial assignment (Y/N) Y
```

The computer will then display the menu of solution methods. Select the pairwise exchange
option and request 15 trials as shown below. (Note that depending on the speed of the
personal computer model that you are using, this step may take somewhat longer).

```
              *** SOLUTION METHOD ***


              Number of trials:   15
```

208

The computer will pause for a few seconds and then displays the output report as shown below.

```
                    Problem Title: IRREGULAR PLAN

Number of Trials:  15          No. of Successful Trials:  9
Best Assignment Found on Trial:  14
Aggregate Layout Value:  72

        Department        Row           Column
        ----------        ------        ------
        DEP1              3             4
        DEP2              3             3
        DEP3              2             1
        DEP4              1             2
        DEP5              1             1
        DEP6              3             1
        DEP7              4             1
        DEP8              4             3
        DEP9              4             4
```

```
                    Problem Title: IRREGULAR PLAN

Number of Trials:  15          No. of Successful Trials:  9
Best Assignment Found on Trial:  14
Aggregate Layout Value:  72

        Department        Row           Column
        ----------        ------        ------
        DEP10             2             3
        DEP11             2             4
        DEP12             1             4
        DEP13             1             3
        DEP14             2             2
        DEP15             3             2
        DEP16             4             2
```

As seen from the above output report, the new layout is much more efficient than the previous one. The aggregate value of the layout is 72 and the best assignment was found during trial 14 and there were nine successful trials.

EXAMPLE 3 - USER EXCHANGE

You may improve the above solution still further by studying the resulting layout. For example, the current location for department DEP7 is (4,1) and that of department DEP6 is (3,1). Departments 6 and 7 have an adjacency rating of "X" which is undesirable. You may exchange the location of department DEP6 with another department that does not have an "X" rating with DEP7. As seen from Table 8-1, department DEP12 has an "A" rating with DEP7. Use the SOLVE option to explore the consequence of this exchange as described below.

Move the pointer to the SOLVE option and select the Display Output sub-option. The computer will ask if you wish to use the results of the last run as initial solution. Press <ENTER> to do so (screens not shown here). The computer will then display the menu of the solution methods. Move the bar down to the User Exchange and press <ENTER>. The computer will display the following screen.

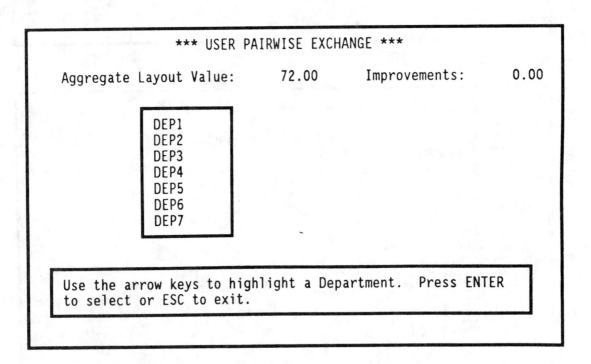

Move the bar down to department DEP6 and press <ENTER>. The computer will mark DEP6 as the first department selected and ask you to select the second department as shown below.

```
*** USER PAIRWISE EXCHANGE ***

Aggregate Layout Value:        72.00      Improvements:        0.00

            ┌─────────────┐
            │ DEP1        │
            │ DEP2        │
            │ DEP3        │
            │ DEP4        │
            │ DEP5        │
            │ DEP6*       │
            │ DEP7        │
            └─────────────┘

    ┌────────────────────────────────────────────────────┐
    │ Use the arrow keys to highlight another department. Press │
    │ ENTER to select or ESC to exit.  First department has been │
    │ marked with (*).                                    │
    └────────────────────────────────────────────────────┘
```

Move the pointer down to DEP12 and press <ENTER>. The computer will perform the pairwise exchange and reports the results as shown below.

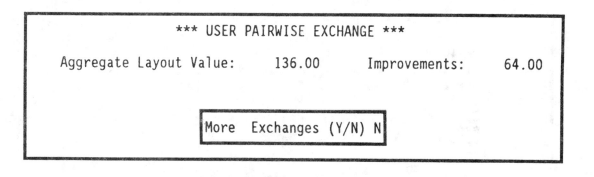

```
*** USER PAIRWISE EXCHANGE ***

Aggregate Layout Value:        136.00      Improvements:        64.00


            ┌──────────────────────────┐
            │ More   Exchanges (Y/N) N │
            └──────────────────────────┘
```

Press <ENTER> to exit from the User Exchange solution option and display the final solution as shown below.

```
                    Problem Title: IRREGULAR PLAN

Number of Trials: 15        No. of Successful Trials: 9
Best Assignment Found on Trial: 0
Aggregate Layout Value:  136

        Department      Row         Column
        ----------      ------      ------
        DEP1            3           4
        DEP2            3           3
        DEP3            2           1
        DEP4            1           2
        DEP5            1           1
        DEP6            1           4
        DEP7            4           1
        DEP8            4           3
        DEP9            4           4
```

```
                    Problem Title: IRREGULAR PLAN

Number of Trials: 15        No. of Successful Trials: 9
Best Assignment Found on Trial: 0
Aggregate Layout Value:  136

        Department      Row         Column
        ----------      ------      ------
        DEP10           2           3
        DEP11           2           4
        DEP12           3           1
        DEP13           1           3
        DEP14           2           2
        DEP15           3           2
        DEP16           4           2
```

As seen from the above solution, the aggregate value of the proposed layout is 136. Note also that the dummy departments have been assigned to the fictitious locations as requested by the input data.

The above solution appears to be a reasonably good layout. It does not contain any adjacent department pair with an undesirable rating "X". However, there is no guarantee that this solution in an optimal solution because the solution methods which were applied were all heuristics.

PROBLEMS

1. For the following departmental pair preference rating list for an eight department facility, develop a reasonable departmental layout for a departmental configuration consisting of two rows and four columns.

Departmental Pair	Preference Rating	Departmental Pair	Preference Rating
1-2	I	3-4	A
1-3	E	3-5	O
1-4	E	3-6	I
1-5	A	3-7	X
1-6	X	3-8	U
1-7	O	4-5	O
1-8	U	4-6	U
2-3	I	4-7	O
2-4	U	4-8	U
2-5	X	5-6	X
2-6	A	5-7	I
2-7	E	5-8	U
2-8	U	6-7	I
		6-8	E
		7-8	A

2. In problem 1, pre-assign department 3 to location (2,3). Solve the problem using 10 random trials and 5 pairwise exchanges.

3. Consider the first six departments in problem 1. Assign these six departments to the following grid layout:

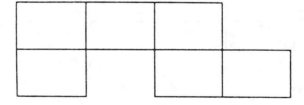

Use 10 random trials and 10 pairwise exchange trials.

213

4. The Fairport Machine Shop planned to move from three different dispersed locations to a new building. Its eight departments were to be laid out on a 4x2 grid in the new building with nearness priorities (adjacency ratings) as shown in the table below. Determine a reasonable layout design for the machine shop.

Departmental Pair	Preference Rating	Departmental Pair	Preference Rating
1-2	I	3-4	A
1-3	E	3-5	O
1-4	E	3-6	I
1-5	A	3-7	X
1-6	X	3-8	U
1-7	O	4-5	O
1-8	U	4-6	U
2-3	I	4-7	O
2-4	U	4-8	U
2-5	X	5-6	X
2-6	A	5-7	I
2-7	E	5-8	U
2-8	U	6-7	I
		6-8	E
		7-8	A

5. Consider the adjacency ratings presented in Fairport Machine Shop (above problem). Assign the eight departments to the following floor space.

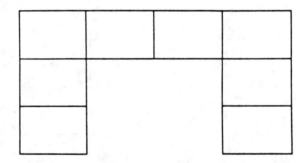

6. Solve problem 5, assume that department 1 must be located at a corner.

7. A small college campus with nine classroom-faculty office buildings needs to be designed so that the amount of traffic over longer distances is minimized. It is difficult to determine the exact amount of traffic between buildings but a listing of nearness priorities (adjacency ratings) has been developed and is shown in the matrix below. The buildings are identified as buildings 1 to 9. Find an appropriate layout design.

	1	2	3	4	5	6	7	8	9
1	-	A	U	O	A	U	O	U	A
2		-	I	E	U	I	I	O	O
3			-	U	A	U	U	A	I
4				-	E	O	E	U	U
5					-	I	U	I	U
6						-	E	U	A
7							-	O	I
8								-	E
9									-

8. Assign the nine buildings in the above problem to the following grid space.

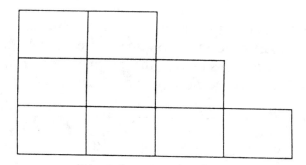

215

9. Assign the eight departments, with the adjacency ratings presented below, to the following grid.

A D F	B G	C E H

	1	2	3	4	5	6	7	8
1	-	I	0	A	E	U	I	A
2		-	0	E	X	A	I	U
3			-	A	I	0	A	X
4				-	U	0	0	E
5					-	X	I	0
6						-	U	A
7							-	U
8								-

10. The Nouret Chocolate Company is designing a new plant with six departments. The locations of the six departments on a 2x3 grid is quite critical as represented by the nearness ratings (adjacency constraints) shown in the matrix below. The departments are identified by the letters A, B, C, D, E and F. Develop the layout for the company.

	A	B	C	D	E	F
A	-	0	X	A	0	A
B		-	I	E	U	X
C			-	X	A	I
D				-	A	U
E					-	I
F						-

216

11. The Nouret Chocolate Company decides to add three departments, identified as departments G, H and I to the proposed plant being developed in problem above. The new plant will be a 3x3 grid and the nearness ratings of the three departments in relation to each other and in relation to the six departments in the existing plan is shown below. Find a reasonably good layout.

	A	B	C	D	E	F	G	H	I
G	X	A	I	A	I	U	-		
H	0	U	I	X	U	X	A	-	
I	I	0	U	A	0	U	X	0	-

12. Assign the nine departments of problem 11 to the following floor-space:

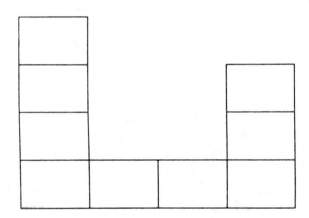

217

13. The tenth floor of a hexagonal office tower, with elevators in the center of the tower was layed out as shown below. The eight room locations are to be allocated to seven laboratories and one office. The rooms are of approximate equal size so that the

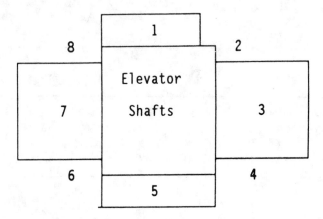

laboratories A, B, C, D, E, F and G and office H can be allocated to any one of the eight rooms. The nearness priorities of the seven laboratories and office are shown in the matrix below. Develop best location layout.

	A	B	C	D	E	F	G	H
A	-	A	I	X	E	E	O	E
B		-	U	O	I	O	I	X
C			-	I	X	U	A	I
D				-	I	I	I	I
E					-	X	U	X
F						-	U	U
G							-	A
H								-

14. Suppose the office in the hexagonal building above must be located adjacent to laboratories C and F. How would you change the nearness ratings shown in the problem above. Will the requirement change the best layout found before?

218

CHAPTER 9

LINE BALANCING

INTRODUCTION

The assembly line balancing technique is widely used in assembly line operations to balance the workloads of stations positioned along an assembly line. The objective is to produce a specified number of units of output with a minimum of worker idle time.

The most common applications of line balancing are found in manufacturing operations such as automobile assembly, television set assembly, etc. However, there are also a number of assembly line balancing applications in the growing service industry. Two examples of this are the order preparation in fast food industries and the processing of blood donors at blood donation sites.

The techniques developed for assembly line balancing do not always produce optimal solutions, because of the high degree of complexity as well as the numerous possible task combinations. The solution methods used are therefore heuristic in nature which means they produce good solutions, but not necessarily optimal solutions.

The computer solution methods to be illustrated here consist of four different versions of heuristic methods.

ILLUSTRATION OF ASSEMBLY LINE BALANCING TECHNIQUES

The technique will be illustrated with an example. Figure 9-1 shows a network of tasks that need to be performed in the order indicated. That is task 1 must be completed before task 2 can be started. Similarly, task 3 must be completed before task 4 can be started. Before task 6 can be started both tasks 4 and 5 must be completed. Hence, the network shows the eight tasks along the assembly and the order in which the tasks must be performed. Of course, there are certain tasks that can be performed independent of each other. For instance, tasks 1, 2, and 5 are independent of tasks 3 and 4.

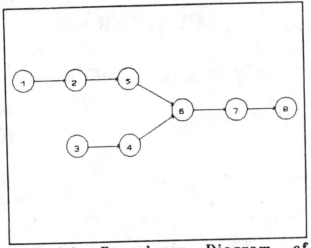

Figure 9-1: Precedence Diagram of Assembly Line Tasks

Each task takes a specified time for its completion. Although, theoretically, any task could take any amount of time, in order to aid the assembly line balancing process it is desirable to have each task take a similar amount of time. Longer tasks therefore should be broken up into smaller tasks, if feasible.

Table 9-1 lists the eight tasks, the time each task takes to do and the immediate predecessor of each task. The immediate predecessor is the preceding task that must be completed first before the task under consideration can be started. Note that the total time for all eight tasks amounts to 11.8 minutes.

The objective of the assembly line balancing technique is to assign the eight tasks to work stations along the assembly line in such a way that the required output volume is completed in time with a minimum amount of collective station time. Station time needs to be minimized because it determines the cost of production. Any idle station time increases the cost of the overall production process.

Based on the above, we therefore have for any assembly line product, a total task time which consists of the sum of all the task times. We also have collective station time which consists of the number of stations required to complete the assembly of the product multiplied by the station time which takes the longest. The station which takes the longest time to complete the assigned task(s) determines what is called the cycle time of the assembly line. The cycle time is the speed with which products roll off the assembly line.

Task	Immediate Predecessor	Task Time (Minutes)
1	-	1.2
2	1	1.2
3	-	1.8
4	3	1.6
5	2	1.3
6	4, 5	2.0
7	6	1.4
8	7	1.3
	TOTAL	11.8

Table 9-1: Precedence Diagram Summary Table - Example Problem

From the total task time and the collective station time we can determine the efficiency of the assembly line. Efficiency of the assembly line is determined by the formula,

$$Efficiency = 1 - \frac{Total\ Idle\ Time}{Collective\ Station\ Time}$$

For the example problem there are eight tasks with a total idle time of 4.16 minutes. Suppose that collective station time is 16.0 minutes, then the efficiency of the assembly line is,

$$Efficiency = 1 - \frac{4.16}{16} = 0.74\ or\ 74\%$$

There are a variety of heuristics to position tasks to work stations on an assembly line. We shall use four different heuristic rules in the computer program. Each rule will be applied and whichever rule produces the best result, that is the rule which provides the highest efficiency, will be utilized. The four heuristic rules are:

1. Position longer tasks to station before shorter tasks. To apply this rule we must approximate the location of the station on the basis of whether a task is early in the sequence, late in the sequence, or is in the middle of the sequence. In other words there is no fixed rule for selecting the station.

2.   Place the task which has the largest number of following tasks before placing other tasks. Since the first task is followed by many other tasks it is nearly always positioned to the first station. Subsequent tasks are then positioned to stations that follow the first station.

3.   Position the task which has the larger number of preceding tasks before positioning other tasks.

4.   Position the task which has the higher positional weight before other tasks, where positional weight is the task time plus the task times of all of the followers.

Note that, in all of the above four heuristics, all assigned tasks must be preceded by their predecessor tasks.

SOLUTION OF ASSEMBLY LINE BALANCING EXAMPLE

We shall now apply the solution method to the example. Suppose that required output volume in one shift is 140 units. Also suppose that there are 420 minutes of assembly line time available in one shift. Then the required cycle time will be 420/140 = 3 minutes. Hence, the maximum cycle time is 3 minutes. It can, of course, be shorter if that is the way the task positioning works out.

Rule 1 will be applied first. It specifies that the longest task be assigned to a work station first. The two feasible candidates are Tasks 1 and 3. We select the one with the larger task time. Task 3, having a task time of 1.8 minutes, is assigned to work station 1 (see Table 9-2). The next 2 candidate tasks are 1 and 4. Task 4 cannot be included since its task time is larger than the remaining time for station 1 (i.e. 3 - 1.8 = 1.2 min). We assign task 1 to this station; the remaining time is then 3 - (1.8 + 1.2) = 0 minutes. We open a new station, number 2. There are two feasible candidates to be assigned, tasks 2 and 4. We select task 4 because it is longer. The remaining station time is 3 - 1.6 = 1.4 minutes. Next, we assign task 2 to station 2. The remaining station time is now 3 - (1.6 + 1.2) = .20 minutes. Since no more feasible candidates exist, we open station 3. There is only one feasible candidate, task 5. We assign this task to station 3. Now task 6 becomes a candidate. But its task time is larger than the remaining station time, so we open station 4 and assign task 6 to station 4. The remaining time for this station is 3 - 2 = 1 minutes, which is smaller than the time for task 7. Therefore, we open station 5 and assign task 7 and then task 8 to this station.

Work station	Task	Task time (minute)	Remaining time (minute)	Station time (minute)
1	3	1.8	1.20	
	1	1.2	0.00	3.0
2	4	1.6	1.40	
	2	1.2	0.20	2.8
3	5	1.3	1.70	1.3
4	6	2.0	1.00	2.0
5	7	1.4	1.60	
	8	1.3	0.30	2.7

Table 9-2: Task Assignment Based on Longest Task First

This process assigns the eight tasks to five work stations. The maximum work station time is 3.0 minutes for station 1. The lowest work station time is for station 3 with only 1.3 minutes. The efficiency of the task assignment is,

$$Efficiency = \left(1 - \frac{3.2}{(5)(3.0)}\right)100 = 78.67\%$$

For the next assignment example we shall use the second assignment rule. It requires that the task which has the largest number of following tasks be positioned first. From the precedence diagram we can observe that task 1 has the largest number of following tasks. It is positioned first to station 1 as shown on Table 9-3. The next assignment produces a tie with tasks 2 and 3. Whenever a tie occurs, the task with the lowest sequential number is assigned first. Hence, task 2 is assigned to station 1 which is feasible because the combined time of tasks 1 and 2 is 2.4 minutes. This, therefore satisfies the maximum cycle time rule. Task 3 is then assigned to station 2. The next assignment finds a tie between tasks 4 and 5. Task 4 is positioned first and is assigned to station 3. Task 5 is then assigned to station 3. We next continue assigning tasks 6, 7, and 8 and find that they can all be assigned to five stations.

Work station	Task	Task time (minute)	Remaining time (minute)	Number of Follower Tasks
1	1	1.2	1.80	5
	2	1.2	0.60	4
2	3	1.8	1.20	4
3	4	1.6	1.40	3
	5	1.3	0.10	3
4	6	2.0	1.00	2
5	7	1.4	1.60	1
	8	1.3	0.30	0

Table 9-3: Task Assignment Based on Largest Number of Follower Tasks

The efficiency of the task assignments based on the largest number of following tasks is,

$$Efficiency - \left(1 - \frac{3.2}{(2.9)(5)}\right)100 - 77.93\%$$

Note that the efficiency is slightly less than in the previous assignment. Actual cycle time is 2.9 minutes and idle time has remained at 3.2 minutes (based on maximum cycle time of 3.0 minutes).

The next step is to position the tasks according to the largest number of preceding tasks. It produces an efficiency of 61.73 percent as shown on Table 9-4. In this case actual cycle time is 2.7 minutes and total idle time is 6.2 minutes because 6 stations were required.

Finally, the last assignment rule using positional weights is applied. It produces an efficiency of 78.67 percent and is therefore tied with the first rule. It also generates an assignment that is slightly different than the first rule as shown on Table 9-5.

Work station	Task	Task time (minute)	Remaining time (minute)	Number of Preceding Tasks
1	1	1.2	1.80	0
	2	1.2	0.60	1
2	5	1.3	1.70	2
3	3	1.8	1.20	0
4	4	1.6	1.40	1
5	6	2	1.00	5
6	7	1.4	1.60	6
	8	1.3	0.30	7

Table 9-4 : Task Assignment Based on Largest Number of Preceding Tasks

Work station	Task	Task time (minute)	Remaining time (minute)	Weight
1	1	1.2	1.80	8.4
	3	1.8	0.00	8.1
2	2	1.2	1.80	7.2
	4	1.6	0.20	6.3
3	5	1.3	1.70	6.0
4	6	2	1.00	4.7
5	7	1.4	1.60	2.7
	8	1.3	0.30	1.3

Table 9-5 : Task Assignment Based on Largest Positional Weight

EXAMPLE 1 - THE CASE OF RADIO HUT

Radio Hut is planning to add a new brand of AM radio for marketing in its overseas stores. Radio Hut Plant #3 in Flint, Michigan has 420 minutes of unused capacity per day which can be re-allocated for the production of the new Talkman AM Radio. The management has determined that in order for Talkman to earn a reasonable profit, the line should produce 200 units per day. The production process involves 16 tasks as shown below.

Task	Description	Time (min.)	Predecessors
1	Put Ckt board on jig	0.36	-
2	Insert IC #1	0.24	1
3	Insert IC #2	0.44	1
4	Insert IC #3	0.60	1
5	Solder IC connectors	1.50	2,3,4
6	Attach board to frame	1.20	5
7	Attach speaker to frame	1.10	6
8	Connect speaker wires to board	0.85	6,7
9	Solder speaker connectors	0.60	8
10	Plug antenna terminals	0.30	9
11	Attach battery terminals	0.50	10
12	Attach phone terminals	0.50	10
13	Inspect unit visually	1.00	11,12
14	Test circuits for integrity	0.60	13
15	Attach top Cover	0.20	14
16	Box unit and instructions	0.50	15

Figure 9-2 presents the precedence diagram for the stated 16 tasks. You have been asked to determine a balanced assembly line for this new product and identify the number of workers needed.

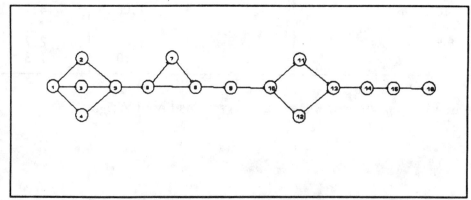

Figure 9-2: Precedence Diagram for the Talkman AM Radio

To solve the above problem, load the DSSPOM into the computer and select the Line Balancing program. After a few seconds the computer will load the program and display the Line Balancing Menu. Select the INPUT option by moving the pointer one level to the right and press <ENTER>.

The program responds by invoking the data entry process and requests a problem title. Type "AM RADIO" and press the <ENTER> key. The next query involves the number of tasks. Type "16" and press <ENTER>. The next two queries relate to the desired output in units and the available production time in minutes. Enter 200 and 420, respectively. The completed initial data entry screen is presented below.

```
Problem title: AM RADIO

Enter number of tasks: 16

Enter the desired number of units per day:  200
Enter daily production time (minutes per day):   420




  ┌─────────────────────────────────────────────────────┐
  │ Enter problem parameters as requested.  Press RETURN to │
  │ accept, or ESC to exit.   Maximum problem size is 30 tasks, │
  │ each having up to five predecessors.  Task times should be │
  │ within 0 and 999.                                   │
  └─────────────────────────────────────────────────────┘
```

The program will resume the data entry process by asking if it should continue with the task definition process as shown below.

```
┌──────────────────────────────────────────┐
│ Continue with task definition (Y/N) Y │
└──────────────────────────────────────────┘
```

Press <Y> to continue the task definition process using the spread sheet editor. The program initializes the spread sheet editor by defining 16 rows. The default task names are Task1, Task2, etc, and the times as well as the number of predecessors are set to zero.

Enter the task definitions one row at a time. Make sure that the number of predecessors (column C) for each task is entered correctly. The completed spread sheet is presented below.

	A	B	C	D	E	F	G	H
								⊢READY⊢
A1 'Task								
	Task	Task	No of	Pred.	Pred.	Pred.	Pred.	Pred.
1	Task	Task	No of	Pred.	Pred.	Pred.	Pred.	Pred.
2	Label	Time	Pred.	One	Two	Three	Four	Five
3	JIG-CKT	0.36	0					
4	IC-#1	0.24	1	1				
5	IC-#2	0.44	1	1				
6	IC-#3	0.60	1	1				
7	SOLD-IC	1.50	3	2	3	4		
8	BOARD	1.20	1	5				
9	SPEAKER	1.10	1	6				
10	SP-W...	0.85		6	7			
11	SOLD-SP	0.60	1	8				
12	ANTENNA	0.30	1	9				
13	BATTERY	0.50	1	10				
14	PHONE	0.50	1	10				
15	INSPECT	1.00	2	11	12			
16	CHK-CKT	0.60	1	13				
17	PUT-TOP	0.20	1	14				
18	WARP	0.50	1	15				

After completing the spread sheet data entry process, press <F10> to keep the data and exit the spread sheet.

You may now obtain a hard copy printout of the input data by moving the pointer to the PRINT option and press <ENTER>. Be sure that the printer is ON and Ready. Obtain the printout and study it carefully to make sure there are no data entry errors. You may proceed to save the problem on disk for future use. Move the pointer to the FILE option and select "Save current file" sub-option then press <ENTER>. The program will ask for a DOS file name. Select a proper name and use a related suffix such as "BAL" to imply line balancing.

You are now ready to solve the problem. Move the pointer to the SOLVE option and select the "Display Output" sub-option then press <ENTER>. The program will pause a few seconds and then present the following solution options menu.

```
Largest processing time first
Largest number of following tasks first
Largest number of preceding tasks first
Highest positional weight first
```

```
Use the arrow keys to highlight the solution method, press
ENTER to select or ESC to exit.
```

As mentioned earlier, the program provides four heuristic solution procedures to choose from. Select the "Largest processing time first" solution option be pressing the <ENTER> key.

The program will pause a few seconds and then report the first output report as shown below.

```
                    Problem Title: AM RADIO

    Total task times              10.49   minutes

    Minimum cycle time             1.50   minutes

    Maximum cycle time             2.10   minutes

    Minimum number of stations        5
```

As seen from the above report, the total task times for the sixteen tasks is 10.49 minutes. The longest task requires 1.50 minutes which constitutes the minimum cycle time. Based on the availability of 420 minutes of production time and a desired output of 200 units, the calculated maximum cycle time is 2.10 minutes and this requires a minimum of 5 work stations. Note however that the actual number of work stations used depends on the task precedence relationships and may exceed this value.

229

Press <ENTER> to continue with the solution process and obtain the next output report as shown below.

Problem Title: AM RADIO

Work station	Task Name	Task Time (min)	Remaining Time (min)	Station Time (min)
1	JIG-CKT	0.36	1.74	0.36
	IC-#3	0.60	1.14	0.96
	IC-#2	0.44	0.70	1.40
	IC-#1	0.24	0.46	1.64
2	SOLD-IC	1.50	0.60	1.50
3	BOARD	1.20	0.90	1.20
4	SPEAKER	1.10	1.00	1.10
	SP-WIRES	0.85	0.15	1.95
5	SOLD-SP	0.60	1.50	0.60
	ANTENNA	0.30	1.20	0.90

Problem Title: AM RADIO

Work station	Task Name	Task Time (min)	Remaining Time (min)	Station Time (min)
	BATTERY	0.50	0.70	1.40
	PHONE	0.50	0.20	1.90
6	INSPECT	1.00	1.10	1.00
	CHK-CKT	0.60	0.50	1.60
	PUT-TOP	0.20	0.30	1.80
7	WARP	0.50	1.60	0.50

The above output reports present the task assignments and number of stations used. For this problem, the 16 tasks have been grouped into 7 stations. The task grouping consists of: tasks 1-4 assigned to station 1, task 5 to station 2, task 6 to station 3, tasks 7 and 8 to station 4, tasks 9, 10, 11, and 12 to station 5, tasks 13,14, and 15 to station 6, and task 16 to station 7. The report also contains remaining station time which is the difference between cycle time and cumulative task times assigned to each station. Press the enter key to continue the solution report as shown below.

```
Problem Title: AM RADIO


Actual cycle time  1.95   minutes

Total work station idle time =     4.21   minutes

Assembly line efficiency    69.16   percent
```

The above report indicates that the actual cycle time, the longest station time, is 1.95 minutes. The total idle time, over all stations, is 4.21 minutes (based on maximum cycle time of 2.1 minutes) which results in the line efficiency of about 69 percent. The line efficiency is obtained as follows:

$$Efficiency - \left(1 - \frac{4.21}{(7)(1.95)}\right)100 - 69.16\%$$

It should be noted that in certain references, instead of using the actual cycle time, the maximum cycle time (in this case 2.10 minutes) is used. The use of actual cycle time results in under-estimating the line efficiency. For example, if in the above equation, you use the maximum cycle time, the line efficiency is about 71.36 percent.

The above reports indicate that, Radio Hut should construct an assembly line with 7 stations (usually for each station there is one worker, hence the number of stations represent the number of employees needed) and assign the 16 tasks to the stations as indicated above. Because the actual observed cycle time is about 1.95 minutes, it is possible to produce 420/1.95 = 215 radios per day.

EXAMPLE 2 - RADIO HUT REDUCES PRODUCTION

Five years ago, Radio Hut adopted your proposal and developed a seven station assembly line which produced the Talkman AM Radio. Talkman became one of the most popular AM radios and sold beyond its projected demand. However, within the last nine months, sales have decreased drastically due to competition and Radio Hut is considering a production cut. In particular, the management is considering a reduction in production by as much as 50 percent to 100 units per day. Further, the production time is also cut back to 360 minutes per day. This reduction is presumed to have a significant impact on the assembly line configuration. Help the management solve its problem.

The revised production amount has an impact on the desired cycle time and in turn, on the number of stations needed. To solve the problem, move the pointer to the EDIT option and press the <ENTER> key. The computer will begin the edit process by placing the pointer in the title field. Change the title to "TALKMAN II" and press <ENTER>. Since the number of tasks has not changed, press <ENTER> to accept the current value. Change the desired output to 100 and the daily production time to 360 minutes. The task definition has not been changed, therefore when asked to revise the task definition, press <N>. The completed edit process is shown below.

```
Problem title: TALKMAN II

Enter number of tasks: 16

Enter the desired number of units per day:  100

Enter daily production time (minutes per day):   360




┌─────────────────────────────────────────────┐
│  Continue with task definition (Y/N) N       │
└─────────────────────────────────────────────┘
```

You are now ready to solve the revised problem. Move the pointer to the SOLVE option and select the "Display Output" sub-option. The computer will display the menu of the four heuristic solution procedures. Press the <ENTER> key to select the first option (this process is the same as in Example 1 and is not shown here). The computer will pause a few seconds and then display the following output report.

```
                    Problem Title: TALKMAN II

Total task times              10.49   minutes

Minimum cycle time             1.50   minutes

Maximum cycle time             3.60   minutes

Minimum number of stations       3
```

This report indicates that the cycle time is 3.60 minutes with the minimum number of stations equal 3. Press <ENTER> to continue. The next output is shown below.

```
                    Problem Title: TALKMAN II

                         Task      Remaining    Station
    Work        Task     Time        Time         Time
    station     Name     (min)       (min)       (min)
    -------     -------  --------  ----------   -------
    1           JIG-CKT   0.36        3.24         0.36
                IC-#3     0.60        2.64         0.96
                IC-#2     0.44        2.20         1.40
                IC-#1     0.24        1.96         1.64
                SOLD-IC   1.50        0.46         3.14
    2           BOARD     1.20        2.40         1.20
                SPEAKER   1.10        1.30         2.30
                SP-WIRES  0.85        0.45         3.15
    3           SOLD-SP   0.60        3.00         0.60
                ANTENNA   0.30        2.70         0.90
```

```
                    Problem Title: TALKMAN II

                         Task      Remaining    Station
    Work        Task     Time        Time         Time
    station     Name     (min)       (min)       (min)
    -------     -------  --------  ----------   -------
                BATTERY   0.50        2.20         1.40
                PHONE     0.50        1.70         1.90
                INSPECT   1.00        0.70         2.90
                CHK-CKT   0.60        0.10         3.50
    4           PUT-TOP   0.20        3.40         0.20
                WARP      0.50        2.90         0.70
```

As seen from the above solution, the revised problem requires only 4 stations instead of the original 7. The increase in the cycle time (from 2.1 minutes to 3.6 minutes) has made it possible for more tasks to be grouped into the same station. Press <ENTER> for the next report as shown below.

```
Problem Title: TALKMAN II


Actual cycle time  3.5   minutes

Total work station idle time =      3.91  minutes

Assembly line efficiency    72.07   percent
```

The revised solution has an actual cycle time of 3.5 minutes and a line efficiency of about 72 percent. The revised solution implies that the desired rate of output of 100 units can be achieved by reconfiguring the line and assigning the 16 tasks to 4 stations.

PROBLEMS

1. For the assembly line problem depicted by the precedence diagram below, develop a balanced assembly line for the case where 440 minutes are available per shift. Required output is 250 units per shift, and task times shown are in minutes.

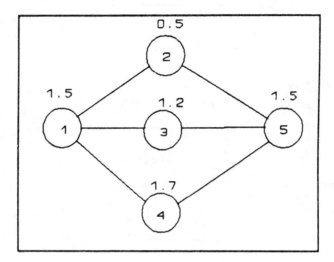

2. Assign the tasks to work stations for the assembly line problem depicted in the precedence table below. There are 400 minutes per shift and required output is 420 units.

Task	Task Time in Minutes	Predecessor Task
1	0.9	None
2	0.7	None
3	0.3	1
4	0.8	2, 3
5	0.6	4
6	0.4	5
7	0.2	6
8	0.5	7

3. For the assembly line problem depicted by the precedence diagram below, develop balanced assembly lines. For an eight hour shift there are 420 minutes of work station time available. Required output per shift is 200 units in August, September and October and 100 units for the rest of the year. Task times are shown in minutes.

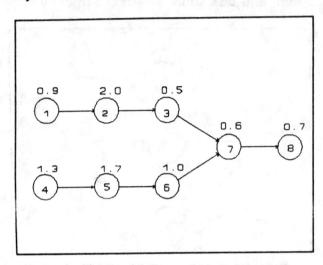

4. Assign the tasks to work stations for the assembly line problem depicted in the following precedence table. There are 410 minutes per shift and required output is either 120 units or 280 units. Solve for both output levels.

Task	Task Time in Minutes	Predecessor Task
1	0.3	None
2	0.5	1
3	0.4	None
4	1.4	2, 3
5	0.2	None
6	0.9	5
7	0.4	4, 6
8	1.3	7

236

5. Bigalow Food Company produces packaged food and is planning to begin production of a new menu item. An assembly line is to be developed that will produce 10 units per 8 hour workday. The tasks, times, and precedence requirements are shown below.

a) Draw the corresponding precedence diagram.
b) Determine the work stations by selecting the longest task first. Give the efficiency of the line.
c) How well balanced is the line?
d) Solve the problem using the other 3 heuristic rules. Which method gives the best efficiency of the line?

TASK	TIME (min.)	PREDECESSOR
A	27	--
B	30	A
C	10	A
D	17	A
E	30	B
F	33	B
G	7	D
H	11	G
I	26	G
J	15	I

6. Shown below are the tasks, times, and precedence requirements for the work required to assemble a tricycle. The company wants to produce 83,200 trikes a year. Assume a 5 day, 8 hour a day work week.

a) Draw the precedence diagram with the task times included.
b) Determine the work stations, cycle time, efficiency rate of a balanced line using highest positional weight.

TASK	TIME (min)	PREDECESSORS
A	.6	--
B	.9	--
C	.7	--
D	1.1	A
E	1.0	B
F	.6	C
G	1.2	D
H	.4	F
I	.6	H,E
J	.7	G,I

7. A large manufacturer of clay masks is planning to add a new line of stands for the masks. They have called you in to balance the production process. A minimum of 450 stands must be produced per 8 hour day. The tasks, times, and predecessors are given below.

a) Draw the precedence diagram.
b) Formulate a balanced line based on the longest task first.
c) How many stations are required? What is the resulting cycle time?
d) Is the efficiency satisfactory?

TASK	TIME (hrs)	PREDECESSOR
A	2.0	--
B	2.2	A
C	2.1	--
D	3.1	B,C
E	1.9	--
F	2.6	E
G	2.1	D,F
H	3.0	G

8. Sunwell Plastics is developing an assembly line to produce a plastic household product. It plans to produce 400 units per 410 minute shift. The tasks, task times and predecessors are shown below. Rebalance line for output of 280 units per shift.

Task	Task Time in Seconds	Predecessor
1	18	-
2	36	-
3	24	-
4	48	1
5	42	2
6	18	3
7	54	4
8	6	6
9	18	8,6
10	24	7,9

9. The Elma Appliance Company manufactures small household appliances. The company is developing a new assembly line for a new food processor. The tasks, task times and predecessor tasks are shown below. What is the maximum output per 400 minute shift? Rebalance the line for 250 units per shift.

Task	Task Time in Seconds	Predecessor
1	25	-
2	15	-
3	5	1
4	9	1
5	11	2
6	15	2,4
7	20	5
8	5	7
9	11	5
10	15	8
11	7	8
12	5	10

10. Clark Furniture Manufacturing (CFM) assembled a line of furniture on an assembly line. CFM decided to do a time study of the thirteen tasks required to assemble one unit on the assembly line. The tasks, task times and predecessor tasks are given below. Required output is 400 units and 420 minutes per shift are available. Rebalance line for output of 220 units per shift.

Task	Task Time in Seconds	Predecessor
1	17	1
2	19	1
3	21	1
4	27	2
5	16	2,3
6	9	3,4
7	11	6
8	27	7
9	8	7
10	14	7,8
11	19	7,9
12	22	11
13	17	11

11. Chambers Manufacturing was modifying its assembly line for its middle line of snow blowers. The tasks, task times and predecessor tasks are shown below. Required output was 500 units per 390 minutes shift. Rebalance the line for output of 300 units per shift.

Task	Task Time in Seconds	Predecessor
1	28	1
2	25	1
3	10	2
4	12	2
5	17	2,3
6	25	4
7	10	4
8	5	6,7
9	8	7
10	9	7
11	18	9,10
12	21	11
13	9	11
14	16	11

12. The Arcade Toy Company produces battery-driven motorized toy vehicles for children. One of its products, a single seater car, is to be assembled on a new assembly line. The tasks, task times, and predecessors are shown below. Develop a balanced line for a required output of 500 units per 410 minute shift. Rebalance the line for output of 300 units per shift.

Task	Task Time in Seconds	Predecessor
1	35	-
2	25	-
3	13	-
4	19	1
5	21	1
6	25	1
7	30	2,3
8	11	3
9	22	5
10	25	5
11	17	6,7
12	11	8,9
13	14	11
14	19	11
15	21	12

13. Plainview Electronics produces electronic devices and will begin assembly of a new model device in about two months. An assembly line is under development and the tasks need to be balanced across the necessary work stations on the line. The work day amounts to 400 minutes per shift and required output is 600 units per shift. The tasks, task times, and predecessors are shown below. Balance the assembly line as well as possible. Rebalance the line for 240 units per shift.

Task	Task Time in Seconds	Predecessor
1	31	none
2	34	none
3	14	1
4	21	2
5	34	3
6	39	3
7	11	5
8	12	5
9	9	5
10	32	6,7
11	25	8
12	17	9
13	19	11
14	14	11
15	30	14
16	8	14

CHAPTER 10

AGGREGATE PLANNING

INTRODUCTION

Aggregate production planning is an operations planning method which allows the evaluation of future work schedules for one or more products, especially evaluation of the desirability and need for overtime and/or sub-contracting. The method is also referred to as "multi-item, multi-period production scheduling."

A production manager typically has to consider the alternative of changing regular time production through layoffs or hiring and the utilization of idle time or overtime. With varying demand levels and high inventory carrying costs it is not easy to develop a production schedule for a future time period which will simultaneously minimize production costs and inventory holding costs.

The aggregate production planning model described in this chapter intends to provide the production manager with the operating results of various production schedules. Typically, a production manager looks at the demands forecasts of one or more products (or items) for the next six months and attempts to develop a feasible production schedule. If the demand forecast is relatively constant on a week to week basis then the problem is rather straight-forward. However, demand usually varies from week to week, and sometimes substantially. It is primarily for the latter problem that the aggregate production planning model is developed.

Suppose monthly demand for two products varies from a low of 100 units to a high of 500 units over a five month period as shown in Table 10-1. The two products use the same production resources and per-unit consumption of the resources are the same. The production resources includes regular time production and overtime production as shown in Table 10-1. Regular time production capacity varies over time and overtime production capacity is 25% of regular time. The production, inventory, and backorder costs are presented in Table 10-2. The problem is to determine a production schedule for these two products which minimizes the total cost of production, inventory, and backorder.

One alternative for solving the above problem is to satisfy the demands through regular time production first and then, for any additional demands through overtime. Table 10-3 presents an example of a production schedule.

Month	Demand Forecasts		Production Capacity	
	Product 1	Product 2	Regular Time	Over Time
1	500	200	800	200
2	500	300	600	150
3	300	400	400	100
4	100	250	400	100
5	100	150	400	100
Total	1500	1300	2600	650

Table 10-1: A Two-Product Production Planning Problem

Regular Time Cost ($/Unit)	$30.00
Overtime Cost ($/Unit)	$45.00
Inventory Cost ($/Unit/Period)	
Product 1	$ 6.00
Product 2	$ 9.00
Backorder Cost ($/Unit/Period)	
Product 1	$10.00
Product 2	$15.00

Table 10-2: Production and Inventory Costs

Production Schedule

| Month | Product 1 | | | Product 2 | | |
	Regular Time	Over Time	End-Inventory	Regular Time	Over Time	End-Inventory
1	500	0	0	300	200	300
2	500	0	0	100	100	200
3	300	0	0	100	100	0
4	100	0	0	250	0	0
5	100	0	0	150	0	0
Total	1500	0	0	900	400	500

Table 10-3: A Production Schedule for the Two-Product Problem

The method of developing the production schedule is rather ad-hoc and there is no guarantee that it will produce an optimal production schedule. The algorithm in DSSPOM utilized to solve the production scheduling problem however, is an exact method and will find the optimal solution. The method can solve problems with variable production capacities, and production costs. Backordering is also allowed. DSSPOM can solve problems with up to four products and 12 periods.

EXAMPLE 1 - A TWO PRODUCT PROBLEM

In this example you will solve the two-product production scheduling problem presented earlier in this chapter. Load DSSPOM into the computer and select the Aggregate Planning module. After a few seconds the computer will load the program and display the Aggregate Palnning Menu. Move the pointer to the INPUT option and press <ENTER>. The program will begin the data entry process by placing the pointer in the title field. Type "AGGREGATE PLANNING" and press <ENTER>. The initial data entry screen is presented below.

```
┌──────────────────────────────────────────────────────────┐
│                                                          │
│    Problem title: AGGREGATE PLANNING                     │
│                                                          │
│    Number of periods:   5                                │
│                                                          │
│    Number of products:   2                               │
│                                                          │
│    Allow  backorders: Y                                  │
│                                                          │
│    ┌────────────────────────────────────────────────┐   │
│    │ Enter problem parameters as requested.  Press RETURN to │
│    │ accept, or ESC to exit.   Maximum problem size is 12 periods │
│    │ and 4 products.                                  │   │
│    └────────────────────────────────────────────────┘   │
│                                                          │
└──────────────────────────────────────────────────────────┘
```

Enter 5 for the number of periods and 2 for the number of products. For this example problem, assume that backorder (or backlog) is allowed. Enter "Y" for this question and press <ENTER> as shown above.

The computer will then ask if you are ready to begin the spread sheet data entry for the demands and production capacities as shown below.

```
┌──────────────────────────────────────────────────────────┐
│ Continue with the cost and requirements (Y/N) Y          │
└──────────────────────────────────────────────────────────┘
```

Press <ENTER> to begin the spread sheet data entry process. The computer will display the initial spread sheet as shown below.

```
┌──────────────────────────────────────────────────┤READY├─┐
│A1                                                        │
│        A       B       C       D     E     F      G      H │
│1                    Capacity                      Cost    │
│2     Resources R-Time O-Time Sub-Con        R-Time O-Time Sub-Con │
│3     Period1     .      .      .              .      .      . │
│4     Period2     .      .      .              .      .      . │
│5     Period3     .      .      .              .      .      . │
│6     Period4     .      .      .              .      .      . │
│7     Period5     .      .      .              .      .      . │
│8                                                         │
│9        '                                                │
└──────────────────────────────────────────────────────────┘
```

Entering the Production Capacities

The spread sheet editor for this problem has three separate sections (two of which are shown above). The first section entitled "Capacity" is designed for entering the regular time, overtime, and sub-contract capacities for various periods. Initially, all of the cells in this section contain periods "∧" (The use of the "∧" character is to center the cell entry). The periods have special meanings to the program. *In particular, for a problem in which the production capacity (such as regular time) does not change over time, you need not enter all of the data. Just enter the fixed value for the first time period and leave the remaining entries as "∧".* The program will interpret this as other time periods having the same production amount. Note that the use of a "0" instead of a period will not work.

Begin the data entry process by moving the pointer to cell B3 and type 800 then press <ENTER>. Next move the pointer to cell B4 and type 600 and press <ENTER>. Enter the regular time production capacities for all of the five periods.

Next proceed to enter the overtime production capacities. Move the pointer to cell C3 and type 200 then press <ENTER>. Move the pointer down to cell C4 and type 150 then press <ENTER>. Enter the remaining three overtime capacities in the same form. For this problem, no subcontracting is allowed, hence leave the column (column D) associated with sub-contracting empty.

Entering the Production Costs

The second section of the spread sheet editor is assigned to production costs (see above). The periods "." in this section work the same way as in section one. That is, in a problem where production costs remain constant through time, you only need to enter the cost for the first period. Since in this solved example, the production costs do not vary with time, you may take advantage of this provision.

Move the pointer to cell F3 and type 30 then press <ENTER>. Then move the pointer to cell G3 and enter 45 then press <ENTER>. The costs for the remaining periods will be set to these two values. Since this problem does not involve sub-contracting, leave the third column of this section empty. The completed spread sheet is shown below.

246

```
G3    45                                                              ┤READY├
           A          B         C         D       E        F        G        H
1                              Capacity                            Cost
2       Resources  R-Time    O-Time    Sub-Con          R-Time   O-Time   Sub-Con
3       Period1      800       200       .              30.00    45.00
4       Period2      600       150       .               .        .        .
5       Period3      400       100       .               .        .        .
6       Period4      400       100       .               .        .        .
7       Period5      400       100       .               .        .        .
8
9
```

Entering the Demand Forecasts

The third section of the spread sheet involves the demand forecasts. You can move to this section of the spread sheet by pressing the <TAB> key. Alternatively, you may press the right arrow key several times. The initial spread sheet for the third section is shown below.

```
D3   ^.                                                              ┤READY├
          D         E         F         G        H        I        J        K
1                                      Cost
2       Sub-Con             R-Time   O-Time   Sub-Con  Demands   Prod1    Prod2
3        .                  30.00    45.00      .      Period1     .        .
4        .                    .        .        .      Period2     .        .
5        .                    .        .        .      Period3     .        .
6        .                    .        .        .      Period4     .        .
7        .                    .        .        .      Period5     .        .
8                                                      Hold-Cost  0.00     0.00
9                                                      Back-Cost  0.00     0.00
```

As seen from the above display, the upper part of the third section is reserved for the demand forecasts for the two products. The lower portion consists of two rows. One is used for entering the holding costs, and the second row is for back-order costs.

Move the pointer to cell J3 to enter the demand forecast of product 1 in period 1. Type 500 and press <ENTER>. Next move the pointer to cell J4 and enter 500 and press <ENTER>. Enter the remaining three demand forecasts for product 1 in the same form. Then move the pointer to cell K3 and enter the demand forecast of product 2 in period 1. Enter the remaining four forecasts in the same manner.

After entering all of the demand forecasts, proceed with the data entry by entering the holding costs and back-order costs. Move the pointer to cell J8 and enter 6 and press <ENTER>. Then move the pointer to cell K8 and enter 9 then press <ENTER>. To enter the back-order costs, move the pointer to cell J9 and enter 10 then press <ENTER>. Next move the pointer to cell K9 and enter 15 followed by <ENTER>. The completed spread sheet is shown below.

K9	**15**							**READY**
		D	E	F	G	H	I	J	K

	D	E	F	G	H	I	J	K
1				Cost				
2	Sub-Con		R-Time	O-Time	Sub-Con	Demands	Prod1	Prod2
3	.		30.00	45.00	.	Period1	500	200
4	.		.	.	.	Period2	500	300
5	.		.	.	.	Period3	300	400
6	.		.	.	.	Period4	100	250
7	.		.	.	.	Period5	100	150
8						Hold-Cost	6.00	9.00
9						Back-Cost	10.00	15.00

After completing the spread sheet data entry, press <F10> to exit from the spread sheet editor and keep the data in memory.

You may now obtain a hard copy printout of the input data by moving the pointer to the PRINT option and press <ENTER>. Be sure that the printer is on and ready before you proceed. You can also save the problem on the disk for future references. If so, move the pointer to the FILE option and select the "Save current file" sub-option by pulling the bar down one level. Press the <ENTER> key to select. The program will display the current drive and sub-directory and asks you to enter a file name. Enter an appropriate DOS file name.

You are now ready to solve the problem. Move the pointer to the SOLVE option and select the Display Output sub-option and press <ENTER>. The computer will pause for a few seconds and then report the optimal production schedule as shown below.

```
                    Problem Title: AGGREGATE PLANNING
                    *** Production Schedule ***

                         Product: Prod1
Period     Reg-Time      Over-Time     Sub-Cont.      Demand      Invent.
  1          600.0          0.0                        500.0       100.0
  2          400.0          0.0                        500.0         0.0
  3          100.0          0.0                        300.0      -200.0
  4          150.0          0.0                        100.0      -150.0
  5          250.0          0.0                        100.0         0.0
```

Press a key to obtain the production schedule for product 2 as shown below.

```
                    Problem Title: AGGREGATE PLANNING
                    *** Production Schedule ***

                         Product: Prod2
Period     Reg-Time      Over-Time     Sub-Cont.      Demand      Invent.
  1          200.0          0.0                        200.0         0.0
  2          200.0        100.0                        300.0         0.0
  3          300.0        100.0                        400.0         0.0
  4          250.0          0.0                        250.0         0.0
  5          150.0          0.0                        150.0         0.0
```

As seen from the above solution reports, the optimal production schedule for the two products consists of a combination of resources utilizing regular time, overtime, inventory, and back-orders. All of the demands for product 1 have been satisfied through regular time production, inventory on hand, and back-ordering. The demands for product 2 have been met by using regular time and overtime production. For this product, no back-order or on hand inventory has been used.

The Aggregate Layout program also reports the various cost components of the schedule. Press any key to proceed with the cost reports. The computer will ask if you wish to see the cost reports. Press <ENTER> to see the reports as shown below.

```
                   Problem Title: AGGREGATE PLANNING
              *** Cost Report: By Product ***

      Product: Prod1

      Regular Time Production Cost      45000.00
      OverTime Production Cost              0.00
      Sub-Contracting  Cost                 0.00
      Inventory Carrying Cost             600.00
      Back-Order Cost                    3500.00

      Product Sub-Total Cost            49100.00
```

The first report is for product 1. It indicates that the cost of regular time production is $45,000, and no overtime and/or sub-contracting have been used. The inventory carrying cost is $600 and back-order cost is $3,500 with the total cost being $49,100. Press any key to obtain the cost report for the second product as shown below.

```
                   Problem Title: AGGREGATE PLANNING
              *** Cost Report: By Product ***

      Product: Prod2

      Regular Time Production Cost      33000.00
      OverTime Production Cost           9000.00
      Sub-Contracting  Cost                 0.00
      Inventory Carrying Cost               0.00
      Back-Order Cost                       0.00

      Product Sub-Total Cost            42000.00
```

The costs for product 2 consists of $33,000 for regular time, $9,000 for overtime for a total of $42,000. For this product no inventory or back- order were used and therefore these costs are 0. Press a key to continue with the summary of cost figures as shown below.

```
┌──────────────────────────────────────────────────────────────────┐
│                 Problem Title: AGGREGATE PLANNING                  │
│                                                                    │
│     *** Cost Report: Summary ***                                   │
│                                                                    │
│                                                                    │
│     Regular Time Production Cost        78000.00                   │
│     OverTime Production Cost             9000.00                   │
│     Sub-Contracting  Cost                   0.00                   │
│     Inventory Carrying Cost               600.00                   │
│     Back-Order Cost                      3500.00                   │
│                                                                    │
│     Overall Total Cost                  91100.00                   │
│                                                                    │
│                                                                    │
└──────────────────────────────────────────────────────────────────┘
```

The above results indicate that the overall regular time production cost is $78,000, overtime production cost amounts to $9,000, inventory carrying cost is $600, and back-ordering costs $3,500. The total cost of production schedule is $91,100.

EXAMPLE 2 - USING SUB-CONTRACTS

In this example you will consider the use of sub-contracting to provide additional production capacity. Consider the two-product problem in Example 1. Now suppose that the products may be sub-contracted for $48 per unit and that sub-contract capacity is 100 units per period.

To solve the above problem, move the pointer to the EDIT option and press the <ENTER> key several times to invoke the spread sheet editor and edit the problem data in Example 1. The initial screen, before the edit process is shown below.

```
┌──────────────────────────────────────────────────────────┤READY├─┐
│A1                                                                 │
│       A       B       C       D     E     F      G       H        │
│1              Capacity                     Cost                   │
│2   Resources R-Time O-Time Sub-Con      R-Time O-Time Sub-Con     │
│3   Period1     800    200    .           30.00  45.00    .        │
│4   Period2     600    150    .           30.00  45.00    .        │
│5   Period3     400    100    .           30.00  45.00    .        │
│6   Period4     400    100    .           30.00  45.00    .        │
│7   Period5     400    100    .           30.00  45.00    .        │
│8                                                                  │
│9                                                                  │
└──────────────────────────────────────────────────────────────────┘
```

Note that the dots (periods) have been replaced by their proper values. To enter the sub-contract capacity, move the pointer to cell D3 and type 100 then press <ENTER>. As before, you need not enter the capacities for the remaining four periods since the dots will be interpreted as having the same value as in period 1. Move the pointer to cell H3 and type 48 and then press <ENTER>. The edit process is complete so, press <F10> to keep the data in memory and exit from the spread sheet editor. The completed spread sheet is shown below.

								READY
H3	48							
	A	B	C	D	E	F	G	H
1			Capacity				Cost	
2	Resources	R-Time	O-Time	Sub-Con		R-Time	O-Time	Sub-Con
3	Period1	800	200	100		30.00	45.00	48.00
4	Period2	600	150	.		30.00	45.00	.
5	Period3	400	100	.		30.00	45.00	.
6	Period4	400	100	.		30.00	45.00	.
7	Period5	400	100	.		30.00	45.00	.
8								
9								

You are now ready to solve the problem. Move the pointer to the solve option and select the Display Output sub-option. The computer will pause for a few seconds and then display the production schedule as shown below.

Problem Title: AGGREGATE PLANNING
*** Production Schedule ***

Product: Prod1

Period	Reg-Time	Over-Time	Sub-Cont.	Demand	Invent.
1	600.0	0.0	0.0	500.0	100.0
2	400.0	0.0	0.0	500.0	0.0
3	100.0	0.0	100.0	300.0	-100.0
4	150.0	0.0	0.0	100.0	-50.0
5	150.0	0.0	0.0	100.0	0.0

```
                    Problem Title: AGGREGATE PLANNING
                   *** Production Schedule ***

                         Product: Prod2
Period     Reg-Time     Over-Time     Sub-Cont.     Demand     Invent.
   1         200.0          0.0          0.0         200.0        0.0
   2         200.0        100.0          0.0         300.0        0.0
   3         300.0        100.0          0.0         400.0        0.0
   4         250.0          0.0          0.0         250.0        0.0
   5         150.0          0.0          0.0         150.0        0.0
```

As seen from the above output report, the production schedule for product 1 is slightly different than that in Example 1. In particular, the regular time production in period 5 is 150 units which is 100 less than the schedule in Example 1. Instead, the 100 units have been sub-contracted in period 3. Note that the 100 units was used as back-order in Example 1. Apparently, it is more cost effective to sub-contract the 100 units in period 3 than to back-order it two periods. The cost report should indicate the difference. Press a key to continue and press <ENTER> to see the cost report as shown below.

```
                    Problem Title: AGGREGATE PLANNING
                   *** Cost Report: By Product ***

        Product: Prod1

        Regular Time Production Cost        42000.00
        OverTime Production Cost                0.00
        Sub-Contracting  Cost                4800.00
        Inventory Carrying Cost               600.00
        Back-Order Cost                      1500.00

        Product Sub-Total Cost              48900.00
```

```
                    Problem Title: AGGREGATE PLANNING
                 *** Cost Report: By Product ***

    Product: Prod2

    Regular Time Production Cost        33000.00
    OverTime Production Cost             9000.00
    Sub-Contracting  Cost                   0.00
    Inventory Carrying Cost                 0.00
    Back-Order Cost                         0.00

    Product Sub-Total Cost              42000.00
```

As seen from the above report, the cost values for product 2 is the same as in Example 1. The total cost for product 1 is $48,900 which is $200 less than that in Example 1. The lower cost is due to the smaller regular time production cost ($42,000 instead of $45,000), and back-order cost ($1,500 instead of $3,500). The sub-contract cost for this schedule is larger ($4,800 compared with 0 in Example 1) but is offset by the lower regular time and back-order costs. This difference which amounts to $200 is reflected in the overall cost as shown below.

```
                    Problem Title: AGGREGATE PLANNING

       *** Cost Report: Summary ***


    Regular Time Production Cost        75000.00
    OverTime Production Cost             9000.00
    Sub-Contracting  Cost                4800.00
    Inventory Carrying Cost               600.00
    Back-Order Cost                      1500.00

    Overall Total Cost                  90900.00
```

As seen from the above output report, the overall cost of production for both products is $90,900 which is $200 less than that in Example 1.

PROBLEMS

1. The demand forecast for a product, over a six-month period, consists of 100, 350, 200, 300, 350, and 400 units for months one through six, respectively. The regular time capacity is 250 units per month and overtime capacity is 20% of regular time. Regular time production cost is $50 per unit and overtime cost is 10% over the regular time. The inventory carrying cost is $6 per unit per month and backorder cost is $12 per unit. Find the optimal production schedule.

2. In problem 1, suppose that no back-ordering is allowed. Find the optimal production schedule.

3. In problem 1, suppose that the demand forecasts and the regular time production cost is adjusted for inflation. In particular, let the inflation rate be 2% per month. Revise the regular time production costs accordingly and solve the problem.
Hint: Assume that the production cost in each month is 2% more than in the previous month.

4. Suppose that there is an initial inventory of 100 units available in problem 1. Find the optimal production schedule. Hint: Reduce demand forecast in month 1 by 100 units.

5. The Premain Company provides preventative maintenance and minor repair service at a fixed charge for clients within a 20 mile radius. The company's customers have seasonal businesses and try to postpone some maintenance until their slow season. This results in a seasonal demand for Premain's services. The number of jobs forecasted for the 4 quarters of next year are 720, 940, 820, and 1060, respectively. The typical service call requires one hour, including travel and paperwork. Employees are paid $10.00 per hour, and the typical employee provides 480 hours of direct work per quarter. Based on the nature of the business, it is not possible to service units before they fail. Overtime is allowed up to 25% of regular time at a cost of 50% higher than regular time.

Skilled workers who are reliable enough to make these service calls are scarce and Premain wants to provide job security to those it can attract. Give an appropriate production schedule, along with the associated cost for Premain. Begin with 2 workers and find the optimal schedule. Hint: Use a very large positive number for inventory cost.

6. Tyson Motor Company has the following demand forecast for the next year, expressed in six bi-monthly periods:

PERIOD	PRODUCT A	PRODUCT B	PRODUCT C
1	250	300	450
2	270	300	500
3	350	300	500
4	430	300	450
5	500	300	400
6	400	300	400
Total	2,200	1,800	2,700

The regular time and overtime production capacities are:

PERIOD	Regular Time	Over Time
1	1000	200
2	1000	200
3	900	180
4	900	180
5	1000	200
6	1000	200
Total	5,800	1,160

Regular time cost is estimated at $10 per unit and increases by 10% in each period. Overtime cost is fixed at $20 per unit with inventory carrying cost equal $2.00 for Product A, $2.50 for B, and $3.00 for C. Back-order cost is 20% higher than inventory carrying cost plus regular time production cost. Find the optimal production schedule.

7. In problem 6, suppose that up to 100 units can be sub-contracted in each period. Further, let the sub-contract cost be 150% of regular time cost. Find the optimal production schedule.

8. Videotek Enterprises is producing two brands of video telephones for the home market. Quality is not quite as high as it could be at this point, but the selling price is high and Videotek has the opportunity to study the market response while spending more time on research and development.

At this stage, Videotek needs to develop an aggregate production plan for the following year. You have been retained to assist the managers in this task.

Monthly demand for the two brands A and B are given below. The manufacturing labor cost is $75 per unit for Brands A and B. Inventory holding costs are $7 per unit per month for each brand. Backorder costs amount to $20 per unit for Brand A and $40 per unit for Brand B.

Ten labor hours are required per telephone set and the work day is 8 hours. Assume 20 working days each month, except for August when the plant closes for 2 weeks vacation. VideoTek employs five workers and each is allowed 25% of overtime. Overtime cost is estimated at 20% in excess of manufacturing cost.

Expected Demand in Units

MONTH	A	B
JANUARY	40	40
FEBRUARY	60	40
MARCH	60	50
APRIL	40	40
MAY	30	30
JUNE	25	25
JULY	20	20
AUGUST	20	20
SEPTEMBER	30	20
OCTOBER	50	40
NOVEMBER	60	40
DECEMBER	50	60

9. In problem 8, suppose that backorder is not permitted. Add as many workers as needed to develop an optimal feasible production schedule.

10. Jobe Industries is expanding its product line to include a new model, XT-40. It will be produced on the same equipment as Jobe's other products and the objective is to meet the demand. The demand forecast in units for the next four months is 800, 600, 900, and 1150, respectively.

Because the model XT-40 deteriorates quickly, there is a large loss in quality, and, consequently, a high carryover cost into subsequent periods. Each unit of the XT-40 carried over into future months costs $7.50 per month per unit.

Production can take place during regular hours or during overtime. The rate of pay for regular time is $6 per hour and overtime is time and a half. Workers are under union contract and work 20 days per month. Each unit requires 5 hours to build.

The available production capacity in units for regular time and overtime is:

PERIOD

	1	2	3	4
Regular	700	700	700	700
Overtime	105	175	210	245

Find an optimal production schedule.

11. In problem 10, assume that XT-40 can be sub-contracted at a cost of $45 and the sub-contract capacity is 20% of regular time capacity. Find the optimal schedule.

CHAPTER 11

INVENTORY ANALYSIS

INTRODUCTION

The six inventory models to be presented below are used in the determination of optimal purchase or production lot sizes. By optimal lot sizes we refer to minimum cost lot sizes where costs consist of set up or ordering cost, inventory holding costs, and shortage costs if appropriate. The case of quantity discounts and the stochastic demand model will also be covered. Data that needs to be entered in order to help solve the six inventory models consist of annual demand, annual production rate, purchase price per unit, holding cost per unit, shortage cost per unit, set up or order cost per unit, number of days per year, quantity discounts, and demands during lead time with associated frequencies.

The six inventory models consist of; the economic purchase lot size model, without back orders and without shortages allowed; the economic purchase lot size model with backorders and shortages allowed; the production run size model without backorders and shortages allowed; the production run size model with back orders and shortages allowed; the quantity discount model; and the stochastic demand model. Below we shall discuss each of the six inventory models in detail. In the first five models it is assumed that annual demand is deterministic.

ECONOMIC PURCHASE LOT SIZE MODEL

The economic purchase lot size model assumes that there are no shortages. In other words, as soon as the inventory is depleted there will be an immediate replenishment of the inventory with a new lot size of inventory. It is also assumed that the inventory is used up at a constant rate.

The above assumptions are illustrated in Figure 11-1. Note that the assumed economic lot size of Q = 400 units is used up every two weeks for an annual demand of (26)(400) = 10,400 units. As soon as the economic lot size of 400 units is used up, a replenishment shipment of 400 additional units arrives for the next two week period.

The formula for the economic purchase lot size without backorders and shortages is,

$$Q^* = \sqrt{\frac{2DS}{H}}$$

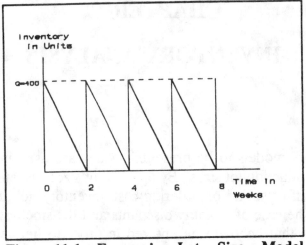

Figure 11-1: Economic Lot Size Model Without Backlog

where Q^* is the optimal lot size in units,

  D is annual demand in units
  S is ordering cost per order in dollars
  H is inventory holding cost per unit per year in dollars
  C is acquisition cost per unit in dollars.

The formula is derived by minimizing the total cost (TC),

$$TC - \frac{QH}{2} + \frac{DS}{Q} + CD$$

Hence, the optimal lot size will increase as annual demand (D) or ordering cost (S) increases. Similarly, the optimal lot size will decrease as the inventory holding cost (H) increases.

EOQ MODEL WITH BACKORDERS AND SHORTAGES

The economic purchase lot size model with backorders and shortages assumes that shortages are allowed and any units short will be delivered upon receipt of the inventory replenishment order. For each unit short there is an inventory shortage cost based on the length of time the unit is short. Otherwise, the assumptions underlying this inventory model are the same as the economic purchase lot size model without backorders and shortages.

260

The shortage model is illustrated in Figure 11-2. Note that in the non- shortage model the maximum inventory level was equal to the economic purchase lot size. In the shortage model the maximum inventory (I_M) is less than the economic purchase lot size (Q^*). The amount that is backordered and short in each order cycle amounts to $Q^* - I_M$ units. If the economic purchase lot size (Q^*) amounts to 400 units and maximum inventory is 360 units then 40 units can be backordered or shorted.

The formula for the economic purchase lot size with backorders and shortages allowed is,

$$Q^* = \sqrt{\frac{2DS}{H}} \sqrt{\frac{(B+H)}{B}}$$

where B is the shortage cost per unit per year in dollars.

Note that the first part of the above formula is identical to the formula for the economic purchase lot size. The second part of the above formula modifies Q^* to take account of the backorders and shortages.

The formula to determine the maximum inventory level is,

$$I_M = \sqrt{\frac{2DS}{H}} \sqrt{\frac{B}{(B+H)}}$$

From the above two formulas, we can derive the backorder or shortage level. It is determined by the formula,

$$Q^* - I_M = \sqrt{\frac{2DS}{H}} \left[\sqrt{\frac{(B+H)}{B}} - \sqrt{\frac{B}{(B+H)}} \right]$$

The above formulas are derived from the total cost (TC) formula,

$$TC = \frac{I_M^2 H}{2Q} + \frac{DS}{Q} + CD + \frac{(Q-I_M)^2 B}{2Q}$$

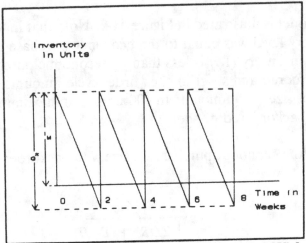

Figure 11-2: Economic Lot Size Model With Shortage

The amount of demand that can be backordered or shorted will depend largely on the relationship between inventory holding cost (H) and shortage cost (B). If H is about equal to B then the amount backordered will be about equal to the maximum inventory level. The larger H is in relation to B the larger will be the backordered units. Similarly the smaller H is in relation to B the smaller will be the allowed backordered units.

PRODUCTION RUN SIZE MODEL WITHOUT SHORTAGES

In the production run size model, the replenishment of inventory is not instantaneous but gradual, at a constant rate equal to production. It is assumed in this model that as soon as the inventory level reaches zero, a production run is started up to replenish the depleted inventory.

The above scenario can be seen in Figure 11-3. As in the previous model, the production run size (Q) will be larger than the maximum inventory (I_M). However, Q cannot be shown on the graph. At time 0, production is started, and between time 0 and 2, inventory is replenished at the production rate P minus the demand rate D for a net inventory replenishment rate P-D. From time 2 to time 3 the accumulated maximum inventory (I_M) is depleted at the demand rate D until all inventory is used up and the production process is started up again. Hence, between time 2 and time 3 there is no production taking place. Presumably, the production equipment will be idle or engaged in producing another product.

The formula for the economic production run size model is,

$$Q^* = \sqrt{\frac{2DS}{H}} \sqrt{\frac{P}{P-D}}$$

262

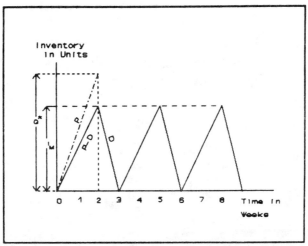

Figure 11-3: Production Run Size Model Without Backlog

where S is the production line set up cost per set up in dollars, and P is the annual production rate in units per year. All other symbols are identical to those used in the other models. The production rate is the rate of production which will produce P units per year if the production line were utilized continuously.

The formula for determining the maximum inventory level (I_M) is,

$$I_M - \sqrt{\frac{2DS}{H}} \sqrt{\frac{(P-D)}{P}}$$

Both formulas are derived from the total cost (TC) formula,

$$TC - \frac{I_M H}{2} + \frac{DS}{Q} + CD$$

You may observe that this formula is identical to the economic purchase lot size model except for the first term, where I_M instead of Q is used. Also note that I_M is related to Q^* by the formula,

$$I_M - \frac{Q^*(P-D)}{P}$$

PRODUCTION RUN SIZE MODEL WITH BACKLOG

The production run size model with backorders or shortages is illustrated in Figure 11-4. Note that backorders and shortages are allowed and, as a result, the economic production run size (Q) is substantially higher than the maximum inventory (I_M).

The formula for the economic production run size is,

$$Q^* = \sqrt{\frac{2DS}{H}} \sqrt{\frac{(B+H)}{B}} \sqrt{\frac{P}{(P-D)}}$$

In this case as well as in the previous model, the production rate P must be larger than the demand rate D.

The formula for the maximum inventory level (I_M) is,

$$I_M = \sqrt{\frac{2DS}{H}} \sqrt{\frac{B}{(B+H)}} \sqrt{\frac{(P-D)}{P}}$$

In this model and in the previous model, the amount of backordering or shortages allowed will depend on the relationship between the inventory holding cost (H) and the shortage cost (B). The higher B, the lower will be the backorders or shortages allowed.

ECONOMIC LOT SIZE WITH QUANTITY DISCOUNTS

The quantity discount model enables you to find the optimum purchase lot size if the purchase price depends on the number of units ordered at a time. Suppose the purchase price is $5.00 per unit if you order from 1 to 99 units; if you order from 100-499 units the price drops to $4.95 per unit and if you place an order of 500 units or more the price drops to $4.90 per unit. In the above situation, we must consider the purchase price in the optimal purchase lot size decision. The number of units at which the price changes is called the price break. In the above example price breaks occur at 99 and 499 units.

The quantity discount model only applies to purchase lot sizes with no shortages. The DSS model calculates the optimal lot size for a given price and then checks if the calculated lot size agrees with the purchase price. If it does not, the computer model will recalculate the optimal lot size until both the lot size and purchase price agree.

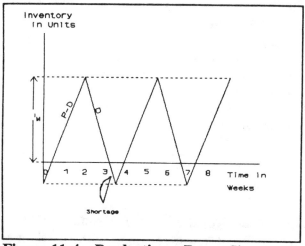

Figure 11-4: Production Run Size with Backlog

STOCHASTIC DEMAND MODEL WITH LEAD TIME

The stochastic demand model evaluates and balances the holding and shortage costs for varying re-order point and safety-stock levels with the objective of minimizing the total costs. Application of the model requires a listing of the demands during lead time. That is, a table of demands with respective frequencies of demand must be supplied to the computer. This demand and frequency data is based on either demand estimates, or a historical tabulation of demand data with historical frequencies. An example of such demand and frequency data is shown on Table 11-1. Also required is a specification of the approximate annual demand as well as the number of days per year on which the data is based.

Based on that input data, the computer then provides a summary of several reorder points and the resultant safety stock, inventory holding costs, inventory shortage costs, and total costs. Based on the tabulated total costs, an optimal solution is selected which provides the optimal re-order point and the optimal safety stock.

EXAMPLE 1 - THE BASIC EOQ MODEL

This example involves the use of the basic economic order quantity (EOQ) model to find an optimal order policy. Suppose that the demand for a product is 5000 units per year and it has a purchase price of $10. The product is small but quite fragile. Consequently, the supplier charges $100 for shipping and handling regardless of the order size. It takes 3 days for an order to arrive. The holding (inventory carrying) cost of this product is $1.00 per unit per year and no backlog is permitted.

To solve the above problem, load the DSSPOM program and select the Inventory Analysis program from the Main Menu. After a few seconds, the computer will display

265

the Inventory Analysis main menu. Move the pointer to the INPUT option. This option has three sub-options as shown below.

```
┌─────────────────────────────────────────────────────────────┐
│                                                               │
│   Input  Edit  Print  File  Solve  Quit                       │
│   ┌─────────────────────────────┐                             │
│   │ Lot/Run Size Models          │                            │
│   │ EOQ with Discount            │                            │
│   │ Discrete Demand Dist.        │                            │
│   └─────────────────────────────┘                             │
│                                                               │
└─────────────────────────────────────────────────────────────┘
```

Because the problem at hand involves the basic EOQ model, press the <ENTER> key to select the first choice. The computer will continue with the data entry process. You will be asked to enter the relevant parameters one at a time. For the parameters for which you do not have a value, press the <ENTER> key to input a zero. For this problem assumes that there are 365 days per year. The completed data entry screen is presented below.

```
┌──────────────────────────────────────────────────────────────┐
│                                                                │
│   Problem title: BASIC EOQ                                     │
│                                                                │
│   Enter number of days per year: 365                           │
│   Enter annual demand:    5000                                 │
│   Enter annual production rate (0 if none):      0             │
│   Enter purchase price in dollars per unit:      10            │
│   Enter setup or order cost in dollars per order:    100       │
│   Enter the Lead-Time in days (0 if none):   3                 │
│   Enter holding cost in dollars per unit per year:      1      │
│   Enter unit shortage cost in dollars/year (0 if none):     0  │
│                                                                │
└──────────────────────────────────────────────────────────────┘
```

After completing the data entry process, obtain a hard copy print-out of the input data. Examine the print out carefully for any typing mistakes. If there are any errors, move the pointer to the EDIT option and press <ENTER>. The computer will place the pointer back on the title field and resume the edit process. Edit the data as needed and correct any errors.

You may also wish to save the problem on disk for future use. To do this, move the pointer to the FILE option and select the "Save Current File" sub-menu. The computer will ask you to enter a DOS file name. Use a proper suffix such as "INV" in the file name for ease of recognition in future.

You are now ready to solve this basic EOQ problem. Move the pointer to the SOLVE option and select the "Display Output" sub-option. The computer will solve the problem and provide the following report.

```
                  Problem Title: BASIC EOQ

      Economic purchase lot size model with no shortage:

   Days between orders              73.0
   Optimal order quantity is      1000.0
   ReOrder Point is                 41.1
   Annual holding cost            500.00
   Annual order cost              500.00
   Purchase price               50000.00


   Total cost                   51000.00
```

As seen from the above report, the optimal order quantity for this product is 1000 units at a time. This implies five orders per year, or every 73 days. The order cost is $500 (five orders at $100 each), the annual holding cost is $500, and the total annual cost is $51000. Because the lead time is three days, the order should be placed when the inventory level reaches 41.1.

EXAMPLE 2 - THE BASIC EOQ MODEL WITH BACKLOG

Consider the above example, but now suppose that backlog is permitted with the shortage penalty cost at $4 per unit. To solve this problem, move the pointer to the EDIT option and press the <ENTER> key. The program will resume the edit process by advancing the pointer to the title field. Change the title to "EOQ WITH SHORTAGE" and press <ENTER>. Press the <ENTER> key seven times to accept the current values of other parameters and to reach the shortage cost inquiry. Change the shortage cost to 4 and press <ENTER>. The completed edit screen is shown below.

```
Problem title: EOQ WITH SHORTAGE

Enter number of days per year: 365
Enter annual demand:   5000
Enter annual production rate (0 if none):      0
Enter purchase price in dollars per unit:      10
Enter setup or order cost in dollars per order:      100
Enter the Lead-Time in days (0 if none):   3
Enter holding cost in dollars per unit per year:      1
Enter unit shortage cost in dollars/year (0 if none):      4
```

You are now ready to solve the problem. Move the pointer to the SOLVE option and select the "Display Output" sub-option. Press the <ENTER> key to solve the problem as shown below.

```
┌─────────────────────────────────────────────────────────────┐
│            Problem Title: EOQ WITH SHORTAGE                   │
│                                                              │
│        Economic purchase lot size model with shortage :      │
│                                                              │
│   Days between orders              81.6                      │
│   Shortage period is               16.3                      │
│   Re-Order Point is                41.1                      │
│   Optimal order quantity is      1118.0                      │
│   Maximum inventory level is      894.4                      │
│   Maximum shortage is             223.6                      │
│   Holding   cost                  357.77                     │
│   Setup     cost                  447.21                     │
│   Shortage cost                    89.44                     │
│   Purchase price                50000.00                     │
│                                                              │
│   Total cost                    50894.43                     │
│                                                              │
└─────────────────────────────────────────────────────────────┘
```

As seen from the above output report, the optimal order policy has slightly changed. In particular, now the optimal order quantity is 1,118 units every 81.6 days. This policy causes a shortage period of about 16.3 days in every cycle. The various cost components are: $357.77 for inventory holding cost; $447.21 for order cost; and $89.44 for shortage cost. The total annual cost including purchase price is $50,894.43.

EXAMPLE 3 - THE PRODUCTION RUN SIZE MODEL

This example involves the use of the production run size model to solve an inventory problem in which items are being produced as well as consumed. As an example problem, suppose that in Solved Example 1, instead of purchasing the product you produce it. Further, suppose the maximum production rate is 7000 units per year and that the setup cost is the same as the order cost and is equal to $100. The number of days per year is 365 and the inventory holding cost is $1.00 per unit per year with a unit production cost of $10 (note that the data is intentionally kept the same as in Example 1 to provide for a comparison). The lead time is set to 0 for this example.

To solve this problem, move the pointer to the INPUT option and select "Lot/Run Size Models" sub-option and press the <ENTER> key. If you have just begun with this exercise, the computer will immediately begin the data entry process. However, if you are continuing from the previous example, the computer will display a warning message, indicating that there is another model in the memory. It will then ask you if the current model should be discarded. This solved example, is a continuation of the previous one, therefore the following message is displayed.

```
┌─────────────────────────────────────────────────────────┐
│ Erase current model and begin a new one (Y/N) Y         │
└─────────────────────────────────────────────────────────┘
```

Press <Y> to erase the current model and continue with the new example problem. The computer will then present a new data entry screen, requesting the relevant parameters one at a time. The completed data entry screen is shown below.

```
┌───────────────────────────────────────────────────────────────┐
│   Problem title: PRODUCTION RUN                               │
│                                                               │
│   Enter number of days per year: 365                         │
│   Enter annual demand:    5000                               │
│   Enter annual production rate (0 if none):    7000          │
│   Enter purchase price in dollars per unit:        10        │
│   Enter setup or order cost in dollars per order:    100     │
│   Enter the Lead-Time in days (0 if none):    0              │
│   Enter holding cost in dollars per unit per year:      1    │
│   Enter unit shortage cost in dollars/year (0 if none):    0 │
│                                                               │
│  ┌─────────────────────────────────────────────────────────┐ │
│  │ Enter problem parameters as requested.  Press RETURN to │ │
│  │ accept, or ESC to exit.                                 │ │
│  └─────────────────────────────────────────────────────────┘ │
│                                                               │
└───────────────────────────────────────────────────────────────┘
```

You are now ready to solve the problem. Move the pointer to the SOLVE option and select the "Display output" sub-option. The computer will pause for a few seconds and then display the following output report.

```
┌─────────────────────────────────────────────────────────────┐
│               Problem Title: PRODUCTION RUN                 │
│                                                             │
│        Production run size model with no shortage :         │
│                                                             │
│   Days between production runs   136.6                     │
│   Length of run is                97.6                     │
│   Optimal run size is           1870.8                     │
│   Re-Production Point is           0.0                     │
│   Max inventory level is         534.5                     │
│   Annual holding cost is         267.26                    │
│   Annual setup    cost is        267.26                    │
│   Purchase price       is      50000.00                    │
│                                                             │
│   Total cost is                50534.52                    │
│                                                             │
│                                                             │
└─────────────────────────────────────────────────────────────┘
```

The above report indicates that the optimal policy in this case is to produce 1,870.8 (or about 1,871) units at time. The resulting cycle is 136.6 days with 97.6 days of production. The maximum inventory is 534.5 units, having an annual cost of $267.26 with a setup cost of $267.26. The total annual cost, including cost of production, is $50,534.52.

EXAMPLE 4 - PRODUCTION RUN SIZE MODEL WITH BACKLOG

This solved example is similar to the previous example, except that in this example backlog is permitted. Again, the cost of backlog is $4 per unit.

To solve the above problem, move the pointer to the EDIT option and press the <ENTER> key to begin the edit process. Keep the parameters the same as in Solved Example 3 by pressing the <ENTER> key eight times (to accept the current data for the eight parameters). Change the shortage penalty cost to 4 and press <ENTER>. The completed data edit screen is shown below.

```
Problem title: PRODUCTION RUN

Enter number of days per year: 365
Enter annual demand:    5000
Enter annual production rate (0 if none):    7000
Enter purchase price in dollars per unit:       10
Enter setup or order cost in dollars per order:       100
Enter the Lead-Time in days (0 if none):    0
Enter holding cost in dollars per unit per year:       1
Enter unit shortage cost in dollars/year (0 if none):       4
```

You are now ready to solve the problem. Move the pointer to the SOLVE option and select the Display Output sub-option by pressing the <ENTER> key. The computer will pause for a few seconds and then display the following solution report.

270

```
            Problem Title: PRODUCTION RUN

        Economic run size model with shortage :

Days between production runs      152.7
Shortage period is                 30.5
Re-Production Point is              0.0
Optimal run size is              2091.7
Maximum inventory level is        478.1
Maximum shortage is               119.5
Holding  cost                     191.24
Setup    cost                     239.05
Shortage cost                      47.81
Purchase price                 50000.00

Total cost                     50478.09
```

As seen from the above report, the optimal policy for this problem is to produce up to 2091.7 in each run, resulting in a cycle of length 152.7 days. The maximum inventory is 478.1 units and the maximum shortage is 119.5 units. The inventory holding cost is $191.24 with a annual setup cost of $239.05. The shortage penalty cost amounts to $47.81 per year with a total annual cost, including production cost, of $50,478.09.

EXAMPLE 5 - EOQ MODEL WITH QUANTITY DISCOUNTS

This example involves solving an EOQ problem in which the purchase of larger batches qualifies for unit price reduction. Consider for example the following price table with volume discounts.

Order Quantity	Unit Price ($)	Holding Cost*
0 - 99	5.00	1.00
100 - 199	4.80	0.96
200 - 399	4.60	0.92
400 - 699	4.40	0.88
700 -	4.00	0.80

* Holding cost is in $ per unit per year and is 20% of unit price.

The above table indicates that if the order size is from 0 to 99 units, the unit price will be $5.00. For orders between 100 and 199, a discount of $0.20 is provided and the unit price is therefore $4.80. Additional increase in the size of the order qualifies for further discounts in the purchase price as shown in the table. Other relevant information for this problem include annual demand equal to 2000 units, setup or order cost equal to $50, and the number of days per year is assumed to be 365.

To solve the above problem, load the DSSPOM program and select the Inventory Analysis from the Main Menu. When presented with the Inventory Menu, move the pointer to the INPUT option and select the "EOQ with Discount" sub-option by pulling the bar down one level and press the <ENTER> key.

The computer will begin the data entry process by displaying a message about the special structure of this problem. The requirement for the EOQ with discounts model is that the order ranges be contiguous and span the positive Q axis.

Enter a proper title for this problem and press the <ENTER> key to continue with the data entry process. The computer will ask the number of days per year, followed by annual demand, setup or order cost, and the number of price break ranges. The completed initial data entry screen is presented below.

```
Problem title: EOQ WITH DISCOUNTS

Enter number of days per year: 365
Enter annual demand:   2000
Enter setup or order cost in dollars per order:      50

Enter the number of pricebreak ranges (up to 20):   5




  ┌──────────────────────────────────────────────────────┐
  │ Enter problem parameters as requested.  Press RETURN to │
  │ accept, or ESC to exit.  Quantity discount model:   Note │
  │ that the pricebreak-ranges must be continuous and span   the │
  │ positive  Q-axis.  The first (lowest) range must start at 0 │
  │ and the last (highest) range should end at infinity. │
  └──────────────────────────────────────────────────────┘
```

Enter a 5 for the number of price ranges and press the <ENTER> key to proceed. The computer will then display the spread sheet data entry screen for the price break information. Note that the "Largest Quantity" for the last range is preset to a very large number. Do not change this number and make sure that the order sizes that you enter are sorted increasingly and will not exceed this number.

Proceed by entering the price break information in the appropriate columns and rows and press the <F10> to keep the data and exit the spread sheet editor. The completed spread sheet is shown below.

```
D7   4                                                            READY
          A          B         C        D
1    Upper      Largest   Holding   Unit
2    Range      Quantity  Cost      Price
3         1        99.0   1.000     5.00
4         2       199.0   0.960     4.80
5         3       399.0   0.920     4.60
6         4       699.0   0.880     4.40
7         5 999999.0      0.800     4.00
```

You are now ready to solve the problem. Move the pointer to the SOLVE option and select the Display Output sub-option. The computer will pause for a few seconds and then report the solution as shown below.

```
                  Problem Title: EOQ WITH DISCOUNTS

          Economic Lot Size with Quantity Discounts:

Order     Range            EOQ        Status        Total cost
----------------         -------      ------        ----------
   0   -  99           447.2136     Infeasible       10447.21
 100   - 199           456.4        Infeasible       10038.18
 200   - 399           466.3        Infeasible        9628.95
 400   - 699           476.7        Feasible          9219.52
 700   -...            500          Infeasible        8400.00
```

The above report indicates that there is one feasible EOQ point in the range of 400 to 699. The total annual cost for this point is \$9,219.52. Because this EOQ point is not in the lowest price range, the total cost of the following break points must be computed and compared with this value. The next display screen will perform the comparison and reports the optimal policy as shown below.

273

```
┌──────────────────────────────────────────────────────────────┐
│                                                                │
│             Problem Title: EOQ WITH DISCOUNTS                  │
│                                                                │
│         Economic Lot Size with Quantity Discounts:            │
│                                                                │
│                                                                │
│     The total cost for the feasible EOQ is     9219.52        │
│                                                                │
│     Since this is larger than the total cost of ordering      │
│         700  units, the optimal order quantity is     700     │
│                                                                │
│                                                                │
└──────────────────────────────────────────────────────────────┘
```

The above report indicates that the cost of ordering 700 units at a time is less than $9,219.52 and therefore the optimal policy is to order 700 units at a time. The next display screen will report the itemized costs components for the optimal policy as shown below.

```
┌──────────────────────────────────────────────────────────────┐
│                                                                │
│             Problem Title: EOQ WITH DISCOUNTS                  │
│                                                                │
│         Economic Lot Size with Quantity Discounts:            │
│                                                                │
│                                                                │
│     Optimal order quantity is      700.0                       │
│     Days between order             127.8                       │
│     Annual holding cost            280.00                      │
│     Annual order   cost            142.86                      │
│     Purchase price                8000.00                      │
│     Total cost                    8422.86                      │
│                                                                │
└──────────────────────────────────────────────────────────────┘
```

The optimal order policy requires an order size of 700 units, to be placed every 127.8 days, at a total annual cost of $8,422.86.

EXAMPLE 6 - STOCHASTIC DEMAND MODEL

The stochastic demand inventory model refers to a problem in which the demand during lead time is not constant (a fixed number of units per day) and varies probabilistically. In this case, demand during lead time is usually estimated via a discrete distribution consisting of the various amounts and associated frequencies of demand during lead time.

Consider a problem in which the annual demand is 1000 units, the lead time is 5 days, and the shortage cost is $10. Holding cost is $5 per unit per year and the order cost is $25. The frequency distribution of the number of units demanded during the specified lead time is summarized in Table 11-1.

Demand During Lead Time	Frequency
10	5
15	15
20	20
25	5
30	4
35	1
Total	50

Table 11-1. Demand Levels During Lead Time and Respective Frequencies

You are now ready to solve the above problem. Load the DSSPOM program and select the Inventory Analysis program. After a few seconds the computer will load the program and displays the Inventory Menu.

Move the pointer to the INPUT option and pull the bar down to the "Discrete Demand Dist." sub-option, then press the <ENTER> key. The computer will proceed with the data entry process. Note that for this problem, production rate is not used and should be assigned 0. The purchase price is also assumed 0. The completed data entry screen is shown below.

```
Problem title: DISCRETE DEMAND

Enter number of days per year: 365
Enter annual demand:   1000
Enter annual production rate (0 if none):     0
Enter purchase price in dollars per unit:     0
Enter setup or order cost in dollars per order:      25
Enter the Lead-Time in days (0 if none):    5
Enter holding cost in dollars per unit per year:    5
Enter unit shortage cost in dollars/year (0 if none):     10


┌─────────────────────────────────────────────────────────┐
│ Enter problem parameters as requested.  Press RETURN to │
│ accept, or ESC to exit.                                 │
└─────────────────────────────────────────────────────────┘
```

After completing the initial data entry screen, the computer will ask if it should continue with the data entry for the demand distribution as shown below.

```
┌─────────────────────────────────────────────────────────────────────┐
│ Continue with the distribution of demand during lead time (Y/N) Y   │
└─────────────────────────────────────────────────────────────────────┘
```

Press <Y> to continue the data entry process. The computer will then ask you to enter the number of observations as shown below.

```
┌─────────────────────────────────────────────────────────────┐
│ Enter number of order quantities during ROP (up to 20):  6 │
└─────────────────────────────────────────────────────────────┘
```

Enter a 6 in this field and press the <ENTER> key to proceed. The computer will then display the spread sheet editor for entering the demand distribution. The completed spread sheet data entry is shown below.

```
C7  1                                                              ┤READY├
            A        B         C
1        Observ.  Demand   Frequency
2           1      10.0       5.0
3           2      15.0      15.0
4           3      20.0      20.0
5           4      25.0       5.0
6           5      30.0       4.0
7           6      35.0       1.0
```

After completing the spread sheet data entry, press the <F10> key to return to the main menu and keep the input data.

You are now ready to solve the problem. Move the pointer to the SOLVE option and select the Display Output sub-option. Press the <ENTER> key to continue the solution process. The solution output report is shown below.

Problem Title: DISCRETE DEMAND
Stochastic Demand Model with Lead-time

Demand during Lead-time	Frequency of demand	Relative Frequency
10	5	0.100
15	15	0.300
20	20	0.400
25	5	0.100
30	4	0.080
35	1	0.020

Average Demand during Lead-time =   19.10 units

The first output report consists of the relative frequency distribution. The relative frequencies represent the fraction of times that the demand assumes the associated value. For example, demand during lead time is 10 units about 10 percent of the time, 15 units 30 percent of the time, etc. Also, the average demand during lead time is 19.10 units.   Press the <ENTER> key to continue with the next report as shown below.

```
┌─────────────────────────────────────────────────────────────────┐
│                  Problem Title: DISCRETE DEMAND                   │
│               Stochastic Demand Model with Lead-time             │
│                                                                   │
│             Summary of Total Costs at Various Reorder Points     │
│                                                                   │
│                                                          Total    │
│     Reorder    Safety      Carrying      Stockout                 │
│      Point     Stock       Cost ($)      Cost ($)       Cost($)   │
│     --------   --------    --------      ---------      --------- │
│                                0.00        910.00         910.00  │
│       10.0       0.0         2.50         460.00         462.50   │
│       15.0       0.0        12.50         160.00         172.50   │
│       20.0       0.9        32.50          60.00          92.50   │
│       25.0       5.9        55.00          10.00          65.00   │
│       30.0      10.9        79.50           0.00          79.50   │
│       35.0      15.9                                              │
│                                                                   │
│                                                                   │
│            Optimal Reorder Point =      30.0 units               │
│            Optimal Safety  Stock =      10.9 units               │
└─────────────────────────────────────────────────────────────────┘
```

The second and final report presents the approximate optimal reorder policy. That is, for this example, the optimal reorder point is when the inventory is at about 30 units with a safety stock of about 10.9 units. This policy approximately minimizes the cost of inventory and stock-out. The solution procedure used here is a heuristic search process and not an exact solution method. The search procedure produces a solution which is sub-optimal but fairly reasonable.

PROBLEMS

1. Economic purchase lot size problem (no shortages) - Suppose demand is 10,000 units per year, order cost per order amounts to $150, and inventory holding cost per year is $15 per unit. Find the optimal purchase lot size.

2. Economic purchase lot size problem (no shortages) - Suppose demand is 160,000 units per year, order cost per order amounts to $300, and inventory holding cost per unit amounts to $1.00. Find the optimal purchase lot size.

3. Economic purchase lot size problem (with shortages) - Suppose demand is 21,000 units per year, order cost per order amounts to $220, inventory holding cost per year is $9 per units and shortage cost per year is $21 per unit. Find the optimal purchase lot size.

4. Economic purchase lot size problem (with shortages) - Suppose demand is 330,000 units per year, order cost is $1,200 per order, inventory holding cost amounts to $4.50 per unit per year, and shortage cost is $2.00 per unit per year. Find the optimal purchase lot size.

5. Optimal production run size (no shortages) - Suppose the annual demand rate is 4,000 units and the annual production rate is 20,000 units. Set up cost is $3,200 per set up and inventory holding cost is $2 per unit per year. Find the optimal production run size.

6. Optimal production run size (no shortages) - Annual production capacity is $240,000 units and annual demand is 20,000 units. Set up cost amounts to $900 per set and inventory holding cost is $3 per unit. Find the optimal production run size.

7. Optimal production run size (with shortages) - Shortage cost amounts to $5 per year per unit and inventory holding cost amount to $1.50 per year per unit. Set up cost is $3,900 per set up, while annual demand is 98,000 units. Production capacity is 640,000 units per year. Find optimal production run size.

8. Optimal production run size (with shortages) - Set up cost to set up a production line with 140,000 units of annual capacity amounts to $960. Annual demand is 68,000 units, inventory holding cost is $6 per unit per year and shortage cost is $1.50 per unit per year. Find optimal production run size.

9. Solve the quantity discount problem, for a product based on a 365-day year. The annual demand for the product is 60,000 units. Order cost per order amounts to $350 and holding cost per unit per year is 25 percent of purchase price. The price list is as shown below.

Lot Size Category	Price
0 - 999	$5
1000 - 4999	4.75
5000 - 9999	4.50
10000 -	4.40

10. Find the optimal reorder point, optimal safety stock and purchase lot size for problem 4. The demand distribution during the five day lead time is shown below. There are 365 days per year.

Demand during Lead Time	Frequency of Demand
350	20
400	40
450	80
500	40
550	20

11. Find the optimal reorder point, optimal safety stock and production lot size for problem 7. The demand distribution during the five day lead time is shown below. There are 365 days per year.

Demand during Lead Time	Frequency of Demand
280	5
290	10
300	30
310	35
320	15
330	5

12. Bleaker Manufacturing's President, faced with rising costs, asked his systems analyst to investigate the production practices of the company's major product line. The analyst found that he had to determine optimal production policy for a production rate of 1500 units per month and annual demand of 10,000 units. Set up cost amounted to $200, and holding cost was $1.50 per unit per month. He was also asked to investigate how much Bleaker could save if the current policy to have a production run once per month were changed to an economic production lot-size policy. What would you advise and why?

13. Determine the minimum cost production cycle for the following group of products, assuming 250 working days per year.

Product Number	Annual Unit Sales (D_i)	Daily Production Run (P_i)	Annual Holding Cost/Unit (IC_i)	Set up Cost per Run (S_i)
1	5000	100	$1.00	$40
2	9000	60	.80	25
3	8000	40	.40	35
4	16000	70	.60	30
5	6000	50	.20	90
6	10000	90	.30	60

14. UNIVERSAL MOTORS (A)

The Cabrolet division of Universal Motors produces and markets automobiles in most parts of the world. Following the sale of its products the Cabrolet division guarantees to its buyers that replacement parts will be available for fifteen years in case of failure and normal wear. Since automobile models change from year to year the fifteen year parts availability placed an enormous burden on the replacement parts operation of the division. Although the replacement parts operation is usually considered the most profitable of all operations in the automobile industry, at the Cabrolet division the profitability of replacement parts had been declining. Jim Knight, the general manager of the operation thought that the profit decline could be attributed to the high set up and start up cost of each batch run.

In the automobile industry it is common practice for the replacement parts operation to order, at the end of a model year, a relatively large supply of those parts that are to be discontinued. Many parts continue from year to year, but some do not. By stock piling these discontinued parts, the replacement parts operation acquired at high volume production cost, replacement parts it could market over the year, or several years, depending on their respective demands. The supply of replacement parts ordered at the end of a model year was determined on the basis of expected demand over the next several years, and on the basis of the economic order quantity formula. Since the economic order quantity formula provided the most economical amount to order, it surprised Mr. Knight that the replacement parts division seemed to expend inordinate amounts on repeat runs. Mr. Knight attributed the decline in profitability to these repeat runs.

John Service, who had worked on a variety of special projects for Mr. Knight, was assigned to investigate the problems associated with the high cost of replacement parts batch runs. Following a thorough investigation he found that:

1. Replacement parts demand forecasting was not very accurate.
2. Start up costs during each replacement parts run was not considered in the economic order quantity calculations.
3. Estimates for set up cost and variable costs were based on two times the costs in effect during the high volume model year run.
4. A capital carrying cost of 50 percent per year was charged to replacement parts inventory.

John Service discussed his findings with engineering, production, and accounting staff and found that historical demand of a similar part was not an accurate prediction of demand. He also found that start up costs were never considered although there was a general awareness that the cost at the beginning of a batch run was much higher than at the end. They felt, however, that the doubling of original costs in the cost estimate should compensate for that. The capital carrying cost was based on the rate of return Cabrolet was earning on its physical assets after accumulated depreciation. The Cabrolet plant had a relatively low book value which, with high earnings, produced an average return on assets of 50 percent. Rate of return on cash holdings was not considered in determining the asset base since all the cash holdings were in the hands of the CENTRAL staff of Universal Motors. At the time, Universal Motors had substantial holdings of cash and convertible securities on which it was earning about 7.5 percent.

John Service decided at that point to investigate some actual data in order to determine how economic order quantities should be calculated. He collected data, shown below, on twelve randomly selected parts and was debating how large the carrying charge should be on the capital invested. He felt 50 percent was much too high; 15 to 25 percent seemed much more reasonable given that Cabrolet was a division of Universal Motors and Universal Motors was earning about 20 percent on its total assets. The set up costs were apparently quite accurate, but the variable costs were only accurate for a short production run of one day and too high for production runs of several days.

Determine economic lot sizes for several levels of holding cost, such as 50%, 35% and 20%. Also consider the two year demand data as demand for a single two year period. Does it change the economic lot sizes?

Cost and Volume Data - Universal Motors

Part Number	Annual Volume Forecast		Set Up Cost per Set Up	Variable Unit Cost
	1989	1990		
03641	900	780	$ 580	$ 5.60
47826	3000	4715	1200	4.20
81428	6000	4975	1470	1.60
05729	4200	3160	960	2.80
46211	28000	22600	2350	0.70
73589	1300	1800	400	5.10
47614	1200	2600	590	3.70
82947	3200	3300	860	8.40
32821	22000	21600	470	1.90
52682	1500	4600	910	3.20
43741	2400	1900	420	6.40
57892	16000	9500	380	2.20

CHAPTER 12

MATERIAL REQUIREMENTS PLANNING

INTRODUCTION

Material requirements planning also known as MRP is a widely used computer-based technique for planning the material flows and production in manufacturing facilities. MRP is an important and necessary tool because of the complexity of product assemblies that consist of many sub-assemblies, components, sub-components and parts. Each product assembly, subassembly, component, sub-component and part has its own lead time which is the time required between the beginning and end of the manufacture of the respective product or product component. Frequent delays occur when sub-components or components have not been ordered or manufactured in time for use in the final product assembly.

A material requirements planning system consists of four modules or files. The first module is the master production schedule (MPS). MPS contain information about the quantities and timing (period of completion) of the various orders for the end-items or finished products. The next important module is the product structure tree, also referred to as the bill of materials (BOM). This file shows how the various parts, sub-components, components, and sub-assemblies fit together to make up the end-items or final assemblies. The third file is the inventory record file (IRF). IRF contains several items of information for every part. These include initial inventory (or on-hand), safety stock, lead time, order policy, setup or order cost, holding (or inventory carrying) cost, and lot-size. The fourth module or file is called scheduled receipts and is optional. That is, if one or more of the components have outstanding orders, from the previous planning horizon, which are scheduled to arrive (or be completed) in the current planning horizon, the timing and quantities of these orders are placed in the scheduled receipts (SR) file. MRP is best illustrated by the example shown below.

Chip Megahertz is the president of Basement Unlimited Supplies (BUS) Inc., a mail-order personal computer (PC) retailer. BUS offers two popular models of personal computers, FD-PC and HD-PC at discounted prices. BUS purchases various parts, needed for FD-PC and HD-PC, from several wholesale outlets around the country and assembles the PCs. Chip is about to develop a time-phased plan for the next three months. At present he has two orders for the FD-PC of 50 and 70 units and two orders for the HD-PC of 10 and 30 units as shown in Figure 12-1.

End item	Week 1	2	3	4	5	6	7	8	9	10	11	12
FD-PC								50				70
HD-PC						10				30		

Figure 12-1: Master Production Schedule for BUS Inc.

The MPS lists the number of units of each final product assembly that must be ready for delivery by specific dates. The dates are usually shown by week number as shown in Figure 12-1. Each week number, of course, corresponds to a specific date. For instance, week 8 could mean November 15, 1990. Note that 50 completed units of FD-PC must be ready for delivery in week 8 and 70 units must be ready in week 12. Since all components have lead times, they must of course be ready earlier than the week 8 and week 12 dates.

Model FD-PC includes a CPU (with the power supply), two floppy disk drives (FDD), and a monochrome monitor (MOM). HD-PC includes the same CPU, a color monitor (COM), and disk storage assembly (DSA). The disk storage assembly consists of one FDD and one 20 Meg hard disk drive (HDD). Figure 12-2 shows the product structure trees for FD-PC and HD-PC.

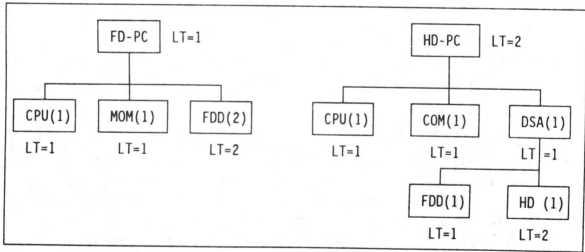

Note: **Number in parenthesis is quantity needed per unit of parent**
LT is lead time

Figure 12-2: **Product Structure Trees for FD-PC and HD-PC**

Also shown is the lead time (LT) in weeks required for each component or product assembly. For example, the lead time for FD-PC is one week which indicates that once all of

285

the parts for building a unit are available, it takes one week to assemble, test, and ship the unit.

BUS purchases the CPUs and FDDs from Disks Repairs Unlimited Systems (Disks_R_US), a wholesale supplier of computer components. However, Disks_R_US sells the CPUs in boxes of 10 each and the FDDs in boxes of 30 each. Other components may be purchased at odd units depending on the quantity needed. Additional information such as safety stock, units on hand, annual demand, order cost, holding cost, lot size and order policy (to be discussed below) collectively referred to as the inventory record file(IRF), is presented in Table 12-1.

Item	On-hand (units)	Safety Stock (units)	Order Policy	Annual Demand (units)	Order Cost ($)	Hold. Cost ($)	Lot Size (units)
FD-PC	7	3	LFL	600	100	50	-
HD-PC	5	3	LFL	200	150	75	-
CPU	10	5	LOT	850	30	10	10
MOM	5	0	LFL	650	40	5	-
FDD	20	10	LOT	2500	50	10	30
COM	5	0	LFL	210	40	5	-
DSA	0	0	LFL	200	10	25	-
HDD	6	4	LFL	210	10	15	-

Table 12-1: Inventory Record File for BUS Inc.

The annual demand for several components exceeds the total quantity needed to assemble the two end items. These additional units are either sold separately or are used for servicing the units which are under guarantee. Holding cost is in dollars per unit per year. Order cost is in dollars per order and represents charges for shipping and handling. For assembled items (e.g., disk storage assembly), order cost represents setup cost. Annual demand, holding cost, and order cost are required for items ordered according to the period order quantity (POQ) policy. They are also used in determination of the annual operating costs.

Safety Stocks

As seen from Table 12-1, several items such as FD-PC require a certain number of units (in this case 3) be carried as safety stock. Safety stocks are usually carried as a hedge against delays in the delivery of ordered items or shipments containing one or more defective items. For a problem to be consistent, the units on hand must be greater than or equal to the safety stock.

Order Policy

The column entitled "Order Policy" refers to the method by which an item is ordered. For instance, the CPUs and FDDs must be ordered in batches of 10 and 30, respectively. This method of ordering is called "Lot Size" (LOT) ordering and require the lot-size to be known a priori. Other items may be ordered according to the number of units needed. This method of ordering is referred to as lot-for-lot (LFL) or net-requirement ordering.

The MRP program also provides a third order method referred to as "period order quantity" or POQ. Whereas LFL order policy usually has high setup or order cost but low holding cost, LOT ordering has low setup or order cost but high holding cost. POQ balances ordering and holding costs and is described below.

Suppose that annual demand is denoted by D, setup or order cost is S, and inventory holding cost is H dollars per unit per year. The classical economic order quantity, which minimizes total annual costs of ordering or setup and inventory holding is given as,

$$EOQ = \sqrt{\frac{2DS}{H}}$$

Further, let NET denote the total net requirements during the planning horizon T. The planning horizon is typically 12 weeks (periods) long. The maximum T for DSSPOM is 26 weeks. The average net requirement, μ_{NET}, is then,

$$\mu_{NET} = \frac{NET}{T}$$

Next determine *POQ*, the number of average net requirements, $\mu_{NET,}$ in one EOQ, is

$$POQ = \frac{EOQ}{\mu_{NET}}$$

POQ is then rounded up to the next integer. The POQ order policy is then to place an order for *POQ* weeks (or periods) worth of net requirements upon encountering the first positive net requirement. This order policy requires that annual demand, unit holding cost, and setup (or order) cost be known a priori.

Low Level Coding

The MRP module requires that all components and sub-components be assigned an identification (ID) number. The ID number assigned to each item identifies that item in a special way. That is, the ID number identifies the component number and level, in the structure tree, at which that item is used. Tree levels are numbered sequentially from top to bottom, with top level (or end items) components having a single digit ID. Sub-components, at next lower level, making up the end items should have ID numbers which are two digits and begin with the digit 1. Components at the third level of the tree (level 2) should have two digit numbers with the first digit being 2. To avoid unnecessary errors, the MRP module automatically assigns ID numbers to the end items. These IDs should not be altered.

In a case where the same component is used in one or more end items, at different levels of the tree, the product structure tree must be revised, using a technique referred to as *low level coding*. In short, low level coding involves lowering a sub-component (in the tree) such that it is used at the same level in all of the components, sub-components, and end items. In the example presented above, FDD is used in both FD-PC and HD-PC, at different levels and therefore must be *low level coded*. Figure 12-3 represents the revised product structure trees after low level coding of FDD.

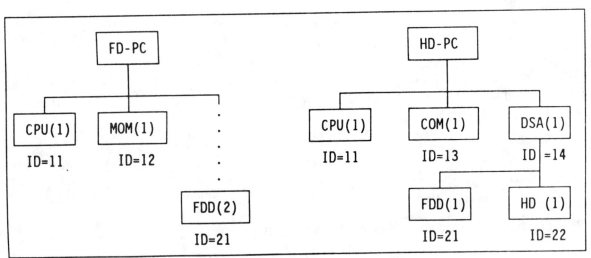

Figure 12-3: Product Structure Trees after Low Level Coding

As seen from Figure 12-3, all items have been assigned ID numbers, consistent with the method described above. The end items FD-PC and HD-PC have no ID numbers because the MRP module will automatically assign them numbers 1 and 2. Note that the first digit of the

ID number identifies the tree level at which the component is used. It is *extremely important* that when you enter the bill of materials (or product structure tree) into the computer, begin with the top level, enter all of the end items first. Then continue with items in the next lower level (level 1) and enter all of the components at this level. Then enter the components at the next level and so on. No sub-component should appear in BOM in such a way that its parent component falls below it in the list. If this occurs, the MRP output will most likely be erroneous.

EXAMPLE 1 - CASE OF BUS, INC.

In this example you will use the MRP module to solve the above problem. Load DSSPOM into the computer and select the MRP module. Move the pointer to the INPUT option and press the <ENTER> key. The data input process will begin by asking for inputs for the MPS, followed by BOM, followed by IRF. The data entry for the scheduled receipts (SR) is optional and is used only when such information is available.

The initial data entry for MPS consists of problem title, the number of end items, the number of periods in the planning horizon, and the number of periods in a year as shown below.

```
Problem title: BUS INC.

Number of end-items (products):  2

Number of periods in planning horizon:  12

Number of periods per year:  52


┌─────────────────────────────────────────────────────────┐
│ Enter problem parameters as requested.  Press RETURN to  │
│ accept, or ESC to exit.  Maximum problem size is 5 end-items │
│ (products) and  26 periods, MPS quantities should be within │
│ 0-9999.                                                  │
└─────────────────────────────────────────────────────────┘
```

The number of periods per year is used in the computations of the operating costs. This number is 52 for a weekly planning horizon and 12 for problems with a monthly planning horizon.

After pressing the <ENTER> key, the computer will begin the spread sheet data entry process for the master production schedule (MPS) file. Note that in the MRP module, MPS is referred

289

to as a 'file'. However, the information in MPS is maintained in the memory and not a disk file. When a problem is saved on disk, all of the information related to the same problem is stored in the same disk file.

The MPS for this solved example is shown in Figure 12-1. Enter this information into the spread sheet. The completed spread sheet is shown below.

```
                                                              ┤READY├
C1  'HD-PC
          A              B          C
1    Period           FD-PC      HD-PC
2    Period1            0          0
3    Period2            0          0
4    Period3            0          0
5    Period4            0          0
6    Period5            0          0
7    Period6            0          10
8    Period7            0          0
9    Period8            50         0
10   Period9            0          0
11   Period10           0          30
12   Period11           0          0
13   Period12           70         0
```

After completing the data entry for MPS, press <F10> to keep the data in the memory and continue with the BOM file.

The information needed for the BOM file consists of the total number of components and the maximum number of sub-components of any component. It can be found by counting the number of components (not including the two main assemblies) and the maximum number of subcomponents per component shown in Figure 12-2. The total number of components in this case is 8 and the maximum number of sub-components is 3. Enter this information into the computer as shown below. Remember to low-level code first.

```
Total No. of Components (including end-items):    8

Maximum number of sub-components of any component:  3



Enter problem parameters as requested.  BOM must have been
low level coded so that every sub-component is placed after
its parent item in the list.  Maximum number of components
is 25, maximum number of sub-components (of any component)
is 4.
```

The computer will then resume the data entry process for the BOM by displaying the spread sheet editor again. Begin the data entry by first entering the structure of the two end items. Move the pointer to cell A3 and enter FD-PC. Now move the pointer down to cell A4 and enter HD-PC. The computer has assigned ID numbers 1 and 2 to FD-PC and HD-PC, respectively. Move the pointer to cell C3 and enter 11 which is the ID for CPU (see Figure 12-3).

Next move the pointer one cell to the right (cell D3) and enter 1, the number of CPUs needed for one FD-PC. Move the pointer to the right again and enter 12 (the ID number for MOM). Press the <ENTER> key and move the pointer to the right again. Type 1 and press <ENTER>.   Enter the remaining information relating to the BOM. Be sure that the order of the components entered into the BOM file is consistent. That is, the row corresponding to each component must always precede its sub-components. The completed spread sheet is presented below.

E3 12						READY
	A	B	C	D	E	F	G
1			Sub-1	Quant/	Sub-2	Quant/	Sub-3
2	Component	ID	ID	Parent	ID	Parent	ID
3	FD-PC	1	11	1	12	1	21
4	HD-PC	2	11	1	13	1	14
5	CPU	11	.	.	.	.	.
6	MOM	12	.	.	.	.	.
7	COM	13	.	.	.	.	.
8	DSA	14	21	1	22	1	.
9	FDD	21	.	.	.	.	.
10	HDD	22	.	.	.	.	.

In the above display, the information relating to the quantity needed per unit of parent for sub-component 3 (Sub-3) is not shown. After completing the data entry for the BOM file, press <F10> to keep the data in memory and continue with the data entry for inventory record file.

The items of information needed for the inventory record file (IRF) includes on-hand stock, safety stock, lead time, order policy (or method), annual demand, holding cost, setup or order cost, and lot size. Enter this information for each component. The completed spread sheet is presented below.

```
                                                                    ╣READY╠
A1
           A          B      C        D       E      F      G       H       I
1                            On-     Safety  Lead   Ord    Annual  Setup   Hold.
2   Component         ID     Hand    Stock   Time   Mth    Demand  Cost    Cost
3   FD-PC             1      7        3       1      LFL    600     100     50
4   HD-PC             2      5        3       2      LFL    200     150     75
5   CPU               11     10       5       1      LOT    850     30      10
6   MOM               12     5        0       1      LFL    650     40      5
7   COM               13     5        0       1      LFL    210     40      5
8   DSA               14     0        0       1      LFL    200     10      25
9   FDD               21     20       10      2      LOT    2500    50      10
10  HDD               22     6        4       2      LFL    210     10      15
```

In the above display screen, the column for lot-size is not shown. The components with non-zero lot-sizes are CPU (lot size of 10) and FDD (lot size of 30). Press the <F10> to keep the data in the memory. The computer will ask if you wish to enter the scheduled receipts. Since there are no scheduled receipts available at this time, press <N> followed by <ENTER> to end the data entry process.

You may now save the model on disk for future use. To save the model, move the pointer to the FILE option and select the Save Current File sub-option then press <ENTER>. The computer will display the current drive and sub-directory and requests a file name. Enter an appropriate DOS file name and use the suffix MRP to indicate that the file contains an MRP problem.

You may also obtain a hard copy printout of the problem. The print option for this module, unlike other modules, has four sub-options as shown below.

```
Input  Edit  Print  File  Solve  Quit
                  ┌─────────────────────┐
                  │ Master Schedule     │
                  │ Bill of Materials   │
                  │ Inventory File      │
                  │ Scheduled Receipts  │
                  └─────────────────────┘
```

To print any of the four MRP components, highlight the option and press <ENTER>. The computer will ask you to make sure that the Printer is On and Ready. Press <ENTER> to proceed with the print option as needed.

You are now ready to solve the problem. Move the pointer to the SOLVE option and select the Display Output sub-option. The computer will display the solution menu as shown below.

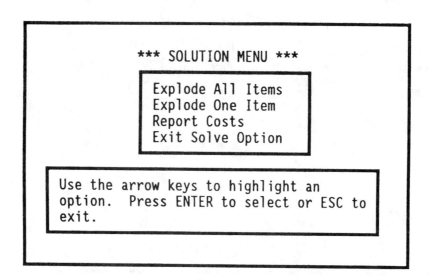

Begin the solution process by requesting the Explosion reports for the two end items first. Move the pointer to the Explode One Item option and press <ENTER>. The computer will display another menu containing the list of all of the components and sub-components as shown below.

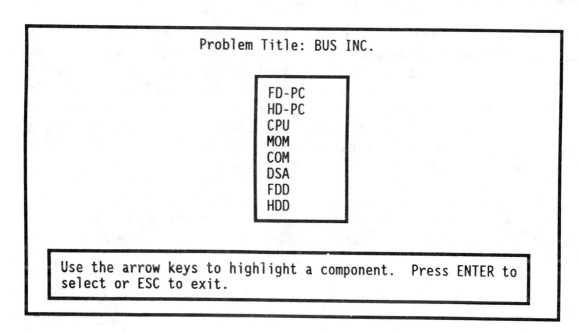

Move the pointer to FD-PC and press <ENTER>. The computer will display the explosion report for FD-PC as shown below.

```
┌─────────────────────────────────────────────────────────────────────────┐
│                      Problem Title: BUS INC.                              │
│    Item: FD-PC          Lead time:      1      Demand:        600         │
│      ID: 1              Lot  Size:      0      H-Cost:      50.00         │
│  Method: LFL              Safety:       3      S-Cost:     100.00         │
│                                                                           │
│             Gross      Sched.     On-        Net     Planned   Planned    │
│  Period   Required    Receipt    Hand    Required   Receipt   Release     │
│    1          0          0        7          0          0         0       │
│    2          0          0        7          0          0         0       │
│    3          0          0        7          0          0         0       │
│    4          0          0        7          0          0         0       │
│    5          0          0        7          0          0         0       │
│    6          0          0        7          0          0         0       │
│    7          0          0        7          0          0        46       │
│    8         50          0        3         46         46         0       │
│    9          0          0        3          0          0         0       │
│   10          0          0        3          0          0         0       │
│   11          0          0        3          0          0        70       │
│   12         70          0        3         70         70         0       │
└─────────────────────────────────────────────────────────────────────────┘
```

As seen from the above report, the first three lines of the report consist of the various statistics for the end item FD-PC. These include its name, ID number, method of ordering, lead time, lot size, safety stock, annual demand, holding cost and setup cost.

The lower portion of the report is the timed phase (or explosion) report for FD-PC. It indicates that the gross requirements for this item consist of 50 units in period 8 and 70 units in period 12. There are no scheduled receipts. The on hand inventory is 7 units which are carried to the end of period 7. The first positive net requirement occurs in period 8 for 46 units. The gross in this period is 50 units, adding 3 units as safety stock results in 53 units. Subtracting the inventory of 7 units results in the net being 46 units. Since FD-PC is ordered according to net requirements (or lot-for-lot), the planned order receipts is for 46 units in period 8. The item has a lead time of 1 week, hence the first planned order release is for 46 units in period 7.

The second gross requirement for this item occurs in period 12 for 70 units. With inventory of 3 units, safety stock equal to 3 units, the net is 70 units in period 12. The computation of the planned receipts and planned releases are similar to those of the first order.

Press the <ENTER> key to return to the Solution Menu. Move the pointer to Explode One

Item option again and press <ENTER>. When the menu of the components is displayed, move the pointer to the HD-PC and press <ENTER> (the process is not shown here). The computer will pause for a few seconds and then displays the explosion report for HD-PC as shown below.

```
                    Problem Title: BUS INC.
   Item: HD-PC          Lead time:    2      Demand:      200
     ID: 2              Lot  Size:    0      H-Cost:    75.00
 Method: LFL               Safety:    3      S-Cost:   150.00

           Gross    Sched.    On-      Net    Planned   Planned
 Period  Required  Receipt   Hand   Required  Receipt   Release
    1        0        0       5        0        0         0
    2        0        0       5        0        0         0
    3        0        0       5        0        0         0
    4        0        0       5        0        0         8
    5        0        0       5        0        0         0
    6       10        0       3        8        8         0
    7        0        0       3        0        0         0
    8        0        0       3        0        0        30
    9        0        0       3        0        0         0
   10       30        0       3       30       30         0
   11        0        0       3        0        0         0
   12        0        0       3        0        0         0
```

As seen from the above report, the first gross requirement for HD-PC is for 10 units in period 6. There are no scheduled receipts. The on hand inventory is 5 units which is carried to the end of period 5. The first positive net requirement for this item occurs in period 6 for 8 units. This end item is also ordered according to LFL method, hence the first planned receipts is 8 units in period 6. HD-PC requires two weeks to assemble and test (lead time) which results in the first planned order release of 8 units in period 4. Calculation of the second planned release is similar to the first.

Now press <ENTER> to return to the Solution Menu again. The next item of interest is the explosion report for FDD. This item is used in both FD-PC and HD-PC. Move the pointer to the Explode One Item option and press <ENTER>. When represented with the list of all components, move the pointer to FDD and press <ENTER> (process not shown here). The explosion report for FDD is shown below.

```
┌─────────────────────────────────────────────────────────────────┐
│                   Problem Title: BUS INC.                         │
│    Item: FDD           Lead time:    2        Demand:     2500     │
│      ID: 21            Lot Size:    30        H-Cost:    10.00     │
│  Method: LOT             Safety:    10        S-Cost:    50.00     │
│                                                                   │
│           Gross    Sched.    On-         Net    Planned   Planned  │
│  Period  Required  Receipt   Hand    Required   Receipt   Release  │
│    1        0        0        20         0         0         0      │
│    2        0        0        20         0         0         0      │
│    3        8        0        12         0         0         0      │
│    4        0        0        12         0         0         0      │
│    5        0        0        12         0         0        120     │
│    6        0        0        12         0         0         0      │
│    7       122       0        10        120       120        0      │
│    8        0        0        10         0         0         0      │
│    9        0        0        10         0         0        150     │
│   10        0        0        10         0         0         0      │
│   11       140       0        20        140       150        0      │
│   12        0        0        20         0         0         0      │
└─────────────────────────────────────────────────────────────────┘
```

The first gross requirement consists of 8 units in period 3. This gross requirement is the first planned order releases for disk storage assembly (DSA) component which occurs in period 3 (DSA has a 1 week lead time). Initially, 20 FDDs are available which are carried through the end of period 2. The 8 units needed in period 3 are taken out of the inventory which results in the remaining inventory equal 12 units. Since this is still larger than the safety stock of 10 units, no order is needed in this period.

The next gross requirement is for 122 units (92 units for 46 FD-PCs and 30 units for 30 HD-PCs) in period 7. The net requirement is 122 - 12 = 110 units plus 10 units as safety stock for a total of 120 units. FDDs are ordered in lots of 30 units each. Hence the planned order receipts is 120 units in period 7. With the lead time equal to 2 weeks, the first planned order release is for 120 units in period 5.

Note that the second net requirement is 140 units, ordering according to lots of 30. The next largest multiple of 30 is 150 units which is the second planned receipts.

Press <ENTER> to return to the Solution Menu. Now move the pointer to the Report Costs option and press <ENTER>. The computer will display the cost reports for all of the components as shown below.

```
                    Problem Title: BUS INC.
                   Holding          Setup          Total
     Item           Cost            Cost           Cost
    --------        ----------      ----------     ----------
     FD-PC           61.54          200.00          261.54
     HD-PC           66.35          300.00          366.35
     CPU             19.62          120.00          139.62
     MOM              2.88           80.00           82.88
     COM              1.44           80.00           81.44
     DSA              0.00           20.00           20.00
     FDD             32.31          100.00          132.31
     HDD             15.00           20.00           35.00
```

As seen from the above report, the setup cost for FD-PC is $200 which is for two orders, each at a cost of $100. Also, the holding cost for HD-PC is $66.35 which consists of 5 units carried for 5 weeks at a cost of 5x5x$1.442 = $36.05 (per unit holding cost for HD-PC is $75/52 = $1.442 per week) and 3 units carried for 7 weeks at a cost of 7x3x$1.44 = $30.28, for a total of $66.25.

EXAMPLE 2 - USING POQ TO REDUCE OPERATING COSTS

After examining the cost report in Solved Example 1, Chip Megahertz noticed a rather large difference between the inventory holding costs and order costs for two components namely, MOM and COM. The order costs for these two items equals $80 each. This indicates that there are two planned releases (for each item) during the planning horizon (each item has a order cost of $40). To verify this, Chip decided to examine the explosion report for MOM.

To help Chip look at the desired report, move the pointer to the SOLVE option and select the Display Output sub-option. When presented with the solution menu, choose the Explode One Item option and press <ENTER>. The computer will display the list of all components, highlight MOM and press <ENTER> (process not shown here). The computer will display the explosion report for MOM as shown below.

```
                   Problem Title: BUS INC.
    Item: MOM          Lead time:      1        Demand:      650
      ID: 12           Lot Size:       0        H-Cost:      5.00
  Method: LFL            Safety:       0        S-Cost:     40.00

           Gross    Sched.    On-       Net     Planned    Planned
  Period  Required  Receipt   Hand   Required   Receipt    Release
    1        0        0        5        0          0          0
    2        0        0        5        0          0          0
    3        0        0        5        0          0          0
    4        0        0        5        0          0          0
    5        0        0        5        0          0          0
    6        0        0        5        0          0         41
    7       46        0        0       41         41          0
    8        0        0        0        0          0          0
    9        0        0        0        0          0          0
   10        0        0        0        0          0         70
   11       70        0        0       70         70          0
   12        0        0        0        0          0          0
```

Chip recalled that in his Quantitative Analysis class, several years earlier, the teacher had discussed various methods of ordering inventory items. Looking at the explosion report for MOM and observing the small amount of inventory carried, he wondered if another order policy would be more appropriate. The word POQ did not ring a bell, but anything that would save him some money was fine. Help Chip to find an answer to his 'what if' question.

Note that by using the POQ method, the two planned order releases for MOM in periods 6 and 10 may be grouped together as one order of 111 units. The impact of this approach is that the cost of order decreases from $80 to $40 for just one order. However, the inventory level will increase and will results in additional inventory holding costs. To determine whether the increase in inventory carrying cost is offset by the decrease in the order cost, develop the explosion report for MOM as described below.

Exit from the Solution Menu by moving the bar down to the Exit option and press <ENTER>. Now move the pointer to the EDIT option and select the Inventory File sub-option. You will be presented with the spread sheet editor for IRF. Move the pointer to the cell corresponding to the order method for MOM (cell F6) and enter POQ (be sure to enter POQ all in upper case letters). Next move the pointer down to cell F6 and enter POQ again to change the order policy for item COM to POQ also. The completed spread sheet is presented below.

```
F7  'POQ
        A          B        C        D        E       F      G        H       I
1                          On-      Safety   Lead    Ord    Annual   Setup   Hold.
2     Component    ID      Hand     Stock    Time    Mth    Demand   Cost    Cost
3     FD-PC        1        7        3        1       LFL    600      100     50
4     HD-PC        2        5        3        2       LFL    200      150     75
5     CPU          11       10       5        1       LOT    850      30      10
6     MOM          12       5        0        1       POQ    650      40      5
7     COM          13       5        0        1       POQ    210      40      5
8     DSA          14       0        0        1       LFL    200      10      25
9     FDD          21       20       10       2       LOT    2500     50      10
10    HDD          22       6        4        2       LFL    210      10      15
```

Next press <F10> to keep the changes in memory and exit the spread sheet editor. You are now ready to solve the problem. Move the pointer to the SOLVE option and select the Display Output sub-option. When presented with the solution menu, select the Explode One Item option and press <ENTER>. The computer will display the list of components in a menu. Move the pointer to MOM and press <ENTER>. The explosion report for item MOM will be displayed as shown below.

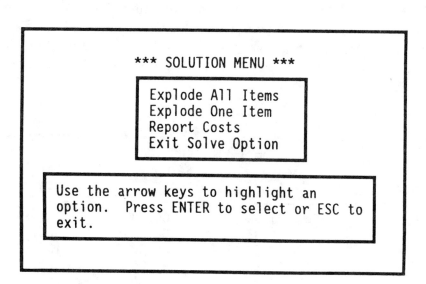

```
           *** SOLUTION MENU ***

          Explode All Items
          Explode One Item
          Report Costs
          Exit Solve Option


   Use the arrow keys to highlight an
   option.  Press ENTER to select or ESC to
   exit.
```

```
                    Problem Title: BUS INC.
    Item: MOM          Lead time:       1      Demand:        650
      ID:  12          Lot Size:        0      H-Cost:       5.00
  Method: POQ           Safety:         0      S-Cost:      40.00

             Gross    Sched.    On-       Net    Planned   Planned
  Period   Required   Receipt   Hand   Required   Receipt   Release
    1          0         0        5        0         0         0
    2          0         0        5        0         0         0
    3          0         0        5        0         0         0
    4          0         0        5        0         0         0
    5          0         0        5        0         0         0
    6          0         0        5        0         0        111
    7         46         0       70       41       111         0
    8          0         0       70        0         0         0
    9          0         0       70        0         0         0
   10          0         0       70        0         0         0
   11         70         0        0        0         0         0
   12          0         0        0        0         0         0
```

As indicated earlier, using the POQ method results in combining the two orders into one. Note that this approach has resulted in 70 units of inventory to be carried for four periods. To determine the impact on the operating costs, press <ENTER> to return to the Solution Menu again. Move the bar to the Costs Report option and press <ENTER>. The computer will display the costs report as shown below.

```
                    Problem Title: BUS INC.
                      Holding        Setup        Total
        Item           Cost          Cost         Cost
       --------     -----------   -----------   -----------
       FD-PC           61.54        200.00        261.54
       HD-PC           66.35        300.00        366.35
       CPU             19.62        120.00        139.62
       MOM             29.81         40.00         69.81
       COM             12.98         40.00         52.98
       DSA              0.00         20.00         20.00
       FDD             32.31        100.00        132.31
       HDD             15.00         20.00         35.00
```

As seen from the above report, the total cost for both MOM and COM has decreased. In particular, the order cost of the revised policy is $40 (for each component) and the holding costs are $29.81 for MOM and $12.98 for COM. These costs compare favorably with the total costs associated with the previous order policy.

Note that the POQ policy may be appropriate for a certain component and result in smaller operating costs but produce sub-optimal results for other components. As a general rule, if an item has a large setup or order cost, small inventory carrying cost, and is being ordered too often, POQ may be a more appropriate order policy.

EXAMPLE 3 - SCHEDULED RECEIPTS

This example will illustrate the use of the scheduled receipts component of MRP system. Suppose that in Example 1, 12 Disk Storage Assemblies are currently being tested and will be ready for use during week 1. Further, Chip had misplaced an order for 20 FDDs which were re-ordered and are scheduled to arrive in week 3. Determine the impact of the above information on the timed phase plans.

The scheduled receipts of an item affect the timed phase plan (explosion report) for that item and all of its sub-components. To illustrate this phenomenon, first solve the problem in its original form and observe the explosion report for DSA, FDD, and HDD. Then add the scheduled receipts and re-solve the problem and compare the solutions as described below.

If you are continuing this example after example one or two, return to the MRP menu first. If you are solving this example for the first time, you need to refer to the data for Example 1 and solve it first. Then return to this example to use the scheduled receipts option.

Move the pointer to the SOLVE option and select the Display Output sub-option. From the solution menu, select the Explode One Item option three times and obtain the report for DSA, FDD, and HDD as shown below.

```
                    Problem Title: BUS INC.
  Item: DSA          Lead time:      1         Demand:        200
    ID: 14           Lot  Size:      0         H-Cost:      25.00
Method: LFL            Safety:       0 ***     S-Cost:      10.00

          Gross    Sched.   On-       Net     Planned   Planned
Period   Required  Receipt  Hand    Required  Receipt   Release
  1         0        0       0         0         0         0
  2         0        0       0         0         0         0
  3         0        0       0         0         0         8
  4         8        0       0         8         8         0
  5         0        0       0         0         0         0
  6         0        0       0         0         0         0
  7         0        0       0         0         0        30
  8        30        0       0        30        30         0
  9         0        0       0         0         0         0
 10         0        0       0         0         0         0
 11         0        0       0         0         0         0
 12         0        0       0         0         0         0
```

```
                    Problem Title: BUS INC.
  Item: FDD          Lead time:      2         Demand:       2500
    ID: 21           Lot  Size:     30         H-Cost:      10.00
Method: LOT            Safety:      10 ***     S-Cost:      50.00

          Gross    Sched.   On-       Net     Planned   Planned
Period   Required  Receipt  Hand    Required  Receipt   Release
  1         0        0       20        0         0         0
  2         0        0       20        0         0         0
  3         8        0       12        0         0         0
  4         0        0       12        0         0         0
  5         0        0       12        0         0        120
  6         0        0       12        0         0         0
  7       122        0       10       120       120        0
  8         0        0       10        0         0         0
  9         0        0       10        0         0        150
 10         0        0       10        0         0         0
 11       140        0       20       140       150        0
 12         0        0       20        0         0         0
```

```
┌─────────────────────────────────────────────────────────────────────┐
│                      Problem Title: BUS INC.                        │
│    Item: HDD          Lead time:      2        Demand:       210    │
│      ID: 22           Lot  Size:      0        H-Cost:     15.00    │
│  Method: LFL             Safety:      4 ***    S-Cost:     10.00    │
│                                                                     │
│            Gross      Sched.     On-        Net     Planned  Planned│
│  Period   Required   Receipt    Hand     Required   Receipt  Release│
│    1         0          0        6          0          0        6   │
│    2         0          0        6          0          0        0   │
│    3         8          0        4          6          6        0   │
│    4         0          0        4          0          0        0   │
│    5         0          0        4          0          0       30   │
│    6         0          0        4          0          0        0   │
│    7        30          0        4         30         30        0   │
│    8         0          0        4          0          0        0   │
│    9         0          0        4          0          0        0   │
│   10         0          0        4          0          0        0   │
│   11         0          0        4          0          0        0   │
│   12         0          0        4          0          0        0   │
└─────────────────────────────────────────────────────────────────────┘
```

Examine the above output reports by observing the planned order releases for the three components. DSA has two orders, an order of 8 units in week 3 and an order of 30 units in week 7. FDD has two orders, an order of size 120 in week 5 and an order of size 150 in week 9. HDD has two orders, one for 6 units in week 1 and another for 30 units in week 5.

Now select the Exit option to return to the MRP menu. Move the pointer to the EDIT option and select the Scheduled Receipts sub-option. The computer will respond by asking you to enter the maximum number of scheduled receipts for any part. In this case, the maximum number is 1 (if there were 2 orders for the same item, it would be 2). Enter a 1 and press <ENTER> as shown below.

```
┌─────────────────────────────────────────────────────────────────────┐
│   Max # of scheduled receipts of any part (0 to 5):   1            │
└─────────────────────────────────────────────────────────────────────┘
```

The computer will then display the spread sheet editor for the scheduled receipts. The first column of the spread sheet contains the names of all of the components and the second column has the ID numbers. The third column is entitled "Prd-1" and is assigned to hold the timing of the scheduled receipt. The fourth column is entitled "Quant" and is to contain the size of the order.

Move the pointer to cell C7 and enter a 1 for the timing of the order for DSA. Press the

<ENTER> and move the pointer to the right and enter 12. Next move the pointer to cell C8 and enter 3. Press <ENTER> and move the pointer to the right one cell and enter 20. Now press <F10> to keep the data in memory and exit from the spread sheet. The completed spread sheet is shown below.

```
                                                            ⊣READY⊢
C8  3
              A        B       C       D
 1   Component       ID     Prd-1 Quant
 2   FD-PC            1     .       .
 3   HD-PC            2     .       .
 4   CPU             11     .       .
 5   MOM             12     .       .
 6   COM             13     .       .
 7   DSA             14     1      12
 8   FDD             21     3      20
 9   HDD             22     .       .
```

You are now ready to solve the problem. Move the pointer to the SOLVE option and select the Display Output sub-option. When presented with the Solution Menu, move the bar to the Explode One Item and press <ENTER> (process not shown here). The computer will display the list of components as before. Move the pointer to DSA and press <ENTER>. The computer will display the explosion report for DSA as shown below.

```
                 Problem Title: BUS INC.
   Item: DSA          Lead time:      1      Demand:        200
     ID:  14          Lot  Size:      0      H-Cost:      25.00
 Method: LFL             Safety:      0      S-Cost:      10.00

           Gross     Sched.    On-       Net      Planned   Planned
 Period   Required   Receipt   Hand    Required   Receipt   Release
   1         0         12       12        0          0         0
   2         0          0       12        0          0         0
   3         0          0       12        0          0         0
   4         8          0        4        0          0         0
   5         0          0        4        0          0         0
   6         0          0        4        0          0         0
   7         0          0        4        0          0        26
   8        30          0        0       26         26         0
   9         0          0        0        0          0         0
  10         0          0        0        0          0         0
  11         0          0        0        0          0         0
  12         0          0        0        0          0         0
```

As seen from the above report, the scheduled receipt of 12 units during week 1 is carried to the end of week 3. 8 units are used to satisfy the requirement of week 4 and the planned order release is no longer needed. Further, the remaining 4 units are carried to week 8 which reduces the net requirement from 30 to 26 units. Press <ENTER> to return to the Solution Menu and select the explosion report for FDD (process not shown here). The explosion report is shown below.

```
                      Problem Title: BUS INC.
     Item: FDD            Lead time:      2        Demand:      2500
       ID: 21             Lot  Size:     30        H-Cost:     10.00
   Method: LOT               Safety:     10        S-Cost:     50.00

              Gross    Sched.    On-      Net     Planned   Planned
   Period   Required  Receipt   Hand   Required  Receipt   Release
     1          0        0       20        0        0          0
     2          0        0       20        0        0          0
     3          0       20       40        0        0          0
     4          0        0       40        0        0          0
     5          0        0       40        0        0         90
     6          0        0       40        0        0          0
     7        118        0       12       88       90          0
     8          0 ·      0       12        0        0          0
     9          0        0       12        0        0        150
    10          0        0       12        0        0          0
    11        140        0       22      138      150          0
    12          0        0       22        0        0          0
```

The scheduled receipt for FDD is 20 units, available at the beginning of week 3. This is added to the inventory of 20 units and carried to week 7. This changes the net requirement to 88 units with the next larger multiple of 10 (lot size) equal to 90 units.

Next obtain the explosion report for HDD as shown below (process not shown here).

```
                    Problem Title: BUS INC.
    Item: HDD          Lead time:      2      Demand:        210
      ID: 22            Lot  Size:      0      H-Cost:      15.00
  Method: LFL            Safety:        4      S-Cost:      10.00

            Gross     Sched.     On-        Net     Planned    Planned
  Period  Required   Receipt    Hand    Required   Receipt    Release
    1         0         0         6          0          0         0
    2         0         0         6          0          0         0
    3         0         0         6          0          0         0
    4         0         0         6          0          0         0
    5         0         0         6          0          0        24
    6         0         0         6          0          0         0
    7        26         0         4         24         24         0
    8         0         0         4          0          0         0
    9         0         0         4          0          0         0
   10         0         0         4          0          0         0
   11         0         0         4          0          0         0
   12         0         0         4          0          0         0
```

As seen from the above report, the gross requirement for HDD is 26 units in week 7. This solution differs from the previous one in that the 8 units needed in period 3 is no longer necessary. Also, in week 7 instead of requiring 30 units, the new requirement is 26 units. The change is due to the scheduled receipts of 12 DSAs in period 1 as described above.

PROBLEMS

1. Consider the following product structure tree.

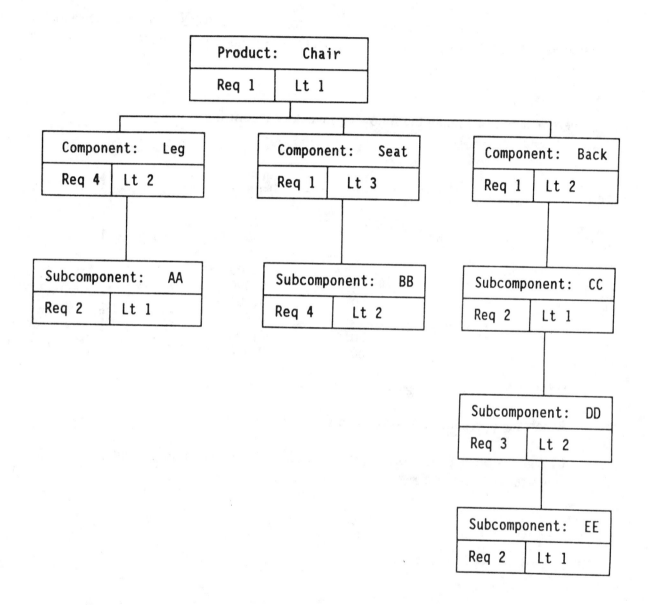

The gross requirements for the end item chair are 300 units in week 8, 400 units in week 10, and 500 units in week 12. Assume that all items are ordered on a lot-for-lot basis and that there are no initial inventories and safety stocks. Develop the explosion report for sub-components DD and EE.

2. Change problem 1 so that there are 500 AAs, 500 CCs, and 500 EEs on hand. Also change the order policy for CC to lot-sizing and use a lot size of 200 units. Develop the explosion report for CC and EE.

3. In problem 2, assume that there is a scheduled receipt of 200 Backs in week 5. Develop the explosion report for items CC and EE. Compare the planned order releases with those in problem 2.

4. Solve problem 1, assuming the following inventory record file.

Item	On Hand	Safety Stock	Order Policy	Annual Demand	Order Cost	Hold. Cost	Lot Size
Chair	100	50	LFL	10,000	10	2	-
Leg	200	50	LFL	25,000	5	1	-
Seat	150	50	LFL	10,000	5	1	-
Back	150	50	LFL	10,000	5	1	-
AA	-	-	LOT	50,000	100	.5	400
BB	-	-	LOT	40,000	100	.5	400
CC	-	-	LOT	20,000	100	.5	500
DD	-	-	LOT	60,000	200	.5	500
EE	-	-	LOT	60,000	200	.5	500

a. Develop the explosion report for items AA, DD, and EE.

b. Report the operating costs of all items.

c. Change the order policy for component Back to POQ, determine the operating cost and compare with that in part b.

5. Consider the following product structure tree.

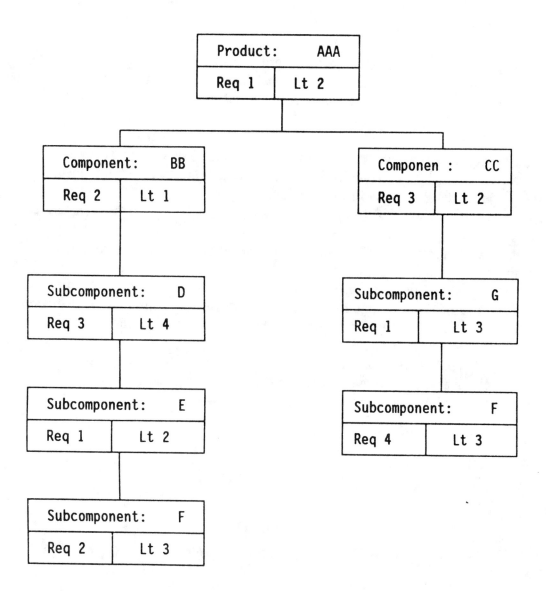

The gross requirements for Product AAA are 400 units in week 10 and 900 units in week 12. There are lot size requirements of 2000 units for subcomponent D, and 500 units for subcomponent G; all other items are ordered according to LFL and no safety stocks are required. Units on hand amount to 600 units for subcomponent D, 1000 units for subcomponent E, 1200 units for subcomponent F, and 500 units for subcomponent G. Develop the explosion report for AAA, BB, CC and F.

6. In problem 5, assume that the scheduled receipts for component F consists of 1000 units in period 4, 1500 units in period 6, and 500 units in period 9. Develop the explosion report for F.

7. In problem 5, assume that F can be ordered according to POQ. Let the annual demand be 50,000 units, setup cost be $200, and holding cost equal $10. Develop the explosion report for F. Is the planned orders release different from that of problem 1. Why?

8. Rad Products, Inc., produces two types of AM/FM cassette players for cars. Both units are identical, but the mounting hardware and finishing trim differ. Model A fits intermediate and full-size cars, while Model B fits small sports cars.

   Rad Products configures the products in the following way. The chassis (radio/cassette unit) is assembled in South America and has a manufacturing lead time of 3 weeks. The mounting hardware is purchased from a local steel company and has a 2 week lead time. The finishing trim is purchased from a Japanese electronics firm with a warehouse in the United States. The finish trim has a lead time of 1 week. Final assembly time may be disregarded since the addition of the trim package and the mounting are performed by the customer.

   Rad Products supplies wholesalers and retailers who place specific orders for both the models up to 9 weeks in advance. These orders, together with enough additional units to satisfy the small number of individual sales, are summarized as follows:

	WEEK								
	1	2	3	4	5	6	7	8	9
Model A				400				600	
Model B					300				200

   There are currently 50 units of each type (of AM/FM player) on hand and no safety stock are required.

a)   Prepare the product structure trees.

b)   Prepare an MRP to meet the demand schedule. Specify the gross and net requirements and the planned order release and receipt periods for the AM/FM cassette players, Model A and B trim units, and the mounting hardware. Assume a LFL order policy.

9. In problem 8, suppose that there are two new orders for the cassette players. They consist of 500 units of Model A in period 12 and 300 units of model B in period 15. Develop the explosion report for all of the items.

10. In problem 9, suppose that the chasis is to be ordered according to lot sizes of 75 units. Further, suppose that there is a scheduled receipt of 100 chassis in period 4. Develop the explosion report for Chassis.

11. Cartoy Manufacturing produces plastic cars for children. The toy cars consist of the body plus 4 wheels. The body consists of a hood, top, base, and 2 sides. Six hundred cars are needed by week 10 and 300 cars are needed in week 12. Current inventory levels and lead times are given below.

a)   Draw a product structure tree for the toy car.

b)   Develop an MRP for the toy cars to meet the required demand. Give net and gross requirements, planned releases, and planned receipts. Assume a lot for lot order policy and assume that no safety stocks are required.

	ON HAND UNITS	LEAD TIME (WEEKS)
Toy Car	200	2
Body Assembly	250	2
Hood	100	2
Top	200	1
Base	350	1
Side	400	2
Wheels	1800	1

12. In problem 11, assume that a safety stock of 50 units is needed for every item. Develop the explosion report for Side and Wheels.

13. In problem 11, assume that there are 3 scheduled receipts for the Toy Car. They include 200 units in week 5, 300 units in week 6, and 200 units in week 7. Develop the explosion report for the Toy Car and compare it with that in problem 11.

14. Foots Shoe Maker produces footwear for women. They are in the process of introducing a new shoe to their vast collection. Before they can actually produce the new shoe, an MRP must be formulated. A pair of ladies shoes, Model 16-67, is made of two units of vinyl and 4 units of rubber. The vinyl is made from 3 units of chemical AA and 4 units of chemical BB. Chemical AB consists of 1 unit each of raw material A and B. The lead time for the purchase/fabrication of each unit is: final assembly takes 2 weeks; raw material A takes 1 week; raw material B takes 2 weeks; chemicals AA and AB each take 1 week; vinyl takes 1 week; and rubber takes 2 weeks. Assume that all components are ordered on a LFL basis.

Fifty pairs of model 16-67 are required in week 10 and 30 pairs are required in week 15.

a) Draw a product structure tree.

b) Develop an MRP planning schedule showing gross and net requirements, order release and receipt dates for the model 16-67, vinyl, and rubber elements.

CHAPTER 13

PROJECT MANAGEMENT

INTRODUCTION

The PERT/CPM technique for project planning is widely used in industry for one-time projects such as building a new plant, installing new machinery, doing a major maintenance job, or similar projects.

Projects that can take particular advantage of the PERT/CPM approach are those that consist of numerous activities where many of the activities must be done sequentially. Large numbers of sequential activities tend to create "bottlenecks" or critical paths. It is the objective of the PERT/CPM technique to identify the critical path and the activities that constitute that critical path. Management can then apply its efforts to alleviate any delays in the activities that are on the critical path and thus ensure that a project will be completed as scheduled.

The terms PERT and CPM have become generic terms for project scheduling. PERT stands for "project evaluation and review technique" and CPM stands for "critical path method." Although some authors ascribe the deterministic approach to one and the stochastic to the other, more common use in recent years is to describe the method as PERT/CPM or CPM/PERT.

ILLUSTRATION OF CPM/PERT TECHNIQUE

The technique can best be illustrated with an example. In Figure 13-1 is a network of activities and events. The lines with the arrows are the activities which take certain time periods (hours, days or weeks) to complete and the nodes that connect each activity are called events. Events are points in time and activities cover elapsed times. For instance, an event is the beginning or end of an activity and an activity takes a certain number of time units to be completed.

The illustrated PERT/CPM network has sixteen activities which are connected by twelve nodes or events. The figures shown alongside each activity are the elapsed times for that activity. No activity can begin until a preceding activity has been completed. For instance, activity 3-6 cannot be started until activity 1-3 has been completed. Similarly, activity 5-8 cannot be started until both activities 2-5 and 4-5 have been completed.

Based on the above precedence requirements we can determine the total elapsed times for each possible path through the network from the first event (node 1) to the last event (node 12).

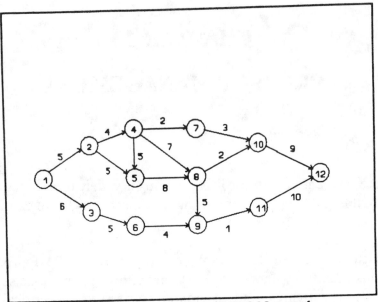

Figure 13-1: Illustrative PERT/CPM Network

The eight possible paths are listed in Table 13-1 with their respective total elapsed times. Note that the elapsed times range from 23 days to 38 days. However, the individual paths only consider precedence requirements along their own respective paths. Hence, the time along the shortest path is rather meaningless. What is important, however, is the time and the path that take the longest, because the longest path is the critical or "bottleneck" path. Any delays in the activities on the longest path will delay the entire project. Hence, the longest path determines the time required to complete the project

PERT THREE PARAMETER ESTIMATE

With three level time estimates it is necessary to estimate three time values for each activity in the CPM/PERT network. The three time values consist of an optimistic time value (shortest), a most likely time value (mode) and a pessimistic time value (longest). The most likely time value is one of the points of central tendency but is not necessarily the midpoint or the average of values.

The average time value can be estimated by the formula,

$$t_a = \frac{t_0 + 4t_m + t_p}{6}$$

where t_a is the average time value, t_o is the optimistic time value, t_m is the most likely time value, and t_p is the pessimistic time value.

314

Path through Network	Elapsed Time
1-3-6-9-11-12	26
1-2-4-7-10-12	23
1-2-4-8-10-12	27
1-2-4-8-9-11-12	32
1-2-4-5-8-10-12	33
1-2-4-5-8-9-11-12	38
1-2-5-8-10-12	29
1-2-5-8-9-11-12	34

Table 13-1: All Possible Paths through Network

We can also estimate the variance of each activity's time by the formula,

$$V = \frac{(t_p - t_0)^2}{36}$$

Suppose we have an activity with an optimistic time estimate of seven days, a most likely estimate of eight days and a pessimistic estimate of 13 days. Based on the above formulas the estimated average time will then amount to 8 2/3 days and the variance will be one day. Since the standard deviation is the square root of the variance, it will also amount to one day.

Suppose we have a CPM/PERT network with three level time estimates as shown in Table 13-2. Also note that each activity except the first two have predecessor activities which must precede them. From the information given in the table we can then construct a network as shown in Figure 13-2. For each activity we determine the average times and the variances as shown in Table 13-3. Based on the average time values we determine the critical path and find that it follows the events 1-2-4-6, and amounts to 22 days. The time along the critical path has a variance of 3.50.

Based on the law of large numbers we can now say that the sum of individual times of each activity along the critical path is approximately normally distributed because it is made up of the sum of three average time values. If we had 30 or more activities along the critical path we could say that the time along the critical path was exactly distributed according to the normal distribution. Similarly, the variance along the critical path is equal to the sum of the variances of each activity on the critical path. It amounts to 3.50. The standard deviation along the critical path then can be found by taking the square root of the sum of the variances along the critical path. It amounts to 1.87 days.

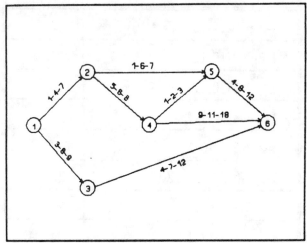

Figure 13-2: PERT Three Level Time Estimates

Activity	Optimistic Estimate	Most Likely Estimate	Pessimistic Estimate	Predecessor Activity
1-2	1	4	7	-
1-3	3	8	9	-
2-4	5	6	8	1-2
2-5	1	6	7	1-2
3-6	4	7	12	1-3
4-5	1	2	3	2-4
4-6	9	11	18	2-4
5-6	4	8	12	2-5, 4-5

Table 13-2: Tabular Array of Three Level Time Estimates

Since ± 1.96 standard deviations covers 95 percent of the area under the normal curve, we can say that the project portrayed by the network can be completed in a time period from 22 - 3.67 days to 22 + 3.67 days, or from 18.33 to 25.67 days with a 95 percent probability.

Activity	Average Time Estimate	Variance	Standard Deviation
1-2*	4.00	1.00	1.00
1-3	7.33	1.00	1.00
2-4*	6.17	0.25	0.50
2-5	5.33	1.00	1.00
3-6	7.33	1.78	1.33
4-5	2.00	0.10	0.33
4-6*	11.83	2.25	1.50
5-6	8.00	1.78	1.33
Total along CP	22.00	3.50**	

Table 13-3: Mean and Variance Time Estimates

*Activities on the critical path.
**Variance of 3.50 is sum of the variances of the activities along the critical path.

PROJECTS WITH TIME-COST TRADEOFFS

The applications of CPM/PERT above are based on normal time estimates. Normal time estimates are based on performing a project during normal work times and using normal work groups. Under certain circumstances it may be necessary to speed up a project. In that case, overtime may have to be instituted and/or work groups may have to be expanded. Speeding up, or crashing, a project is usually not as efficient as doing the project under normal circumstances. Therefore, if a project needs to be speeded up we need to investigate the time- cost trade-offs associated with the speeding up or crashing of the project.

Crashing a project can best be illustrated with an example. Suppose the project represented by the CPM/PERT network in Figure 13-2 has the crash-time- cost parameters as shown in Table 13-4. The normal cost is the cost for completing each activity in the normal time. The total crash cost includes additional costs incurred if the respective activity is speeded up by the maximum amount of time. The crash cost per day is the additional cost incurred if the activity is speeded up by one day. It is assumed that the cost of shortening an activity by the first day is the same as shortening an activity by another day or a third day. If crashing is not possible for an activity (beyond its normal time), the normal time and crash times are the same as well as the normal cost and crash cost.

The critical path for the network is 1-2-4-6 with a total length of 21 days. Hence, if we want to speed up the project by one day at a time we should speed up or crash activities along the critical path, so long as no other critical path develops as we shorten the critical path. In the next section, we will solve this problem using the computer and illustrate the complete crashed project.

Activity Number	Initial Node	Final Node	Normal Time	Crash Time	Normal Cost	Crash Cost
1	1	2	4	3	$100	$500
2	1	3	8	6	$200	$400
3	2	4	6	4	$300	$500
4	2	5	6	4	$400	$800
5	4	5	2	2	$500	$500
6	4	6	11	5	$100	$500
7	5	6	8	6	$400	$800
8	3	6	7	6	$200	$500

Table 13-4: Crash-Time-Cost Parameters

EXAMPLE 1 - DETERMINISTIC ACTIVITY TIMES (CPM)

Consider the CPM/PERT network of Figure 13-2 consisting of 6 events and 8 activities. Further, assume that the activities in this network are deterministic and activity times are the same as the most likely estimates (the activity times are presented in Table 13-4 in the Normal Time column).

The objective of the CPM/PERT program is to find the critical path and the time required to complete the project given the precedence requirements. In order to solve the above problem, select the Project Management program from the Main Menu. Once the Project Management program is loaded, move the pointer to the INPUT option. The Input option includes three sub-options, representing the three project management models as shown in Exhibit 1. Pull the pointer down to the deterministic sub-option and press the <ENTER> key.

```
Input   Edit   Print   File   Solve   Quit
    ┌────────────────────────────────────┐
    │  Deterministic Model (CPM)         │
    │  Probabilistic Model (PERT)        │
    │  CPM with time-cost tradeoff       │
    └────────────────────────────────────┘


        Problem title: CPM EXAMPLE

        Enter number of activities:  8

        Enter number of nodes:  6


    ┌──────────────────────────────────────┐
    │ Continue with activity times (Y/N)  Y │
    └──────────────────────────────────────┘
```

The program will then ask if you wish to continue to enter the network data. Press the <ENTER> key to select "Y". The spread sheet data entry screen is presented below.

```
                                                ┤READY├
 A1  'Activity
         A          B       C        D
 1    Activity    Begin    End    Activity
 2    Label       Node     Node     Time
 3    ARC1          1        2      4.00
 4    ARC2          1        3      8.00
 5    ARC3          2        4      6.00
 6    ARC4          2        5      6.00
 7    ARC5          3        6      7.00
 8    ARC6          4        5      2.00
 9    ARC7          4        6     11.00
 10   ARC8          5        6      8.00
```

After completing the spread sheet data entry, press the <F10> key to exit and keep the data. At this time you should get a hard copy print-out of the model and examine it carefully to ensure that the data is correct. Once the data appears correct, save the model on disk by selecting the "FILE" option and pulling the pointer down to the save sub-option. You will be asked to enter a DOS file name. Use a file name to represent the type of model and for the three character suffix use "PRO" to indicate that the file contains a project management problem. (Note that the use of "PRO" is not mandatory and is just for convenience.) Enter a file name and press the Enter key to save the model.

319

Now select the SOLVE option to solve the problem. You will be presented with the usual three option sub-menu representing the type of output device desired. Select the display output to obtain the solution on the screen as shown below.

```
                      Problem Title: CPM EXAMPLE
                          Event Status Report
                  Earliest        Latest        Slack
                    Time           Time          Time
        Event
        -----       --------      --------      ---------
         1            0.00          0.00          0.00
         2            4.00          4.00          0.00
         3            8.00         14.00          6.00
         4           10.00         10.00          0.00
         5           12.00         13.00          1.00
         6           21.00         21.00          0.00
```

```
                      Problem Title: CPM EXAMPLE
                         Activity Status Report
        Activity   Initial    Final      Slack
        number      node      node        time
        --------   -------   -------     --------
        ARC1*        1         2          0.00
        ARC2         1         3          6.00
        ARC3*        2         4          0.00
        ARC4         2         5          3.00
        ARC5         3         6          6.00
        ARC6         4         5          1.00
        ARC7*        4         6          0.00
        ARC8         5         6          1.00

          Project completion time is :  21

            * -> Activity is on critical path(s)
```

As seen from the above output reports, the critical path consists of the three activities identified as arc 1, arc 3, and arc 7 with a total length of 21 days. The path is identified by activities marked with a star "*". The star is placed next to the associated activity.

EXAMPLE 2 - PERT THREE ESTIMATE PROJECT

Consider the network of Figure 13-2 again. Now suppose that the activity times are probabilistic and have been estimated by the three estimates as shown in Table 13-2. In order to solve this PERT three-estimate problem, select the Project Management program from the Main Menu. Move the pointer to the INPUT option, pull the pointer down to the second sub-option and press the Enter key. The program will ask you to enter the relevant parameters as shown below.

```
Problem title: PERT EXAMPLE

Enter number of activities:  8

Enter number of nodes:  6

┌─────────────────────────────────────────┐
│ Continue with activity times (Y/N) Y     │
└─────────────────────────────────────────┘
```

```
                                              ┤READY├
A1 'Activity
          A        B       C       D       E       F
1     Activity  Begin   End     Best    Modal   Worst
2     Label     Node    Node    Time    Time    Time
3     ARC1       1       2      1.00    4.00    7.00
4     ARC2       1       3      3.00    8.00    9.00
5     ARC3       2       4      5.00    6.00    8.00
6     ARC4       2       5      1.00    6.00    7.00
7     ARC5       3       6      4.00    7.00   12.00
8     ARC6       4       5      1.00    2.00    3.00
9     ARC7       4       6      9.00   11.00   18.00
10    ARC8       5       6      4.00    8.00   12.00
```

Now select the SOLVE option to solve the problem. You will be presented with the usual three option sub-menu representing the type of output device desired. Select the Display Output to obtain the solution on the screen as shown below.

```
Problem title: PERT EXAMPLE

Enter number of activities:  8

Enter number of nodes:  6


┌─────────────────────────────────────────────────────┐
│ Report means and standard deviations (Y/N) Y         │
└─────────────────────────────────────────────────────┘
```

```
                    Problem Title: PERT EXAMPLE

    Activity       Mean       St. Dev.
    --------     --------     --------
    ARC1           4.00         1.00
    ARC2           7.33         1.00
    ARC3           6.17         0.50
    ARC4           5.33         1.00
    ARC5           7.33         1.33
    ARC6           2.00         0.33
    ARC7          11.83         1.50
    ARC8           8.00         1.33
```

As seen from the above output reports, upon request, the program will report the mean and standard deviation for each activity. It then solves the problem using the means as the activity times. For Example 2, the critical path consists of activities 1, 3, and 7 with an average project completion time of 22 days. The output report consists of both the "Event Status Report" and the "Activity Status Report." The event status report indicates which events are critical. The critical events have zero slack time, i.e., their earliest times and latest times are the same (see Exhibit 7). The activity status report indicates which activities are on the critical path and also reports the project completion time.

```
                    Problem Title: PERT EXAMPLE
                       Event Status Report
                  Earliest        Latest          Slack
        Event       Time           Time            Time
        -----     --------       --------        ---------
          1         0.00           0.00            0.00
          2         4.00           4.00            0.00
          3         7.33          14.67            7.33
          4        10.17          10.17            0.00
          5        12.17          14.00            1.83
          6        22.00          22.00            0.00
```

```
                    Problem Title: PERT EXAMPLE
                      Activity Status Report
        Activity  Initial    Final      Slack
        number     node       node       time
        --------  -------    -------    --------
        ARC1*       1          2         0.00
        ARC2        1          3         7.33
        ARC3*       2          4         0.00
        ARC4        2          5         4.67
        ARC5        3          6         7.33
        ARC6        4          5         1.83
        ARC7*       4          6         0.00
        ARC8        5          6         1.83


        Expected project completion time is :   22.00

            * -> Activity is on critical path(s)
```

EXAMPLE 3 - TIME-COST TRADEOFF EXAMPLE

This example involves a project management problem in which time cost tradeoffs are possible. The network structure of Figure 13-2 will be used to illustrate the method. The normal times, crash times, normal costs, and crash costs are presented in Table 13-4. As before, select the INPUT option and pull the pointer down to the Time Cost tradeoff sub-option. Press the <ENTER> key to begin the data entry process as shown below.

```
Problem title: TIME-COST TRADEOFF


Enter number of activities:  8

Enter number of nodes:  6



┌──────────────────────────────────────┐
│ Continue with activity times (Y/N) Y │
└──────────────────────────────────────┘
```

Press the <ENTER> key to proceed with the spread sheet data entry. Below, the completed input data screen is shown.

```
                                                    ╡READY╞
A1 'Activity
        A       B       C       D       E       F       G
1   Activity Begin   End     Normal  Crash   Normal  Crash
2   Label    Node    Node    Time    Time    Cost    Cost
3   ARC1       1       2      4.00    3.00    100.00  500.00
4   ARC2       1       3      8.00    6.00    200.00  400.00
5   ARC3       2       4      6.00    4.00    300.00  500.00
6   ARC4       2       5      6.00    4.00    400.00  800.00
7   ARC5       4       5      2.00    2.00    500.00  500.00
8   ARC6       4       6     11.00    5.00    100.00  500.00
9   ARC7       5       6      8.00    6.00    400.00  800.00
10  ARC8       3       6      7.00    6.00    200.00  500.00
```

If you wish to change the activities' label, use the spread sheet editor to make changes as desired. Once the input data is completed, press <F10> to accept the data and exit from the spread sheet editor.

You are now ready to solve the problem. Move the pointer to the SOLVE option and select the Display Output sub-option. Press the <ENTER> key to proceed with solving the problem. The output screens are shown below.

```
+-------------------------------------------------------------+
|                                                             |
|            Problem Title: TIME-COST TRADEOFF                |
|                                                             |
|                                                             |
|                                                             |
|          +----------------------------------------+         |
|          |  Report crash costs per day (Y/N) Y    |         |
|          +----------------------------------------+         |
|                                                             |
+-------------------------------------------------------------+
```

The first screen (above) shows a query from the program to display the cost of crashing per day for each arc. Press <Y> to obtain this information as shown below.

```
+----------------------------------------------------------------------+
|                                                                      |
|                 Problem Title: TIME-COST TRADEOFF                    |
|                  Crash Cost Per Activity Report                      |
|     Activity   Initial   Final    Normal     Crash     Crash Cost    |
|     number     node      node     time       time      Per  Day      |
|     --------   -------   -----    ------     -----      ----------    |
|     ARC1       1         2        4          3          400.00        |
|     ARC2       1         3        8          6          100.00        |
|     ARC3       2         4        6          4          100.00        |
|     ARC4       2         5        6          4          200.00        |
|     ARC5       4         5        2          2          Infinity      |
|     ARC6       4         6        11         5          66.67         |
|     ARC7       5         6        8          6          200.00        |
|     ARC8       3         6        7          6          300.00        |
|                                                                      |
+----------------------------------------------------------------------+
```

As seen from the above report, the program presents information relating to the cost of crashing each activity. For example, the activity corresponding to ARC4 can be crashed from 6 days (normal time) to 4 days (crash time) at a cost of $200 per day. Note that for an activity (arc) which cannot be crashed, or its duration shortened, the crash cost per day is infinite (e.g., ARC5). At this point, press the <ENTER> key to continue with the solution process as described below.

```
              Problem Title: TIME-COST TRADEOFF

          * * *  Activities on critical path(s) * * *

 Activity  Initial   Final    Normal    Activity  Crash    Crash
  label     node     node      time       time     time     Cost
 --------  -------   -----    ------    --------   -----   -------
 ARC1       1         2         4.0        3.0      1.0     400.00
 ARC2       1         3         8.0        8.0      0.0       0.00
 ARC3       2         4         6.0        4.0      2.0     200.00
 ARC4       2         5         6.0        6.0      0.0       0.00
 ARC5       4         5         2.0        2.0      0.0       0.00
 ARC6       4         6        11.0        8.0      3.0     200.00
 ARC7       5         6         8.0        6.0      2.0     400.00
 ARC8       3         6         7.0        7.0      0.0       0.00
```

The program will first report the set of activities which are critical (a delay in any one of these activities will delay the project completion time). It also reports the normal time, activity time, crash time, and crash cost for each activity. The activity time is the current amount of time (after crashing) that each activity requires. The crash time is the amount of time that each activity has been crashed (or shortened), and the activity cost is the total cost of crashing that activity. For example, activity ARC7 has been crashed from a normal time of 11 days to 8 days (crashed 3 days) at a cost of about $67 per day for a total of $200.

```
┌─────────────────────────────────────────────────────────────────┐
│                                                                   │
│              Problem Title: TIME-COST TRADEOFF                     │
│                                                                   │
│         Optimal time-cost trade off has been achieved             │
│                                                                   │
│    Normal time :  21                                              │
│                                                                   │
│    Crash  time :  6                                               │
│                                                                   │
│    Project completion time :  15                                  │
│                                                                   │
│    Normal cost :     $2200.00                                     │
│                                                                   │
│    Crash  cost :     $1200.00                                     │
│                                                                   │
│    Total cost :      $3400.00                                     │
│                                                                   │
└─────────────────────────────────────────────────────────────────┘
```

The program will then proceed by reporting the total normal time (project completion time in absence of crashing), the total crash time, project completion time (after crashing), and the associated costs. For this solved example, the normal time is 21 days, the project has been crashed by 6 days at a cost of $1200. Total normal cost is $2200; adding the crash cost, the total project cost is $3400. These results indicate that if you decide to complete the project at its normal time of 21 days, it will cost $2200. But if you decide to complete the project earlier, say by 6 days, it will cost an extra $1200.

As with the earlier two models, the computer will display reports of the event status as well as activity status as shown below.

```
┌─────────────────────────────────────────────────────────────────┐
│                    Event Status Report                            │
│              Earliest        Latest          Slack                │
│    Event      Time           Time            Time                 │
│    -----      --------       --------        ---------            │
│     1          0.00           0.00            0.00                 │
│     2          3.00           3.00            0.00                 │
│     3          8.00           8.00            0.00                 │
│     4          7.00           7.00            0.00                 │
│     5          9.00           9.00            0.00                 │
│     6         15.00          15.00            0.00                 │
│                                                                   │
└─────────────────────────────────────────────────────────────────┘
```

```
                      Problem Title: TIME-COST TRADEOFF
                         Activity Status Report
        Activity    Initial    Final    Slack
        number       node      node     time
        --------    -------    -------  --------
        ARC1*         1          2        0.00
        ARC2*         1          3        0.00
        ARC3*         2          4        0.00
        ARC4*         2          5        0.00
        ARC5*         4          5        0.00
        ARC6*         4          6        0.00
        ARC7*         5          6        0.00
        ARC8*         3          6        0.00


            * -> Activity is on critical path(s)
```

As seen from the above results, all activities are marked as critical (or being on some critical path). The reason is that many activities have been crashed to their shortest possible times. This has created multiple critical paths through the network and has caused every activity to be critical. You should use the above data to verify that in fact all paths from start to finish have the same length. Use the activity times reported earlier to determine the length of each path.

PROBLEMS

1. Find the critical path and the critical path time using the CPM/PERT computer program for the following problem.

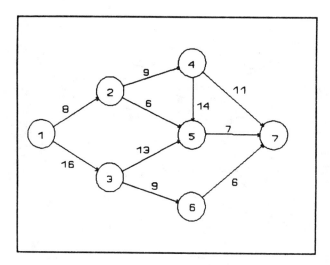

2. Develop the network diagram for the CPM/PERT problem listed below in tabular format.

		Time Estimates		
Activity	Optimistic	Most Likely	Pessimistic	Predecessor Activity
1	5	9	11	-
2	1	2	4	-
3	6	8	9	1
4	4	5	10	1
5	7	8	11	2
6	8	10	15	4
7	9	11	16	3
8	10	15	16	3
9	9	13	16	6
10	5	8	11	8

3. Based on the CPM/PERT network you developed in the above problem, solve the problem using the computer solution procedure.

4. Use the three level time estimates procedure to run the CPM/PERT network shown below.

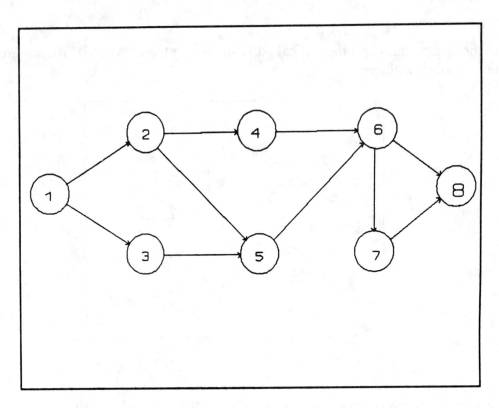

Time Estimates

Activity	Optimistic	Most Likely	Pessimistic
1-2	5	8	9
1-3	11	12	16
2-4	6	9	10
2-5	2	3	4
3-5	7	14	16
4-6	8	9	17
5-6	6	7	8
6-7	8	9	9
6-8	14	15	19
7-8	10	15	16

5. Crash the project in problem 1 with the following crash-time-cost parameters. Crash costs are in addition to normal costs.

Activity	Normal Time	Crash Time	Normal Cost	Total Crash Cost	Crash Cost/ Day
1-2	8	6	$750	$100	$50
1-3	16	13	810	105	35
2-4	9	8	940	45	45
2-5	6	5	635	15	15
3-5	13	11	495	110	55
3-6	9	7	580	40	20
4-5	14	11	875	165	55
4-7	11	11	695	-	-
5-7	7	6	940	40	40
6-7	6	6	710	-	-

6. Develop the CPM/PERT Network for the following deterministic problem and then run the computer solution using the project crashing module. Crash costs are in addtion to normal costs.

Activity	Normal Time	Crash Time	Normal Cost	Total Crash Cost	Crash Cost/ Day
1-2	5	3	$195	$30	$15
1-3	7	6	180	55	55
1-4	8	8	360	-	-
2-5	3	3	345	-	-
2-6	6	5	310	40	40
3-6	4	4	145	-	-
3-7	12	10	460	70	35
4-7	11	8	510	75	25
4-8	4	3	340	10	10
5-9	3	3	135	-	-
6-9	2	2	485	-	-
6-11	1	1	910	-	-
7-10	9	7	415	60	30
8-10	8	7	390	45	45
9-11	7	4	210	150	50
10-11	6	3	265	15	5

7. TROPIC OIL WELL DRILLERS

Tropic Oil Well Drillers struck oil on the latest well they drilled. You have been asked to develop a network and related PERT analysis including a critical path. The project at hand is to mount a pumping unit on the well and install the necessary pipe line to the flow station in order to bring the well into production. For simplicity's sake assume that all tasks go on around the clock. The project can commence with three activities proceeding simultaneously:

a) The concrete slab will be poured at the well location. The supervisor of this activity estimates that it will probably take 11 hours. It may take as little as 9 hours.

b) The pumping unit will be ordered. Since this is done by phone, the time required is negligible (zero). In any event it should not take over an hour.

c) The field gang can commence to cut away the jungle between the low station and the well location. Judging from the distance and trouble involved, this should take 30 hours. With luck as little as 20 hours, but definitely not more than 40 hours.

After the slab has been poured, it should take about 24 hours to set and cure. Since the type of cement is well known and weather conditions in this area do not vary much, it is unlikely that there will be much change in this estimate.

The supply house believes that if everything goes right they can get the unit on location in as little as 3 hours after receiving the order. On the other hand, the road is not in good condition and it may take as much as 9 hours, especially if they have trouble fording the river. Better use 9 hours as the most likely estimate.

Once the slab is in and cured and the unit delivered, a crew can mount the unit on the slab. This job should take 5 hours. If the crew works rapidly it may take only 4 hours. Similar jobs have taken as long as 12 hours.

After the unit is installed, the electrical gang can install the electric motor on the base. At the same time that the electrical gang is working, following installation of the unit, a production crew can install the pumping unit rods. The electrical boss estimates; pessimistic, 5 hours; realistic, 4 hours; optimistic, 3 hours. The production crew says 8 hours likely, 4 hours hopefully and maybe as long as 18 hours.

Meanwhile, back at the jungle trail, as soon as the right of way is cut, a line crew from the electric shop can run wire from a substation at the flow station to the well location at the same time as a pipe line gang is running the necessary flow line. The electric line should take 10 hours to run, as much as 12 hours and as little as 8 hours. The flow line, which is threaded and coupled, should not take too much longer, say 11 hours probable with a maximum of 14 and a minimum of 10 hours.

When the electric motor has been installed and the hot line run from the substation to the location, it will be possible to tie in and test the electric motor. This operation will take an hour, neither more nor less.

As soon as the pumping unit rods and the flow line have been installed from station to location, the well head can be connected to the flow line. This should take about an hour. It won't take less than that and may take as long as 4 hours.

As soon as the electric motor is tested and the well head connected, two final activities may be accomplished simultaneously:

a) On location, the unit must be belted up and the subsurface pump tested. This will likely take 4 hours, may take as little as 1 hour and as much as 10 hours.

b) At the same time, at the flow station, the proper valves must be opened to produce the well to the test bank. Best guess on this is 1 hour. If a pumper can be reached immediately it may take almost no time. On the other hand, it might take 2 hours.

When these tasks are done, the project may be considered complete. Complete the following activities:

1. Compute the expected time and variance for each activity.
2. Draw the arrow diagram; number each event.
3. Determine the critical path(s).
4. Determine the expected time and variance for the completion of the entire project.
5. What is the probability that the job will be complete within 54 hours?

8.   Mr. Smith decided to have his own house built. To complete this project he had analyzed the following activities and had time values estimated for these activities. The first activity consisted of obtaining a loan which included enlisting the services of a legal advisor. He estimated that this would take about 5 weeks, could take as long as 8 weeks but might also be accomplished in 2 weeks.

The next two activities could be done simultaneously. These are purchasing a lot on which to build the house and obtaining an architectural plan and related blueprints. The first activity was expected to take 6 weeks, could take as little as 1 week but might take as long as 11 weeks. The second activity was expected to take at least 6 weeks, possibly 12 weeks, but most likely 9 weeks.

Upon completing the previous two activities, the basement can be excavated. This was expected to take two weeks, no more or less. After the excavation, the basement walls and foundation could be poured, which was expected to take anywhere from 1 to 3 weeks but most likely 2 weeks.

The woodwork activity was next; it was expected to take about 7 weeks, no more or less. The electrical and plumbing work would occur during the foundation and woodwork activity and was not considered part of the network.

Finishing and painting was expected to take 6 weeks, but because of the unpredictability of the weather it would probably take 9 weeks and could take as long as 12 weeks.

   a)   Draw a PERT network with expected time values and standard deviations.
   b)   What is the expected time required for completing the project?
   c)   What is the probability that the project will be completed in 33 weeks or less?

9.   General Hospital Supply Company has received a special order for a number of units of a custom-made product that consists of 2 components, A and B. The product is a non-standard product that the company has never produced before, and the scheduling department has determined that the application of CPM is warranted. A team of manufacturing engineers has prepared the following table:

ACTIVITY	DESCRIPTION	PREDECESSOR	TIME
A	Plan Production	--	6
B	Procure Materials for A	A	15
C	Manufacture Part A	B	10
D	Procure Materials for B	A	16
E	Manufacture Part B	D	11
F	Assemble Parts A & B	C,E	5
G	Inspect Parts	F	3
H	Completed	G	0

   a) Develop a network for General Hospital Supply Company.
   b) State the project completion time and the critical path.

334

10. Trent Leasing Company has employed the services of Serchware Unlimited, a computer software company, to develop an information system to keep leasing and maintenance records on its fleet of moving vans. Two Trent employees and two Serchware employees have formed a project team to decide what needs to be done. They have come up with the following tasks and their estimated optimistic, most likely, and pessimistic times:

ACTIVITY	PREDECESSOR	O	M	P
1. Basic Design	--	3	4	6
2. Detail Design A	1	4	5	7
3. Detail Design B	1	7	9	12
4. Code A	2	6	7	10
5. Code B	3	7	9	11
6. Detail Design C	3	5	6	7
7. Test A & B	4,5	6	7	10
8. Code C	6	3	4	5
9. Test C	4,5,8	2	4	6
10. Documentation	4,5,8	5	6	9
11. Integrate System	7,9	3	4	6
12. Test System	11	6	10	12

   a) Draw the appropriate network based on the above data.

   b) Give the earliest time, latest time, and slack time for each event.

   c) What is the critical path and the project completion time that Trent can expect from Serchware?

11. The H.B. Laboratory Company has manufactured chemistry supplies for many years. Recently, a member of the company's new product research team submitted a report suggesting that the company manufacture a new non-breakable test tube that could withstand extreme heat and cold. Because no other manufacturer has such a product, management hoped that the new product could be manufactured at a reasonable cost.

    H.B. Laboratory's top management would like to initiate a project to study the feasibility of this idea. The end result of the feasibility study would be a report recommending the appropriate action to be taken on the test tube. The project manager has identified a list of activities and a range of times necessary to complete each activity. The information is given below.

   a) Develop a PERT/CPM analysis for this project. Include a project network, calculation of expected times, critical activities, and the expected project completion time.

   b) Compute the probabilities for completing the project by weeks 23, 27, and 29.

ACTIVITY	PREDECESSOR	O	M	P
1. R&D Product Design	--	4	8	12
2. Plan Market Research	--	3	3.5	7
3. Manufacturing Study	1	3	4	5
4. Build Prototype	1	7	8	15
5. Prepare Market Survey	1	3	4	5
6. Develop Cost Estimates	3	3.5	4	4.5
7. Prelim. Product Tests	4	3.5	5	6.5
8. Market Survey	2,5	5.5	6.5	10.5
9. Price & Forecast Report	8	2	3	4
10. Final Report	6,7,9	2	3	4

12. Suppose that you are going to construct a small storeroom with an office. The structure will be used to store computer equipment and will have a large air conditioning system placed in the attic of the storeroom. The equipment cannot be installed until the steel roof frame is in place, but must be installed before the roof is built. The roof frame is to extend down over the top of the exterior cement wall and cannot be installed until the wall is complete. Suppose also that the company has decided that it will not put the asphalt paving around the storeroom until the fence has been erected and the exterior wall of the storeroom is completed. The times for these stages and corresponding activities are given below.

a)   Develop an appropriate network.
b)   Give project completion time and critical path.

STAGE	TIME	PREDECESSOR
1. Install Air Conditioning		
Activities:		
a. Install Electric	7	
b. Install A.C.	3	Install Electric
2. Construct Roof Frame		
Activities:		
a. Dig Floor	2	
b. Pour Floor	3	Dig Floor
c. Erect Steel	4	Pour Floor
3. Place Roof On		
Activities:		
a. Construct Roof	10	
4. Build Exterior Wall		
Activities:		
a. Put Up Walls	5	
5. Pave Around Storeroom		
Activities:		
a. Lay Gravel	2	
b. Pour Asphalt	3	Lay Gravel
c. Roll Asphalt	2	Pour Asphalt
6. Erect Fence		
Activities:		
a. Put Support Posts In	7	
b. Install Fence Panels	6	Put Support Posts In

CHAPTER 14

QUALITY ASSURANCE

INTRODUCTION

Two quality control models will be presented in this chapter. The first model is the acceptance sampling model and the second is the process control model.

When shipments or large numbers of pieces are received by a firm from a supplier it is common to randomly select a number of pieces from the shipment (lot) and inspect the sampled pieces. If more than a specified number of the sampled pieces are defective the entire shipment or lot is rejected, otherwise the lot is accepted. Random sampling reduces the cost of inspection but it does not provide full assurance that the percentage of defectives in the inspected random sample is similar to the percentage of defectives in the entire lot. The acceptance sampling model described in detail below provides considerable information on how closely and under which conditions the results of the random sampling process represent the actual condition of the entire lot.

Process quality control, also called process control, is a statistical sampling process which selects at predetermined frequencies samples from the process output and inspects the pieces in the sample to ensure that they are within process specifications. The process specifications are measured in quantitative terms such as grams of weight, millimeters in diameter, etc. The number of pieces in each sample also is specified beforehand. On the basis of several samples the computer then determines the grand mean of the dimensions of the process output as well as the upper control limit (UCL) and the lower control limit (LCL) of the process mean dimension. Any future sample means then are considered to be acceptable, if their dimensions fall within the upper and lower control limits.

Control charts are also used when the process characteristic is counted, as in number of defective in a batch, rather than measured. The control charts we use for counting number of defective are called attribute control charts. There are two types of attribute control charts, one for the number of defective items in a sample, called the p-chart, and one for the number of defects in a composite unit such as number of spelling errors on a page. This type of control chart we call a c-chart.

Below we shall describe and illustrate both the acceptance sampling and the process control models in more detail.

ACCEPTANCE SAMPLING

The acceptance sampling model provides information on the probability of accepting a lot or shipment as a function of the actual percent or fraction of defectives in the lot for those cases where the number of pieces in the lot (N), the number of pieces in the sample (n) and the maximum number of allowable defective pieces in the sample (c) are specified. That is, let X be the number of defectives in a sample of size n. Then X has a Binomial distribution with parameters n and p, where p is the fraction of defectives. The probability of having x defectives is given as,

$$P[X = x] = \binom{n}{x} p^x (1 - p)^{n-x} \quad x=0,1,...,n$$

To find the probability of having c or fewer defectives in the sample, add P[X = x] for x from 0 to c,

$$P[X \leq c] = \sum_{x=0}^{c} P[X = x] = \sum_{x=0}^{c} \binom{n}{x} p^x (1-p)^{n-x}$$

Based on the above information the quality control analyst can then plot the probability of accepting a lot as a function of the actual percent or fraction of defectives in the lot. The resulting graph which connects the plotted points is called the operating characteristic (OC) curve. Figure 14-1 represents the OC curve for N = 5000, n = 15, and c = 2.Note that the plotted points are spaced .05 fractions or the equivalent 5 percentage points apart. Other spacings of the fraction of defectives are of course also possible.

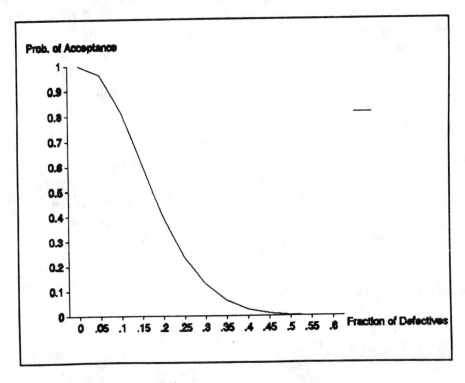

Figure 14-1: Operating Characteristic Curve

338

There are several underlying assumptions that must be satisfied before the operating characteristic curve can be applied. First, the probability of any one item being defective must be independent of any other item being defective. Secondly, the probability calculations of small samples are calculated by using the Binomial probability distribution (as discussed above) while for larger samples (over 20 pieces) the Poison approximation to the Binomial is utilized. That is, let μ = np be the expected number of defectives. Then the probability of x defectives, in a sample of size n, is approximated by,

$$P[X - x] - \frac{\mu^x e^{-\mu}}{x!}$$

The probability of having c or fewer defectives is determined in a similar form to that of the Binomial equation. That is,

$$P[X \le c] - \sum_{x-0}^{c} P[X - x] - \sum_{x-0}^{c} \frac{\mu^x e^{-\mu}}{x!}$$

Utilizing the operating characteristic curve you will discover that the curve will be generally lowered if, (1) the sample size (n) is increased; and (2) the maximum number of allowed defective pieces (c) is decreased. Lowering the curve, of course, means that the probability of acceptance will be reduced for a given fraction of defectives in the entire lot. Similarly, the operating characteristic curve can also be raised by doing the opposite of what was done above.

To determine what is the most desirable operating characteristic curve is not an easy task. However, from the above description and with the use of the computer model you can quickly generate any number of different operating characteristic curves.

To approximate the desirable operating characteristic curve we need to specify what is an acceptable fraction of defectives in a lot. This acceptable level is called the acceptable quality level (AQL). It is shown on Figure 14-2 and is .06 or 6 percent. Connecting the AQL with the OC curve reveals that the Type I error (α) is 10 percent. The Type I error is the probability of rejecting an acceptable lot, that is, a lot which has less than 6 percent of defectives.

It is also necessary to specify a fraction of defectives in a lot beyond which it is totally unacceptable. This fraction is called the lot tolerance percent defective (LTPD), a term coined by statistical quality control people but which is not very descriptive. A more descriptive term would be "unacceptable quality level." However, we shall stay with common practice and use the LTPD term. In the example on Figure 14-2 it is .27 or 27 percent. Connecting the LTPD with the OC curve reveals the type II error (β) which is 20 percent. The type II error is the probability of accepting an unacceptable lot, that is a lot which has more than 27 percent of defectives.

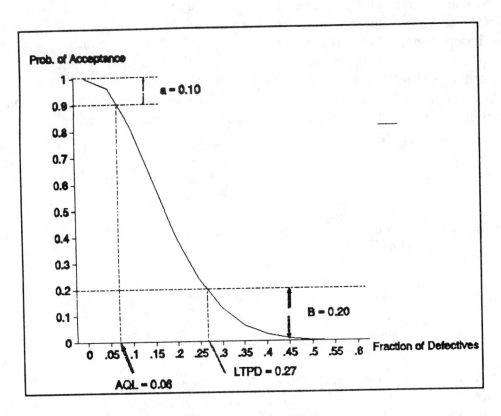

Notes: AQL = Acceptance Quality Level
LTPD = Lot Tolerance Percent Defective

Figure 14-2: Defining Type I (α) and Type II (β) Errors

With the above information we can specify such parameters as acceptable quality level (AQL) and lot tolerance percent defective (LTPD) or parameters for type I error (α) and type II error (β). By varying the sample size (n) and/or the maximum number of defectives allowed in a sample (c) the above specifications can be approximated. Experimentation with the computer model will reveal that relatively large samples are required if both AQL and LTPD are set at low values.

Another useful curve that can be constructed from the data generated for the OC curve is the average outgoing quality (AOQ) of the inspected lots measured in terms of fraction of defectives. The average outgoing quality is found by multiplying the fraction defective of the lot times the probability of acceptance of the lot. The computer model provides the results for each specific increment of the lot fraction defective.

Plotting the calculated values of the AOQ produces the AOQ curve as shown in Figure 14-3. Note that the AOQ values are based on the previous examples. The AOQ curve provides the maximum average outgoing quality level as a function of the lot fraction defective for a specific sampling plan. A sampling plan is a specification of the sample size (n) and the allowed number of defectives (c) in a sample.

340

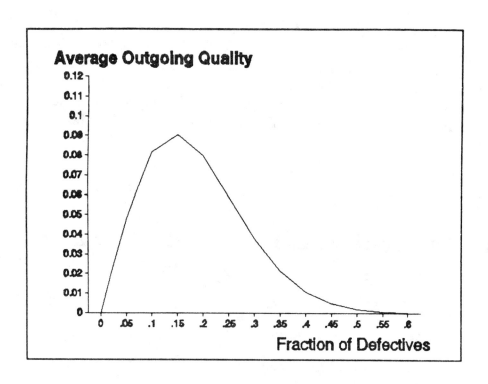

Figure 14-3: Average Outgoing Quality Curve

PROCESS CONTROL OF QUALITY

In process control of quality the main concern is that the process continues unchanged. The statistical control method of process control is designed to identify if the process changes, i.e., goes out of control. For instance, if a box filling process is designed to fill a box so that it contains on average 301 grams and if it is able to do that when the box filling equipment is performing satisfactorily, i.e., is under control, then a statistical control process can be developed to identify when the process changes and either under-fills or overfills the boxes.

In process control we therefore want to identify when a change occurs in the process. To identify a change in the process we take small samples of say 4 or 5 pieces (boxes), calculate the mean of the measurement we are controlling and then compare that mean value with the means of previous samples. It is also common practice to plot the means on a chart which is called a process or quality control chart. A control chart for means has an upper value called the upper control limit (UCL) and a lower value, called the lower control limit (LCL). If the calculated mean of the sample falls within the two limits, that is between the LCL and the UCL then the process is considered to be under control. If it falls outside the limits then we may want to investigate if the process has changed and needs to be adjusted.

To illustrate how the upper and lower control limits are estimated we shall take five samples of five pieces with measurements or observations as shown in Table 14-1. For each sample we calculate the sample mean and record the sample range. For the 25 pieces we also determine the grand mean as shown, and for the five samples we also determine the mean of the range as shown. The next step is to calculate the standard deviation of the sample means which is generally referred to as the standard error of the mean. This standard error will then be used as an estimate of the process standard error. The estimated standard error amounts to 1.57, the grand mean is 58.8, and the range mean is 9.8.

Sample	Observations of Sample Pieces					Total	Sample Mean	Range
1	59	58	57	54	56	284	56.8	5
2	56	52	60	57	55	280	56.0	8
3	58	74	52	79	71	334	66.8	27
4	62	58	59	58	57	294	58.8	5
5	54	55	54	58	57	278	55.6	4
Aggregate Total or Mean						1470	58.8	9.8

Table 14-1: Illustration of Determining Sample Means and Grand Mean

To determine the upper control limits for the sample mean we shall take the grand mean and add to it two standard errors. For the lower control limits of the sample mean we shall take the grand mean and subtract two standard errors. Sample mean control limits with two standard errors will cover slightly over 95 percent of measurements if the process remains in control. If a sample mean falls outside of the control limits there is thus less than a five percent chance that the process is still in control.

For the illustration the control limits then are UCL = 68.08, and LCL = 49.52. In Figure 14-4 the two control limits and the grand mean are plotted on the process control chart and future sample means can be plotted on it for future samples.

When the process variation (standard deviation of the mean) is not available, the mean range (referred to as R-BAR), is used to estimate the variability in sample mean. The equations for the control limits are given as,

$$LCL_{\bar{x}} - M - A_2\bar{R}$$
$$UCL_{\bar{x}} - M + A_2\bar{R}$$

where M is the grand mean and values of A_2 are tabulated in Grant[1].

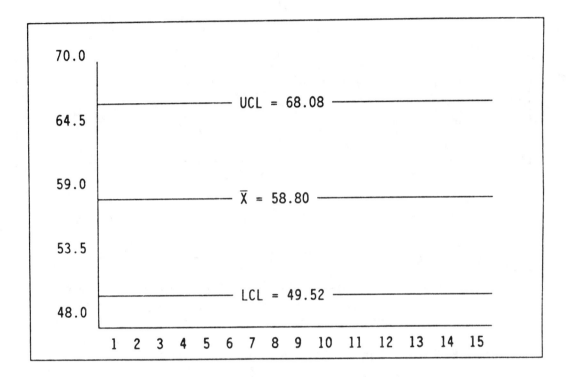

Figure 14-4: Process Control Chart for Sample Means

We can also develop a sample range control chart as shown on Figure 14-5. The mean of the sample range is 9.8. The upper and lower control limits are determined by an interval look up chart which is based on established and accepted quality control procedures (see for example Grant, *et al*). For a sample size of five observations the lower control limit for the range is zero and the upper control limit is based on multiplying the mean of the sample range by 2.11, which then amounts to 20.67. Both the upper and lower control limits of the sample range are based on three standard errors. You can of course also specify other values for the number of standard errors.

PROCESS CONTROL FOR ATTRIBUTES

To determine the control charts for number of defectives in a sample we use the p-chart. Similarly, to control numbers of defects on an assembly, component or system we

---

[1]E. L. Grant and R. Leavenworth, *Statistical Quality Control* (New York: McGraw-Hill, 1964).

use the c-chart.

The theoretical basis for the p-chart is the binomial distribution. However, for large sample sizes the normal distribution is used as an approximation. The p-chart is constructed in the same way as the mean process control chart with both upper and lower control limits.

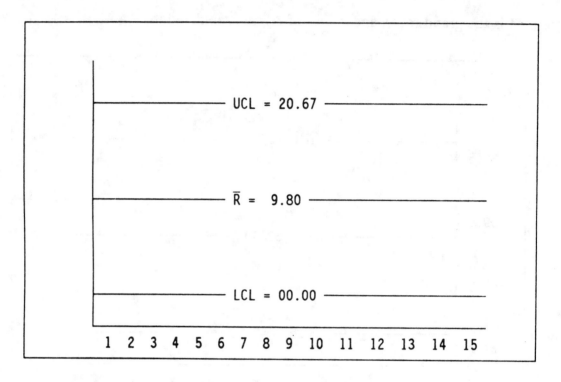

Figure 14-5: Process Control Chart for Sample Ranges

The grand mean or center line on a p-chart is the average of the fraction defectives in the samples on which the center line, p, is based. The standard error of the sampling distribution can be estimated using the formula,

$$\sigma_p = \sqrt{\frac{\bar{p}(1 - \bar{p})}{n}}$$

Upper and lower control limits can then be determined for three standard errors by the formulas,

$$UCL = \bar{p} + 3\sigma_p$$
$$LCL = \bar{p} - 3\sigma_p$$

For example, consider the data presented in Table 14-2. The entries represent the number of defectives in samples of size 10. As seen from the table, the mean number of

344

defectives is 0.133 and the standard error of the mean is 0.107. Using 95% percent control limits, the lower control limit is 0 (the control limit is actually negative but has been replaced with 0) anf the upper control limit is 0.344.

Sample	1	2	3	4	5	6	7	8	9	10	11	12	Mean	STDV
Defective	2	1	3	0	1	2	1	0	2	1	0	3	0.133	0.107

Table 14-2: Number of Defectives for Samples of Size 10

The same procedure as above is used to determine upper and lower control limits for the c-chart. The underlying distribution for the c-chart is the Poisson distribution. It assumes that number of defects occur over some continuous region. The mean number of defects per unit, i.e. spelling errors per page, is then identified as c and the standard error is $\sqrt{c}$. Upper and lower control limits can then be determined for two standard errors by the formulas:

$$UCL - \bar{c} + 2\sqrt{\bar{c}}$$
$$LCL - \bar{c} - 2\sqrt{\bar{c}}$$

For example, consider the data presented in Table 14-3. The entries represent the number of defects per unit. As seen from the table, the mean number of defects is 5.4 and the standard error of the mean is 2.32. Using 3 sigma control limits, the lower control limit is 0 and the upper control limit is 12.37.

Sample	1	2	3	4	5	6	7	8	9	10	11	12	13	14	15	Mean	STDV
Defects	5	4	7	9	2	8	2	5	7	7	8	3	4	6	4	5.4	2.3

Table 14-3: Number of Defects Per Unit

In both the p-chart and c-chart situations the lower control limit cannot be lower than zero. However, the above formulas could actually determine negative values for the lower control limit. If this occurs then set the lower control limit equal to zero.

EXAMPLE 1 - ACCEPTANCE SAMPLING

This example involves the acceptance sampling problem presented earlier in this chapter. To solve the problem, load DSSPOM into the computer and select the Quality Assurance Module. When presented with the Quality Assurance main menu, move the pointer to the INPUT option. For this module, the INPUT option has four sub-options as shown below.

```
┌─────────────────────────────────────────────────────────┐
│                                                          │
│      Input  Edit  Print  File  Solve  Quit               │
│    ┌─────────────────────────────┐                       │
│    │ Acceptance Sampling         │                       │
│    │ X-Bar Chart                 │                       │
│    │ P-Chart                     │                       │
│    │ C-Chart                     │                       │
│    └─────────────────────────────┘                       │
│                                                          │
└─────────────────────────────────────────────────────────┘
```

The menu will initially point to the Acceptance Sampling sub-option. Press the <ENTER> key to select this choice. The program will begin the data entry process by placing the pointer in the title field. Type ACCEPTANCE SAMPLING and press <ENTER>. The remainder of the data entry process is shown below.

```
┌─────────────────────────────────────────────────────────┐
│                                                          │
│   Problem title: ACCEPTANCE SAMPLING                     │
│                                                          │
│   Lot Size:    5000                                      │
│                                                          │
│   Sample Size:       15                                  │
│                                                          │
│   Acceptable Number of Defective:        2               │
│                                                          │
│   Increment For the Fraction of Defective:      .05      │
│                                                          │
│                                                          │
│   ┌─────────────────────────────────────────────────┐   │
│   │ Enter problem parameters as requested.  Press    │   │
│   │ RETURN to accept, or ESC to exit. Sample size    │   │
│   │ must be less than or equal to lot size.          │   │
│   │ Parameter values should be within 0-99999.       │   │
│   └─────────────────────────────────────────────────┘   │
│                                                          │
└─────────────────────────────────────────────────────────┘
```

You may now save the model on disk for future use. To save the model, move the pointer to the FILE option and select the Save Current File sub-option then press <ENTER>. The computer will display the current drive and sub-directory and request a file name. Enter an appropriate DOS file name and use the suffix QLY to indicate that the file contains a quality assurance problem. You may also obtain a hard copy printout of the problem. Move the pointer to the PRINT option and press <ENTER>. The computer will ask you to make sure that the Printer in On and Ready. Press <ENTER> to obtain a printout.

You are now ready to solve the above acceptance sampling problem. Move the pointer to the SOLVE option and select the Display Output sub-option. The computer will pause for a few seconds and then display the solution report as shown below.

```
                   Problem Title: ACCEPTANCE SAMPLING

     Fraction  of    Prob.  of      Average out-
     defective (p)    acceptance     going quality
     -------------    ----------     -------------
     0.0000           1.0000         0.0000
     0.0500           0.9638         0.0482
     0.1000           0.8159         0.0816
     0.1500           0.6042         0.0906
     0.2000           0.3980         0.0796
     0.2500           0.2361         0.0590
     0.3000           0.1268         0.0380
     0.3500           0.0617         0.0216
     0.4000           0.0271         0.0108
     0.4500           0.0107         0.0048
     0.5000           0.0037         0.0018
     0.5500           0.0011         0.0006
```

```
                   Problem Title: ACCEPTANCE SAMPLING

     Fraction  of    Prob.  of      Average out-
     defective (p)    acceptance     going quality
     -------------    ----------     -------------
     0.6000           0.0003         0.0002
     0.6500           0.0001         0.0000
```

As seen from the above output report, the probability of acceptance for a sample from a population with no defective (0 percent) is 1. This probability is 0.9638 when there are 5 percent defective, 0.8159 for 10 percent defective, etc.. The average out-going quality is 0, 0.0482 (or 4.82 percent), 0.0816 (or 8.16 percent) for 0, 5 and 10 percent defective. The average out-going quality represents the expected number of percentage of defective which will be included in the accepted lots. For the above example, this value is maximum for a population in which 15 percent is defective. The plots of the probability of acceptance and average outgoing quality are represented in Figures 14-1 and 14-3.

EXAMPLE 2- PROCESS CONTROL: X-BAR CHART

       In this example you will solve the process control problem presented in **Table 14-1**. Load DSSPOM into the computer and select the Quality Assurance module. After a few seconds the computer will load the program and display the main menu. Move the pointer to the INPUT option.

The program will begin the data entry process by displaying the four sub-options associated with INPUT option. Move the bar down to X-BAR Chart sub-option and press <ENTER>. The computer will resume the data entry process by placing the pointer in the title field. Type "PROCESS CONTROL" and press <ENTER>. The initial data entry screen is presented below.

```
    Problem title: PROCESS CONTROL

    Number of Samples:    5

    Number of Observations in Each Sample:    5


   ┌─────────────────────────────────────────────────┐
   │ Enter problem parameters as requested.  Press RETURN to │
   │ accept, or ESC to exit. Maximum number of samples is 50, │
   │ maximum number of observations (per sample) is 10. │
   └─────────────────────────────────────────────────┘
```

Enter 5 for the number of samples and 5 for the number of observations per sample. The computer will then ask if you are ready to continue with the spread sheet data entry for the observations as shown below.

```
┌───────────────────────────────────────┐
│ Continue with the observations (Y/N) Y │
└───────────────────────────────────────┘
```

Press <ENTER> to begin the spread sheet data entry process. The computer will display the initial spread sheet. Enter the sample observations into their appropriate cells. Begin with the sample observations in the first column (entering data one column at a time is mush easier than one row at a time since you do not need to press the <ENTER> key to move to another cell). Move the pointer to cell B2 and type 59 then press the down arrow key. Then type 56 and press the down arrow key. Enter all the of the observations in column 1. When you reach cell B6, press the <ENTER> key and move the pointer up to cell C2. Next enter the data in column 2 and proceed to enter all of the observations in a similar fashion. The completed spread sheet is shown below.

348

```
┌─────────────────────────────────────────────────────────────┤READY├
│F6  57                                                               │
│         A            B         C         D         E         F      │
│1   Sample       Obser 1   Obser 2   Obser 3   Obser 4   Obser 5     │
│2   Sample 1      59.00     58.00     57.00     54.00     56.00      │
│3   Sample 2      56.00     52.00     60.00     57.00     55.00      │
│4   Sample 3      58.00     74.00     52.00     79.00     71.00      │
│5   Sample 4      62.00     58.00     59.00     58.00     57.00      │
│6   Sample 5      54.00     55.00     54.00     58.00     57.00      │
│                                                                     │
└─────────────────────────────────────────────────────────────────────┘
```

After entering all of the observations, press <F10> to keep the data in memory and exit from the spread sheet data editor.

You may now save the model on disk for future use. To save the model, move the pointer to the FILE option and select the Save Current File sub-option then press <ENTER>. The computer will display the current drive and sub-directory and requests a file name. Enter an appropriate DOS file name and use the suffix QLY to indicate that the file contains a quality assurance problem. You may also obtain a hard copy printout of the problem. Move the pointer to the PRINT option and press <ENTER>. The computer will ask you to make sure that the Printer in On and Ready. Press <ENTER> to obtain a printout.

You are now ready to solve the problem. Move the pointer to the SOLVE option and select the Display Output sub-option and press <ENTER>. The computer will pause for a few seconds and then report the solution as shown below.

```
┌───────────────────────────────────────────────────────────────┐
│              Problem Title: PROCESS MEAN                       │
│                                                               │
│  Control limits for the Sample Mean:                          │
│                              R-BAR      2-Sigma    3-Sigma     │
│        Lower control limit =  53.116     49.52      44.88      │
│        Grand Mean          =  58.800                          │
│        Upper control limit =  64.484     68.08      72.72      │
│                                                               │
│  Control limits for the Sample Range:                         │
│                                                               │
│        Lower control limit =   0.000                          │
│        Mean Range          =   9.800                          │
│        Upper control limit =  20.678                          │
│                                                               │
│        ┌──────────────────────────────────────────┐          │
│        │ Wish to see the sample means (Y/N) Y      │          │
│        └──────────────────────────────────────────┘          │
│                                                               │
└───────────────────────────────────────────────────────────────┘
```

As seen from the above solution reports, the grand mean is 58.8 and the mean range is 9.8.

The sample mean lower and upper control limits, based on R-Bar (mean range formula), are 53.116 and 64.484, respectively. These values indicate that a sample with a mean outside of this range is out of control. The 2-sigma and 3-sigma control limits are somewhat wider. In particular, the 2-sigma lower and upper control limits are 49.52 and 68.08. This interval covers about 95 percent of the sample means (assuming a Normal distribution). Using the 2-sigma control limits will result in more samples to pass inspections. However, the chance of an out-of-control process not being detected (type II error) will also increase.

Similarly, the lower and upper control limits for the mean range are 0 and 20.678. A sample having a range outside of these limits is out of control. You can also request a list of the sample means by providing a positive response to the question displayed at the bottom of the screen. Press <ENTER> to obtain a list of the sample means as shown below.

```
                  Problem Title: PROCESS CONTROL

       Sample            Mean          In Control
     ----------       -----------      ----------
     Sample 1           56.800            Yes
     Sample 2           56.000            Yes
     Sample 3           66.800            No
     Sample 4           58.800            Yes
     Sample 5           55.600            Yes
```

As seen from the above output report, using the R-Bar control limits, the third sample is out of control. The sample mean for sample number 3 is 66.8 which is 4.4 units above the upper control limit.

EXAMPLE 3- PROCESS CONTROL: P-CHART

In this example you will solve a p-chart process control problem. Consider the data presented in Table 14-2, the problem is to determine various intervals for the fraction defective. To solve this problem, Load DSSPOM into the computer and select the Quality Assurance module. After a few seconds the computer will load the program and display the main menu. Move the pointer to the INPUT option and select the P-Chart sub-option then press <ENTER>.

The computer will resume the data entry process by placing the pointer in the title field. Type "P-CHART EXAMPLE" and press <ENTER>. The initial data entry screen is presented below.

```
┌──────────────────────────────────────────────────────────────┐
│                                                                │
│   Problem title: P-CHART EXAMPLE                               │
│                                                                │
│   Number of Samples:  12                                       │
│                                                                │
│   Number of Observations in Each Sample:  10                   │
│                                                                │
│  ┌──────────────────────────────────────────────────────────┐ │
│  │ Enter problem parameters as requested.  Press RETURN to  │ │
│  │ accept, or ESC to exit. Maximum number of samples is 50. │ │
│  └──────────────────────────────────────────────────────────┘ │
│                                                                │
└──────────────────────────────────────────────────────────────┘
```

Enter 12 for the number of samples and 10 for the number of observations per sample. The computer will then ask if you are ready to continue with the spread sheet data entry for the observations as shown below.

```
┌─────────────────────────────────────────┐
│ Continue with the observations (Y/N) Y   │
└─────────────────────────────────────────┘
```

Press <ENTER> to begin the spread sheet data entry process. The computer will display the initial spread sheet. Enter the number of defectives in each sample in column B across from the associated sample number. For example, enter 2 in cell B2 as the number of defectives in the first sample. Then press the down arrow to move the pointer to cell B3. Enter 1 and press the down arrow key again. Enter all of the 12 observations in column B. The completed spread sheet is shown below.

```
                                                    ┤READY├
┌──────────────────────────────────────────────────────────┐
│ A1  ' Sample                                              │
│          A          B                                     │
│ 1      Sample   # of Def                                  │
│ 2     Sample 1      2.00                                  │
│ 3     Sample 2      1.00                                  │
│ 4     Sample 3      3.00                                  │
│ 5     Sample 4      0.00                                  │
│ 6     Sample 5      1.00                                  │
│ 7     Sample 6      2.00                                  │
│ 8     Sample 7      1.00                                  │
│ 9     Sample 8      0.00                                  │
│ 10    Sample 9      2.00                                  │
│ 11    Sample 10     1.00                                  │
│ 12    Sample 11     0.00                                  │
│ 13    Sample 12     3.00                                  │
│                                                          │
└──────────────────────────────────────────────────────────┘
```

After entering all of the observations, press <F10> to keep the data in memory and exit from the spread sheet data editor.

You may now save the model on disk for future use. To save the model, move the pointer to the FILE option and select the Save Current File sub-option then press <ENTER>. The computer will display the current drive and sub-directory and requests a file name. Enter an appropriate DOS file name and use the suffix QLY to indicate that the file contains a quality assurance problem. You may also obtain a hard copy printout of the problem. Move the pointer to the PRINT option and press <ENTER>. The computer will ask you to make sure that the Printer in On and Ready. Press <ENTER> to obtain a printout.

You are now ready to solve the problem. Move the pointer to the SOLVE option and select the Display Output sub-option and press <ENTER>. The computer will pause for a few seconds and then report the optimal production schedule as shown below.

```
Problem Title: P-CHART EXAMPLE

   p-Chart Control limits:

   Mean Number of Defective  =       0.133

   Standard Error of the Mean =      0.107

Interval
percent        80%       85%       90%       95%       99%
--------    --------  --------  --------  --------  --------

Lower Limit  0.0000    0.0000    0.0000    0.0000    0.0000

Upper Limit  0.2715    0.2881    0.3102    0.3440    0.4101
```

As seen from the above solution reports, the mean number of defectives is 0.133 and the standard error of the mean is 0.107. The output consists of five different lower and upper control limits for 80%, 85%, 90%, 95%, and 99% levels. For example, the 95% interval level is 0-0.34 which indicates that, in a sample of size 10, the fraction of defectives must be within 0 and 0.34 (or about 34 percent).

EXAMPLE 4- PROCESS CONTROL: C-CHART

In this example you will solve a c-chart process control problem. Consider the data presented in Table 14-3; the problem is to determine various control intervals for the number of defects per unit. To solve this problem, Load DSSPOM into the computer and select the Quality Assurance module. After a few seconds the computer will load the program and display the main menu. Move the pointer to the INPUT option and select the C-Chart sub-option then press <ENTER>.

The computer will resume the data entry process by placing the pointer in the title field. Type "C-CHART EXAMPLE" and press <ENTER>. The initial data entry screen is presented below.

```
┌─────────────────────────────────────────────────────────┐
│                                                         │
│     Problem title: C-CHART EXAMPLE                      │
│                                                         │
│     Number of Samples:   15                             │
│                                                         │
│   ┌───────────────────────────────────────────────────┐ │
│   │ Enter problem parameters as requested.  Press RETURN to│
│   │ accept, or ESC to exit. Maximum number of samples is 50.│
│   └───────────────────────────────────────────────────┘ │
│                                                         │
└─────────────────────────────────────────────────────────┘
```

Enter 15 for the number of samples. The computer will then ask if you are ready to continue with the spread sheet data entry for the observations as shown below.

```
┌─────────────────────────────────────────────┐
│Continue with the observations (Y/N) Y       │
└─────────────────────────────────────────────┘
```

Press <ENTER> to begin the spread sheet data entry process. The computer will display the initial spread sheet. Enter the number of defects in each unit in column B across from the associated sample number. For example, enter 5 in cell B2 as the number of defects in the first unit. Then press the down arrow to move the pointer to cell B3. Enter 4 and press the down arrow key again. Enter all of the 15 observations in column B. The completed spread sheet is shown below.

```
┌──────────────────────────────────────────────┤READY├
│B16   4
│            A          B
│1       Sample    # of Def
│2      Sample 1       5.00
│3      Sample 2       4.00
│4      Sample 3       7.00
│5      Sample 4       9.00
│6      Sample 5       2.00
│7      Sample 6       8.00
│8      Sample 7       2.00
│9      Sample 8       5.00
│10     Sample 9       7.00
│11     Sample 10      7.00
│12     Sample 11      8.00
│13     Sample 12      3.00
│14     Sample 13      4.00
│15     Sample 14      6.00
│16     Sample 15      4.00
│
└──────────────────────────────────────────────
```

After entering all of the observations, press <F10> to keep the data in memory and exit from the spread sheet data editor.

You are now ready to solve the problem. Move the pointer to the SOLVE option and select the Display Output sub-option and press <ENTER>. The computer will pause for a few seconds and then report the optimal production schedule as shown below.

```
Problem Title: C-CHART EXAMPLE

c-Chart Control limits:

Mean Number of Defective      =      5.400

Standard Deviation of the Mean =      2.324

No. of
Sigmas        1.0     1.5     2.0     2.5     3.0     3.5
--------     -------  ------- ------- ------- ------- -------

Lower Limit   3.08    1.91    0.75    0.00    0.00    0.00

Upper Limit   7.72    8.89   10.05   11.21   12.37   13.53
```

As seen from the above report, the mean number of defects is 5.4 and the standard deviation is 2.324. The output report includes six different control intervals for different sigma values. For example, the control limits associated with 3 sigma values is 0-12.37. This implies that as long as the number of defects in the process is within this range, the process is in control.

PROBLEMS

1. Run the acceptance sampling module and plot the operating characteristic curve and average outgoing quality curve for a batch of 4000 pieces with a random sample of 20 pieces and an allowed number of defectives of 2 pieces. Use fraction of defective increments of 0.05.

2. Run the acceptance sampling module and plot both the operating characteristic curve and the average outgoing quality curve for a batch of 7500 pieces with a random sample of 16 pieces and an allowed number of defectives of 1. Use fraction of defective increment of 0.025.

3. For the observations in the six samples below run the mean and range process control module and plot both the mean and range control charts.

Observations

Samples	1	2	3	4
1	19.4	19.2	18.9	19.7
2	18.0	18.9	19.2	19.3
3	19.6	19.4	19.1	19.0
4	18.6	19.1	18.8	18.9
5	18.4	18.9	18.7	19.0
6	18.8	18.4	18.9	18.7

4. Run the p-chart control chart module for 9 samples each consisting of thirty pieces with 0, 1, 0, 1, 2, 0, 0, 1, 2 defectives per sample. Plot the upper and lower control limits and the p for the 90 percent confidence interval.

5. Run the c-chart control chart module for 12 pages which show spelling errors of 5, 4, 3, 2, 4, 2, 3, 5, 6, 0, 1, 4 errors per page respectively. Plot the upper and lower control limits and the c for two standard errors.

6. Run the p-chart control chart module for 6 samples each consisting of fifty pieces with 2, 3, 5, 0, 4, 1 defectives per sample. Plot the upper and lower control limits and the p for the 85 percent confidence interval.

7. Run the c-chart control chart module for 20 randomly selected yards of cloth which show defects per yard of cloth of 2, 0, 3, 4, 5, 6, 0, 1, 2, 3, 1, 4, 2, 3, 0, 1, 4, 3, 2, 1 defects per yard respectively. Plot the upper and lower limits and the c for three standard errors.

8. Run the acceptance sampling module and plot the operating characteristic curve and average outgoing quality curve for a batch of 4000 pieces with a random sample of 20 pieces and an allowed number of defectives of 2 pieces. Use fraction of defective increments of 0.05.

9. Rockford Manufacturing randomly inspects samples of $n=90$ of a component for one of its wheel assemblies each time a shipment of about 2500 items ($N=2500$) is received. The acceptable quality level (AQL) is 0.02 and lots are rejected if number of defectives in a lot is 3 or more ($C=2$). Develop OC curve. What is probability (β) that a lot will be accepted for LTPD of 0.05? What is α for AQL=0.02?

10. Develop the operating characteristics curve for $N=2600$, $n=80$, $c=2$. What is α if AQL is 0.02 and β if LTPD = 0.06? Plot the average outgoing quality level (AOQL) for 0.02 increments.

11. Develop the operating characteristics curve for $N=1500$, $n=40$, $c=1$. What is α for AQL = 0.03 and β if LTPD = 0.06. Plot the average outgoing quality level for 0.05 increments.

12. Erie county has averaged 2.3 traffic deaths per week during the past twelve months. Develop a c-chart with $\pm$ 2 standard deviations.

13. Grain Belt Cereals monitored its 15 ounce corn flake box packing machine by taking random samples at about 107 minute intervals to ensure the correct weight was packed in each box. Underweight boxes could be construed as cheating the public and overweight boxes would be costly to the company. Below is a listing of 12 recorded samples of four boxes each. Develop a $\bar{x}$ chart and a R chart with $\pm$ 2 standard deviations. Estimate the sample variance from the twelve samples.

Sample		Box Weights		
1	15.08	15.11	15.02	15.09
2	15.02	15.03	15.04	15.06
3	14.99	14.96	14.98	15.01
4	15.00	15.06	15.10	15.06
5	14.96	14.97	14.95	14.93
6	14.98	15.06	15.07	15.01
7	15.02	15.09	15.10	15.11
8	15.05	15.01	14.99	15.03
9	15.01	15.03	15.05	15.05
10	15.02	15.06	15.10	15.09
11	14.98	14.99	14.99	15.01
12	15.01	15.06	15.07	15.11

14. Develop a c-chart with ± 2 standard deviations for the number of arrests per week of the Waterford Police Department. The arrest data for the past 18 weeks is listed below.

Week	Number of Arrests	Week	Number of Arrests
1	11	10	11
2	6	11	9
3	5	12	12
4	19	13	14
5	7	14	16
6	9	15	17
7	11	16	8
8	15	17	12
9	14	18	13

15. For the N.Y. State Department of Transportation's Monroe County Office, develop a p-chart for the number of randomly-selected automobiles which failed annual inspections because of unacceptable tires. Number of randomly selected automobiles number 25 per week.

Week	Number of Failures	Week	Number of Failures
1	2	11	2
2	5	12	0
3	1	13	5
4	0	14	3
5	6	15	2
6	1	16	1
7	3	17	0
8	5	18	2
9	0	19	1
10	1	20	3

19. Grain Belt Cereals monitored its 15 ounce corn flake box packing machine by taking random samples at about 107 minute intervals to ensure the correct weight was packed in each box. Underweight boxes could be construed as cheating the public and overweight boxes would be costly to the company. Below is a listing of 12 recorded samples of four boxes each. Develop a $\bar{x}$ chart and a R chart with ± 2 standard deviations. Estimate the sample variance from the twelve samples.

Sample		Box Weights		
1	15.08	15.11	15.02	15.09
2	15.02	15.03	15.04	15.06
3	14.99	14.96	14.98	15.01
4	15.00	15.06	15.10	15.06
5	14.96	14.97	14.95	14.93
6	14.98	15.06	15.07	15.01
7	15.02	15.09	15.10	15.11
8	15.05	15.01	14.99	15.03
9	15.01	15.03	15.05	15.05
10	15.02	15.06	15.10	15.09
11	14.98	14.99	14.99	15.01
12	15.01	15.06	15.07	15.11

20. Develop a c-chart with ± 2 standard deviations for the number of arrests per week of the Waterford Police Department. The arrest data for the past 18 weeks is listed below.

Week	Number of Arrests	Week	Number of Arrests
1	11	10	11
2	6	11	9
3	5	12	12
4	19	13	14
5	7	14	16
6	9	15	17
7	11	16	8
8	15	17	12
9	14	18	13

21. For the N.Y. State Department of Transportation's Monroe County Office, develop a p-chart for the number of randomly-selected automobiles which failed annual inspections because of unacceptable tires. Number of randomly selected automobiles number 25 per week.

Week	Number of Failures	Week	Number of Failures
1	2	11	2
2	5	12	0
3	1	13	5
4	0	14	3
5	6	15	2
6	1	16	1
7	3	17	0
8	5	18	2
9	0	19	1
10	1	20	3